North Korea

THE BRADT TRAVEL GUIDE

PUBLISHER'S FOREWORD

The first Bradt travel guide was written in 1974 by George and Hilary Bradt on a river barge floating down a tributary of the Amazon. In the 1980s and '90s the focus shifted away from hiking to broader-based guides focusing on new destinations – usually the first to be published on those places. In the 21st century Bradt continues to publish these ground-breaking guides, along with those to established holiday destinations, incorporating in-depth information on culture and natural history alongside the nuts and bolts of where to stay and what to see.

Bradt authors support responsible travel, with advice not only on minimum impact but also on how to give something back through local charities. Thus a true synergy is achieved between the traveller and local communities.

*

Since the day George Bush classified North Korea as part of the 'Axis of Evil', I've wanted to publish a travel guide to it. It was not only a logical conclusion to *Iran* and *Iraq*, but we also knew, as all travellers know, that no government fully represents its citizens, and an evil government often rules some of the kindest, friendliest people on earth. If we have the chance to meet them, even under strict supervision as in North Korea, then we should take this opportunity. Robert Willoughby did this, loved what he saw (mostly), and has put his findings into this book. Even if you don't want to travel to this intriguing country, further knowledge of it should help inform your political opinions.

Happy travelling!

Hilary Bradt

19 High Street, Chalfont St Peter, Bucks SL9 9QE, England
Tel: 01753 893444 Fax: 01753 892333
Email: info@bradt-travelguides.com
Web: www.bradt-travelguides.com

North Korea

THE BRADT TRAVEL GUIDE

Robert Willoughby

Bradt Travel Guides Ltd, UK
The Globe Pequot Press Inc, USA

First published 2003

Bradt Travel Guides Ltd
19 High Street, Chalfont St Peter, Bucks SL9 9QE, England
Published in the USA by The Globe Pequot Press Inc,
246 Goose Lane, PO Box 480, Guilford, Connecticut 06437-0480

British Library Cataloguing in Publication Data
A catalogue record for this book is available from the British Library

ISBN 1 84162 074 2

Photographs
Front cover Robin Tudge (RT)
Text Robin Tudge (RT), Nick Bonner (NB)

Illustrations Robin Tudge
Maps Alan Whitaker

Typeset from the author's disc by Wakewing, High Wycombe
Printed and bound in Italy by Legoprint SpA, Trento

Author

Robert Willoughby blames his wanderlust on his father, who was always coming back from God-knows-where with God-knows-what gifts. Convinced that student life would be the death of him, Robert qualified in 1996 as a TEFL teacher and left his hometown of London for Moscow. Five years later, having worked in the US and all over east Asia, visiting the DPRK and Cambodia for fun, he returned to London, where he qualified and now works as a journalist. Robert Willoughby can be contacted at robertwiloughby@yahoo.co.uk.

CONTRIBUTOR

Robin Paxton contributed sections on the parts of the DPRK other travellers haven't reached, which in this volume consists of all of *Chapter 9: East Coast to the Northernmost Corner*. Robin Paxton is a Singapore-based journalist and at the time of writing is the Asia and Australasia editor of *Metal Bulletin*. He can be contacted at robinpen@hotmail.com; tel: +65 6836 8919.

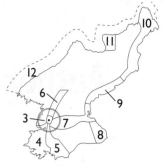

Contents

Acknowledgements

In writing the book, it was rarely possible to gather information by straightforward question and answer; I often felt I had to master the black arts of inference, deduction and logic puzzles. However, the help and encouragement from the following people really changed writing my first book from a laborious task of accumulating and assessing a million post-it notes into a labour of love.

What amazed me when researching this book was not just how one contact led to another, because everybody with anything to do with the DPRK knows everybody else, but the diversity of the contacts contrasted with the exclusivity of their link, making for a fascinating crowd of friends and acquaintances. For me, all are united by a common enthusiasm to share their knowledge and experiences of that country. By plane, fax, phone and email, online, in print and in the pub I have many great people who all proved invaluable one way or another in producing this book, and I haven't been able to include countless people in agencies and embassies.

I must first thank Robin Paxton for his sections on the northern parts of the DPRK. I am also heavily indebted to the ebullient Nick Bonner, without whom much of this book couldn't have been written and whose knowledge, contacts and infectious enthusiasm he so generously imparted. Dr Jim Hoare and Susan Pares donated their time and knowledge of the DPRK from decades of working with and in the country. Those four I cannot thank enough for the generosity with which they contributed to the book.

Many thanks also go to Keith Bennett, who smoothed off a surprising number of corners, and Neil Taylor, who saw what needed clarifying and suggested further leads and fill outs. Thanks to Roger Barrett for his support, information and introductions, and for imparting his pioneering spirit, and the maps he loaned.

Thanks to Pyongyang resident Joanne Richardson and frequent Pyongyang visitor Paul White for their snippets of life in the city. I also have to thank Jon Cannon for so enthusiastically sharing his views and experiences of the DPRK and giving gen about the Chinese side of the fence, for which I also thank Bryan Schmuland for his additions about travelling along China's border. I must also thank Dermot Boyd-Hudson, primarily for his help on explaining and understanding Juche; Dr Philip Edwards, Hall Healy and Angela Choe for their help with the wildlife and DMZ peace park project; and Guy Horne for his Pyongyang Marathon information.

Andrea Godfrey and Rachel Russell brought forth further information and other assistance, and Veronica Malykh and Richard Hunt used their skills to attain those itsy bits just beyond my linguistic reach. Many thanks to Steve and Rowena Samuels for housing me in Beijing during my last DPRK foray, as they had done the time before that, too. Peter Hare and Tiffany You for help on the first DPRK visit, and to that end Michelle Gamelin. Amanda Cooper and Chris Bland read the finished manuscript and gave very valuable comments and questions, Colin Tudge gave good advice, and thanks also to Matt Milton and Jerry Goodman for commenting on the original. I must also thank Laetitia Antonowicz for her unending support, insights and asking the right questions when and where I couldn't throughout the writing of the book, especially those five days when the wheels came off the whole adventure. James McConnachie, who tipped me off about Bradt and commented on the texts. Everyone at Bradt. Thanks to my Ma for putting me up, and putting up with me while I wrote the book during the nuclear winter of my earning ability, and to all my friends and family who listened to me talk of little else until spring finally arrived, and to Robin Tudge, whose help can't be put into words.

Kim Il Sung Friendship Exhibition, Mt Myohyang

Foreword

The Democratic People's Republic of Korea, generally known as North Korea, is by no means an ordinary tourist destination. Not only has its government been traditionally wary of the outside world but the long-lasting state of tension on the Korean peninsula has tended to put off visitors. Yet the country has much to offer. There are spectacular mountain scenes, fast flowing rivers, waterfalls, and fine beaches. The sea is clear and unpolluted. Whatever view one may have of the country's political system, the monuments and vistas of Pyongyang, the capital, are like no others in the world.

All of this is covered in Robert Willoughby's most welcome guidebook, which should meet the needs both of the visitor and of the growing number of longer-term foreign residents. Hitherto, it has been hard to find an adequate guidebook to North Korea. At best, the country has attracted a chapter or two tacked on to much fuller accounts of the Republic of Korea or South Korea. It is true that, once in North Korea, the visitor may find quite good locally produced guidebooks. But even the best of these assumes that all visitors will be part of a guided tour, with no free time. They are far from comprehensive and usually fail to deal with practical matters such as where to eat or how to get around. And they are not always available, even in the bigger hotel bookshops. So to have gathered together in one place both descriptive and practical information is a great benefit. In addition, the reader will find sufficient background material to make any visit enjoyable and more rewarding.

Unless there is some major change in the country's circumstances, visiting North Korea will always be something for only a few. Those few will in future have the benefit of this useful and informative work.

J E Hoare
Chargé d'Affaires, British Embassy, Pyongyang 2001–2002

Introduction

The first time I flew from Beijing to Pyongyang, in the late 1990s, I became aware of going somewhere else, somewhere different, before even getting on the plane. The plane, a compact Air Koryo Ilyushin-62 with an unusually well glazed cockpit, sat parked at the farthest, darkest end of a Beijing terminal wing. It didn't look like a Boeing or Airbus or anything built to fly this last decade; it had engines at the back and a particular swoop to its design. The Koreans waiting to board wore quality suits of sombre-coloured cloth of an oddly uniform, timelessly stylish cut. They talked to each other, not on mobiles, and not to me. I did speak to the other foreigners, all strangers to one another but bound by the common interest and thrill of having any business in North Korea.

Boarding the plane, I saw that in the interior, the colours, shapes, seats, knobs and dials were all stylish in a conservative, '70s kind of way. The in-flight magazine and free copy of the *Pyongyang Times* newspaper wrote of the brilliance and world-encompassing influence of people and ideas I hadn't heard of, with current affairs dominated by wars and empires I thought were finished 50 years ago. The air hostess wheeled the drinks trolley along, laden with beer, cider and mineral water, all of North Korean brands, none that I recognised.

Pyongyang airport looked like any other, except for Kim Il Sung's portrait hanging over it. Myself and the other passengers went through passport control, with the passport officer notably high up in his cubicle. The other side, everyone was met by a driver and car. No throng of taxi men hassling and haggling, no buses. No advertising! Myself and some other strangers who quickly befriended one another on our joint adventure (of being in North Korea) were whisked away in a large car, with driver and guide, around empty hills, through road checkpoints dotted along empty roads. Everything seemed straight out of the opening scenes in Tintin's *Destination Moon*.

Soon, a clean, tall city unfolded before us, and unfold is the word. Many cities unravel, their layouts like random bits of string flung in a box, but Pyongyang unfolds, vistas and boulevards of buildings with sharp lines pan out so neatly as definable sections on a vast plan of the city. We arrived at the hotel, a soaring metallic gantry tower on an island, and entered its cavernous foyer, with its steel frame roof and a glass elevator zooming up and down through it. Here I met everyone I'd met waiting for the plane. You're here too? My my! This wasn't Tintin, but Orwell, and any second, Bond. A Korean Blofeld would appear in the lift, guffawing over the tannoy, 'Ho ho ho! So, Mr Willoughby... or should I say, Mr. Smith?' whereupon the roof would open like a massive steel flower and we would all disappear in a shower of sparks and rocket fumes.

It's easy for the imagination to run riot about North Korea. I first got interested in the place while working in China, itself a country abounding in frontiers for foreigners convinced they're the first to set foot anywhere. It was at Beijing's airport that I noticed flights to Pyongyang on the departures board. So there was a way into the land on the edge of the world, that small pocket of mountains that the Western press was forever wailing to be a worry and a menace, this secretive, hermetic state referred to as Stalinist on the good days, that final bastion of high ideals and base deeds. I got my chance to go as part of a larger delegation, and whilst I remember every single moment, the trip as a whole confirmed some rumours and debunked other myths. A lot of things I had read about the place before going didn't seem true while there, or was I being brilliantly hoodwinked? I realised I didn't really know anything at all worth knowing. So when the grapevine sent a memo that Bradt wanted someone to write a guidebook about North Korea, I jumped at the chance, to find out as much for myself as to try and flash a bit of torchlight into this dark corner of the world.

That said, it hasn't been easy to research. A massive amount of the information in print is incomplete and out of date, and it's an uphill climb to stay on top of recent changes. In the country, a lot of basic information about places, like opening times, prices and phone numbers, were refused. I learned this was because if the person I was asking actually knew, and I was definitely asking the right person, they still wouldn't tell me because they didn't feel entitled to tell me. It was not up to them to decide what I could and couldn't be told, and that rule applies to everything. On a wider note, there are few objective sources about the country, and literature ranges from the extremes of veneration and vitriol.

I've tried to write this book as much for those people who go in with a guide (mainly tourists), as for those who live there or are visitors for other reasons. There are omissions of basic information and broad issues. On the first point, for tourists, questions about times, prices and numbers are largely irrelevant because they're with guides at all times and their itineraries are planned so that museums and what-not can be opened especially for one tour group. Non-tourists are still barred from visiting grand public buildings or museums without guides to take them round, which must be arranged, but parks, the right restaurants and shops can all be visited relatively freely, as can a few outlying temples and museums in outer places – but don't rely on just turning up. As for broader issues, remember that this guide is only useful in the country if it's allowed in, so what I haven't explicitly written about I've included links to; just consider who writes what and for what reason.

I promise I've done my best to provide as much information as possible; to anyone who can plug the obvious gaps, snippets of prices, numbers, times, who can prove something is wrong or something is no longer true, I and Bradt will be exceedingly grateful for your input.

Keep your eyes and mind open, smiles wide and hands waving high – when not shaking the hands of Koreans.

Part One

General Information

Mt Chilbo

NORTH KOREA AT A GLANCE

Location Northeast Asia: China and Russia along northern borders, South Korea (the Republic of Korea, ROK) to south; Japan east across the Sea of Japan

Area 120,540km²

Climate Long, cold winters; short, hot, humid and rainy summers

Population 22,225,000

Capital Pyongyang

Main towns Kaesong, Wonsan, Hamhung, Nampo, Chongjin, Kangye, Sinuiju

Currency Won (1 won = 100 chon)

Official language Korean

Religion Atheist

Ethnic divisions Racially homogeneous; there is a small Chinese community and a few ethnic Japanese

Type of government Authoritarian socialist dictatorship

International telephone code +850

Time GMT +9

Weights and measures Metric

Electricity 220v, 60Hz

Flag Three horizontal bands blue-red-blue with thin white lines dividing them; off-centre-left of the red band is a white circle with a red, five-pointed star.

Kim Il Sung Square, Pyongyang

Background Information

GEOGRAPHY

The Korean peninsula protrudes about 1,000km southwards from northeast Asia, a mountainous outcrop centred squarely between China, Russia and Japan, the latter cupping the peninsula in shelter from the Pacific. The peninsula runs from 43° 00' north, south down to the sea at 33° 06' north, and its 222,209 km² area was, up to 1945, a land mass of one homogenous people in one country: Korea. However, since that time, this country has been bitterly divided into north (the Democratic People's Republic of Korea, DPRK) and south (Republic of Korea, ROK) along a wavy border around the 38th line of latitude. A 238km-long demarcation line snakes from the east to the west coast, coated by a 4km thick band of restricted military activity, namely the De-Militarised Zone or DMZ. But maps from both sides show the DMZ as a faint detail across one country; Pyongyang, the only capital on northern maps, is marked as a village on southern maps that claim the capital as Seoul. This can be confusing, for at least in northern publications, figures exclusively for the northern area slip amid figures for the whole peninsula. For example, the figure for Korea's borders totalling 1,369km in KITC's 'Korea's Tourist Map' excludes the DMZ and the same book states Korea's total area as 222,209.31km², not mentioning that the DPRK is only 120,540km² of that (CIA Factbook). For this section, all figures pertain to the DPRK unless stated for the peninsula.

Besides the DMZ, the DPRK has a 1425km-long northern border with China and a 19km one with Russia. Both borders are 'natural'. The Chinese border follows the 803km River Amnok (or Yalu by its Chinese name) southwest between Sinuiju and Dandong cities to the West Sea and the 548km Tuman River that flows northeast to the Korean East Sea (also called the Sea of Japan), the Tuman's final section comprising the Russian border at Rajin-Songbon. These rivers source approximately two-thirds north along the Chinese border at the vast volcanic Lake Chon on Mt Paektu. From the lake's opposing shores Chinese and Koreans holler at one another in this forum amid a formidable range of mountains, so Korea's northern border is a natural border of igneous walls and river-sized moats.

The DPRK has the monopoly on the peninsula's mountains, which with highlands constitute 80% of the DPRK's land area. Mt Paektu is the peninsula's highest at 2,750m. The DPRK has over 50 mountains above 2,000m, many are grouped in the Hamgyong range that tapers into the wedge-

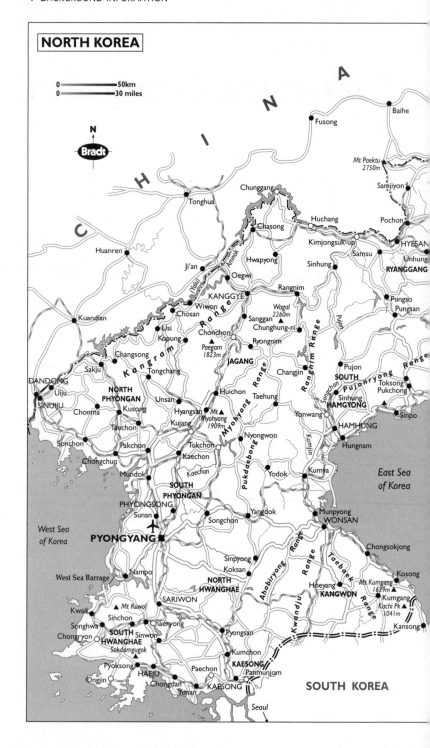

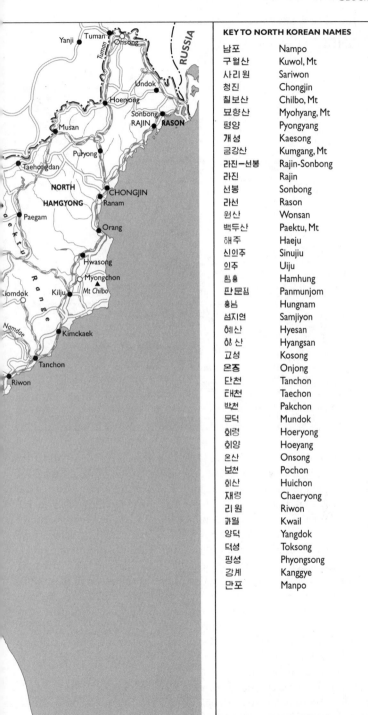

KEY TO NORTH KOREAN NAMES

남포	Nampo
구월산	Kuwol, Mt
사리원	Sariwon
청진	Chongjin
칠보산	Chilbo, Mt
묘향산	Myohyang, Mt
평양	Pyongyang
개성	Kaesong
금강산	Kumgang, Mt
라진-선봉	Rajin-Sonbong
라진	Rajin
선봉	Sonbong
라선	Rason
원산	Wonsan
백두산	Paektu, Mt
해주	Haeju
신의주	Sinujiu
의주	Uiju
함흥	Hamhung
판문점	Panmunjom
흥남	Hungnam
삼지연	Samjiyon
혜산	Hyesan
향산	Hyangsan
고성	Kosong
온정	Onjong
단천	Tanchon
태천	Taechon
박천	Pakchon
문덕	Mundok
회령	Hoeryong
회양	Hoeyang
온산	Onsong
보천	Pochon
희산	Huichon
재령	Chaeryong
리원	Riwon
과일	Kwail
양덕	Yangdok
덕성	Toksong
평성	Phyongsong
강계	Kanggye
만포	Manpo

shape of the country's northeast. In the DPRK's north are the higher and drier hills and plains spiked with needle-leaf and spruce trees. Only feint traces of farmland tuck into the gaps between the hills. The lowland, fertile plains in the southwest and scattered along the island-free east coast hold most of the arable land (and most of the country's 22.2 million people), tended by the orderly groups of houses that are the collectivised or cooperative farms. These neat one-storey brick houses with traditional roofs, or multi-storey concrete cubes, centre vast paddy-fields that roll floor-flat to the horizon. The elaborate hillside terracing seen in southern Asia isn't here, as the water in these thin, muddy strips would quickly freeze in winter and destroy the paddies' delicate structure. Instead, the hillsides are covered with maize, as is every spare strip of earth; in the cities as out in the country, maize protrudes from every orifice. Rice and maize are harvested around October, so spring is for the secondary crops of barley-wheat, wheat, and potatoes. Soya beans, eggplant, red peppers and ginseng are also important.

The seasonal droughts and floods that have always blighted the peninsula's agriculture have worsened partly through extensive deforestation of lowlands' mixed forests of pine and broad leaf, oak and birch. Afforestation is visible in many of the DPRK's nine provinces (Kangwon, Jagang, Ryanggang, North & South Pyongan, North & South Hamgyong, North & South Hwanghae), and around its four 'special cities' (Pyongyang, Nampo, Rajing-Sonbong, Kaesong) that are under central authority. Under the ground, the country's mineral wealth includes soft coal, copper, tungsten, gold and uranium. Place names are suffixed by what the feature is, like Panmun-ri, (*ri* = town, *si* = city), Taedong-gang (*gang* = river), Pothong-dong (*dong* = district), Kumgang-san (*san* = mountain), Moranbong (*bong* = hill).

CLIMATE

The DPRK's warm, temperate climate divides into four seasons, spring (March to May) summer (June to August), autumn (September to November) and winter. The seasons are dry except the monsoon-like rainy season of summer; that over half of Pyongyang's 916mm of annual precipitation falls in July and August is very typical. Typhoons also tour the peninsula's coasts, causing floods and wind-damage The southeast coastal region is the wettest, with Wonsan averaging 1,400mm in annual rainfall. Westerly winds from the Asian landmass make winters cold and dry, getting colder and drier the further north you go. High humidity besides, the DPRK's July temperatures can run up to 25°C in the southwest round Nampo to Pyongyang, while winter in the capital plumbs to –8°C and atop Mt Paektu plummets below –20°C.

NATURE AND CONSERVATION

The DPRK has a few national parks, mainly around mountain sites, as in Mt Chilbo, Mt Paektu, Mt Kuwol, Mt Myohyang and Mt Kumgang, which have varying degrees of religious and historic significance and are sprinkled with temple sites, ruined and restored. In these parks and elsewhere, many cultural sites, particularly old tombs and temples, have been rebuilt following the ravages of war, looting, neglect and falling into official ill-favour. The parks and other sites accumulatively cover thousands of square km, the country overall has only around 580km² of protected land, and the national proportion of pristine land is less than 1% of the total area. Pollution from heavy industry has turned some local ecosystems into alien worlds, and respite has come not by decree but through economic contraction that has cut the output of the polluting factories. However, areas of extreme human impact contrast with areas of extremely sparse human inhabitation, as around Mt Paektu and the mountains leading into the DPRK's northeast.

The DPRK altitude, long latitude and climactic range make it home to a wide variety of flora and fauna found from temperate evergreen forests through broad-leafed deciduous forests up to tundra meadows. Amongst those species indigenous to Korea and to the northern area specifically are wildlife found in Japan, China and Russia, while the DPRK is a grand roosting place for migrating birds. Across Korea can be found black and brown bear, tiger, sable and deer, and often seen soaring over the peninsula are Baikal teal, white-naped crane and white-bellied black woodpecker, while maple and azalea dowse the land in colour. Wildlife-oriented trips can be arranged through tour operators.

HISTORY

'5,000 years of Korean history' is a stock phrase found everywhere in Korean literature. It comes from the following tale:

In the beginning, there was the God Hwan In and his son Hwan Ung, who wanted to govern the earth's people. His father consented and sent him earthwards into the Korean peninsula where he established agriculture and the laws of humanity. A bear and a tiger prayed to Ung to be human. Ung gave them garlic and cloves and told them to avoid sunlight for 100 days. The bear succeeded and transformed into a woman, and later married Ung. In 2,333BC they had a son, Tangun Wanggom, who set up his capital at Pyongyang and called his kingdom Choson (Morning Freshness). So was born Korea, and they ruled for a millennium and a half. This story denotes a Chinese influence: 'Morning Freshness' indicates the peninsula's location relative to ancient China, east where the sun rises, while Wang in Chinese means 'king'.

The more modern alternative history of Korea begins with the first human habitation originating from east and northeast Asia. Remains of 'Ryonggok man' of some 400,000 years age have been found near Pyongyang, as have the remains of man from 40,000 years ago. Culture sites date back to 30000BC, with evidence of ancient Mongolian and Manchurian tribes.

By 6000BC 'combed' pottery and other evidence in unearthed villages suggests sedentary agricultural lives, with domesticated farm animals and huts sunk into the earth. The first dolmens appear from 3000BC, large graves of slabs of stone laid flat across upright stones, possibly also used for ritual sacrifice, with agricultural stone implements found buried around them. Bronze mirrors and daggers date from 1500BC, and mirrors, knives, bells and other ceremonial trinkets with heavy Chinese influence in their design have also been found.

Early records say that by 300BC there were five tribes controlling distinct areas of the Korean peninsula and the adjacent mainland. The largest, most powerful tribe was the Choson, with its capital Wang-hsien-ch'eng near today's Pyongyang. Trade was conducted with the Chinese state of Yan, one of many Chinese warring states, and it was a Yan warlord that took over the Choson. Over a century, Choson expanded from around the Taedong northwards, to the east coast and south to the Han River, building forts all the way.

In China the Han were ascendant and wanted to up the ante from simple trade with the peninsula, preferring tribute and subservience. In 109BC, Han Emperor Wu sent land and sea forces to destroy the Choson, attacking Wang-hsien-ch'eng, and sweeping the peninsula, leaving only the southernmost area free. Wu's gains were absorbed into the Han empire and, combined with Manchurian areas beyond the Yalu and Tuman rivers, were divided into four 'commanderies' under Chinese administration. The biggest commandery, with a population of 400,000, was Lo-lang, (with Pyongyang the capital).

Rice cultivation was introduced, mainly in the south, and a greater variety of sophisticated tools and weapons in iron and bronze were imported. Chinese officials' tombs, large mounds dotted around modern Pyongyang, have contained many sophisticated paintings and artefacts from Han culture.

Chinese rule continued uncertainly for four centuries. Individual tribes could be brought to order, their chieftains sometimes given 'official' status and the bronze seals to prove it as their tribes were exploited for labour and goods. There was generally more subservience than outright resistance, and the tribes were controllable while they were divided and in the vicinity of any commandery barracks. But the hardy Koguryo people, hunters and warriors, were spread across the mountains of northern Korea and eastern Manchuria. Their numerous tribes combined under one 'king' who was thus empowered to resist commandery rule and invade Chinese and northeast Korean regions for food, materials and slaves.

By 37BC, the Koguryo had developed a powerful state, with influence from far into Manchuria to the southern Han River. Dynastical and barbarian invasions debilitated China's grip and the weakened commanderies fell prone to tribal resistance by the 3rd century AD. Tribes in the peninsula's south combined and fought the southern Tai-feng commandery. Both the Lo-Lang and Tai-Feng were cut off when China imploded, and the Koguryo absorbed the Lo-Lang in 313. Meanwhile, two states were forming from the tribes in the peninsula's deepest south. Paekche in the southwest combined from Ma Han tribes, and soon after the Koguryo victory, Paekche abolished Tai-Feng. Southeast, Chin Han tribes united to create the Silla state. Wedged between Silla and Paekche lay the Pyon Han states dominated by Japan (also called Kaya), but it was Silla, Paekche and Koguryo's that formed the seven-hundred year 'Three Kingdoms Period'.

Ancient states: the Three Kingdoms period

The Koguryo was the biggest of the three kingdoms, covering the peninsula's northern half and beyond the rivers Yalu and Tuman. Its expansion west into China halted when the Yen warrior-state raided and ransacked Koguryo in the mid-4th century. So, for easier pickings, Koguryo forces went south, jabbing and clawing territory from Silla and Paekche. Tens of thousands of Koguryo's population were conquered people, including many former officials of Lo Lang, so a strong, military-based government was needed to run the expanding Koguryo. A large fort in Koguryo's capital Pyongyang (since 427) was among many built, while victims of Koguryo's military defeats or surrenders were executed. From Pyongyang the king ruled, served by administrative and military officials. These posts superseded the tribe-chieftain ties, but as the chieftains became Koguryo nobility, they took the top jobs anyway. Their sons were schooled to head this administration with an education derived from Confucian teachings from China, to collect regular tax in grain from the peasants and labour from the slaves and to codify the nation's laws written in the adopted Chinese written language.

Using Chinese written language made China's literary texts accessible, as well as the Confucian philosophy and the full workings of the remnant political structures. From China also came Buddhism in the 4th century AD, with all its glories of architecture and arts. China also continued in its position as a regional player to ally with as the three kingdoms warred among themselves. Hence Chinese culture permeated the three kingdoms throughout their existence.

Paekche's Sino-connections saw it more imbued with Buddhism earlier than the other kingdoms. Paekche's foreign policy was, like Silla's and Koguryo's, a continual series of alliances made to attack or defend the aggressor of the day, but Paekche endured more unwelcome interest from the other two. From the mid-4th to the late 7th century, Koguryo forces compressed Paekche into the peninsula's corner, the Puyo royal family taking the capital south from Hansong to Ungjin to Sabi, leaving behind slain troops and offering tributes of live slaves to appease Koguryo. Apart from sheer size, one problem was that the Puyo, outsiders to the area, were lording over Paekche's indigenous Ma Han, who had unfortunately been suppressed very effectively under commandery rule. The administration was not based on any great loyalty nor had they learned much from Chinese ways of governance. Paekche's main asset was the peninsula's best agricultural land, which the kingdom's slaves cultivated well, but the land was all the more alluring to jealous neighbours.

Silla was the kingdom with the smallest population and land and was clamped between Koguryo and Kaya. From its tribes, the Silla had developed governance from a council of tribal chieftains, a *hwabaek* that discussed great matters of state. Conquered tribes were not made hwabaek, that was only for the victors who chose their joint leader. Therein began the division of power based on clan, developing into a multi-layered social structure of rights and privileges based on kinship, rank and status, ascribed through a hereditary caste system, the bone-rank system. The ruling royal clan was the *songgol* rank (the top) and affiliates of the *chingol* ranks. Regulations dictated the size of one's house and stables, cut of dress and cloth used, and other distinctive ornamentation. This regimented caste system would continue throughout the Silla's existence.

Silla also developed an administrative system of state based on Chinese practice, with the monarch overseeing numerous controlling boards with their own remits over finance, war, personnel, etc. This centralised government drew taxes, labour and troops from the local level through an administrative chain breaking the country down into province, district and county levels. This efficient form of governance, with a stable royal household at its heart, was able to organise Silla's warring so effectively that it averted being totally lost to its neighbours. In the early 600s, the Tang of China were able to refocus on the peninsula, and when taking on Koguryo, Silla took its chance to ally with the Tang and quash conclusively the Koguryo and Paekche threats.

Paekche collapsed, and in 668 Korguryo was pacified. However, the Tang emperor's version of peace was Tang hegemony, something that the Silla hadn't fought long and hard for; it wasn't to be robbed of the spoils this way. Remaining Korguryo aristocrats and their forces were generously welcomed by the Silla in a new front to oust the Tang. A reformed alliance of Silla, Paekche and Korguryo forces, each in distinctive uniforms, set off north, countering Tang attacks with their own crippling assaults, and by the late 670s, the Tang were out.

Unified Silla ... and Palhae

The Silla dominated from the Taedong southwards, but Koguryo's aristocracy were not spent as a group capable of command and rule. With the Malgal tribes, the state of Palhae was formed straddling the Yalu River, so had sea access on both sides, into the Yellow Sea and the Sea of Japan, and as such could forge substantial trade links with the Chinese and Japanese. It thus grew westwards and northwards, placing its capital in Dunhua in today's Jilin Province. For two centuries the state existed and traded, reaching 2,000km across, until the unity of the tribes succumbed to the nuances of internal conflict that makes tribes tribal, and the state couldn't resist the encroaching Qidan in the 10th century.

Meanwhile, the Silla ran their kingdom for many fortuitous years, albeit with a good deal of Chinese influence politically and culturally. A half-century after the Tang were ousted, Chinese suzerainty over the peninsula was re-established. Silla students had already been sent to study Tang governance administration, bringing back further developments on the ethics of Confucianism and its wisdom on the structures and working relations of administration.

Chinese culture permeated Korea through trade, and was carried on through Korean trade into Japan. Trade with China developed links as far away as Iran, and India became a mine of knowledge for Silla's burgeoning love of Buddhism. Buddhism became the national religion and was lavished with gifts of land, slaves and money in the hope that it would protect the state in return. Wood-cut prints of the Buddhist scriptures were housed in magnificent temples built in the royal city and taken cross country high into the fabulous mountain temples and monasteries. A rising tide of literary works from this time was permeated with Buddhist thoughts, and the importing of the religion also imported its associated literature, architecture and paintings that spread across the new territories in what is now considered a golden age of arts.

Silla's territory and population had more than trebled in size, some of which was redistributed amongst the nobles of the victorious side and magnanimously given back to the surrendering tribal chiefs; those chiefs who had professional skills and scholarly understanding were employed in government. As such, the 8th century was marked by relative peace in the kingdom, affording the government much time and prosperity to promote advancements in the arts and sciences. Departments of medicine, mathematics, and astronomy were established, as was a department of translation for the Silla's growing trade network. Goods from textiles, furs, pottery and instruments to advanced iron weapons, silver and gold jewellery were exported.

The capital Kjongju grew to over a million in population with streets 10km in length, with dozens of immense private estates, palaces, monasteries and government buildings, staffed by a ruling class whose provincial lands were tilled by slaves. The Tang had carted off 200,000 into slavery, and slavery continued under the Silla. In the counties, many peasants had their own life-tenancies on land but were still subject to tax and labour service, kept account of on continually updated registers. These dues were collected and concentrated in the provincial capitals delegated to run the regions outside the capital, and became concentrations of power away from the Silla court.

The capital and county distinction grew as the families of the elite moved to the capital, and the Silla kings became more autocratic and determined to distinguish between themselves and their underlings. The hwabaek was finally replaced by Chinese administration, and by the late 700s, civil examinations allowed a few commoners to attain position through ability, threatening the aristocrats' long-standing system of position through birth.

For the aristocracy however, their own allegiance of bone-clan kin-ties to the dynasty became of less value than material wealth, and with peace and prosperity came decadence. Provincial revolts broke out with increasing frequency, starting in King Hyegong's reign (765–779) which ended in his assassination. A succession of coups and massacres marred the reigns of the next 20 kings in the 150 years from 784, marking the Silla's accelerating decline. While the aristocrats connived and conspired, the people on their lands tired of their toils and rising taxation and left, roaming the counties as destitute migrants, forming their own popular rebellions or turning to banditry. A plague of banditry inland accompanied a plague of piracy that afflicted Korea's coasts, exacerbating regional instabilities, so inciting more power struggles which were ever more focused on the throne. The bandits themselves accrued land and slaves and became powerful factions in their own right, such that one bandit, Kungbok, became a king-maker, helping Kim Ujing take the throne, though Kungbok himself was killed in 846 for his own connivance for the throne.

As the Sillan state began to break down in the late 800s and early 900s Paekche re-emerged, and a formidable general called Wang Kon from the former Koguryo region led from 918 a new state around the Taedong, later called Koryo. These states formed with the Silla the 'Later Three Kingdoms' Period' marked by intense inter-state warfare, from which the Koryo came out supreme.

Koryo

Wang Kon, crowned King Taejo in 935, welcomed the fallen Sillan king and his nobles into his court, giving them land and positions in government. Over the next couple of decades, from his new Songak capital (today's Kaesong) near to the troublesome northern border, he launched a systematic offensive of gifts and privileges to bring the provincial barons on-side, tipping the balance in Wang Kon's favour in bringing to heel the castle towns that defied the Silla. Land, privileges and later caste titles rewarded those helping to found

Koryo (the word from which Korea derives) and entice those reluctant to submit. Regional leaders gave familial 'hostages' or kin to the court to ensure loyalty, and Koryo soon spanned all the peninsula up to the Yalu's mouth, from whence its border stretched across to near today's Wonsan. This fortified border was supported by two provinces under military command, connected to Kaesong and the other provinces through new roads and a postal system.

King Taejo's successors developed new government boards, and expanded government-owned factories of raw materials. The career-routes into government were subject to more civil-service examinations taken by students of new Confucian academies, meaning more 'commoners' could attain positions of power and privilege. Privilege principally was the dispensation of land to officials (that returned to the state upon their death), and so the divine rights of the old aristocracy were eroded. Nonetheless, Koryo's social structure was still as regimented as its predecessors and ancestry counted for a great deal, as one new government board dealt with genealogical records. At the top were the Royal Caste, then the military and civil officials' class, called the Yangban. Below them were more grades of profession, down to the Yangmin, or commoners of peasants, and below them, the 'untouchables'. At least eight generations clean of untouchable status had to be proved by would-be officials.

Buddhism was further encouraged with lavish gifts of land, slaves and tax exemptions, until the temples and monasteries became grand concentrations of wealth within a tight hierarchical structure of considerable political and economic power, and its leaders of high aristocratic stock. Monasteries provided welfare for the poor and usurious loans for others, and it was a Buddhist monk that persuaded his brother King Sukchong (1082–96) to scrap barter for a standard coinage. Wood-block printing also revived with a great number of Chinese texts.

On that subject, foreign affairs were as usual dominated by events in China. To be safe, from 1033 a grand wall was built connecting the dozen fortified towns along Koryo's northern border. Following centuries of paying tribute to whichever dynasty held the other side of the wall seemed a sure route to peace, with just a few incursions from the Sung, the Jurchen, the Liao and the Chin.

Then in the early 13th century, the Mongols (also known as the Yuan) came. They'd stormed out of the Gobi Desert, smashed the Chin from power, taking China, Manchuria, then looked south on to the peninsula. Years of battling the Jurchen hadn't prepared the Koryo armies for the Mongols, who washed over the country in a tide of blood. The only glimmer of fortune in these years of ravaging was that the Mongols were poor navy men. This allowed the Koryo court, with the Choe family at the fronts, to take every official and jewel their boats could carry and sail into safe exile on Kanghwa Island. There they lived and prospered for nearly three decades, while the mainland people were enslaved or just massacred. The court used this unreal time to build great palaces and pavilions and recarve the wood blocks for the Tripitika that were burnt in the Mongol invasion. Only in 1258 did the Choe realise that their great service to Buddha wasn't going to remove the Mongols.

A little bloody coup won a new leader, who led the return to the mainland, and through apology, tribute, marriage and familial hostage taking by the Mongols, re-established Koryo as a Mongol vassal state.

Now, through the Mongols, Koryo could prove its heartfelt loyalty to their rulers by pouring all its resources into invading Japan. In 1274 and 1281, hundreds of thousands of soldiers and hundreds of ships and crews were put up for two massive invasions of Japan. Neither succeeded. Notwithstanding the huge economic drain this had on the peninsula, the frustrated Mongols sucked Koryo even drier. Koryo came under complete Mongol control through marriage and appropriation, and for a century, anything the Mongols wanted, they took. The Mongols were not totally parasitical and were partly responsible for the influx of neo-Confucian texts, and the Confucian study of King Chungson (1309–13) at the Mongol capital. This would spell the end of Buddhism's dominance.

For Buddhism was not protecting the state. By the mid-14th century, Japanese pirates, or Wako, were touring and pillaging Koryo shores. In the 14th century, the Mongols were losing control of China as the Ming resurged from the south towards Korea. The Koryo court buckled under factional fights and usurpations, while one general, Ri Songgye, made a name for himself battling the Wako. Sent by pro-Mongol King U to fight the Ming, Ri Songgye considered fighting the Ming to be a futile exercise. Indeed, he decided instead that they would surely be an improvement on the Mongols. So Ri turned his forces on U and deposed him in 1389. An efficient purge followed and, with Ming relations affirmed, Ri Songgye became undisputed Ri Taejo, in 1392.

Ri (also known as the Chosen or Yi) 1392–1910

Ri Taejo moved the capital from Kaesong to the city of Hanyang, renaming it Seoul, or 'capital'. Holders of large estates loyal to the previous dynasty were dispossessed and their lands given to Ri followers. In 1390 Ri had all the old land registry records burnt, creating a clean slate for him to distribute lands as he liked. However, as under the Koryo, dual governance came through military and civil officials, staffed at the top by Yangban. As under the Koryo, society was rigidly structured, with royal caste, yangban of 'merit' and 'minor merit' in a pyramid of power, then numerous sub-strata of professions and yangmin commoners, and at the bottom the untouchables (including now sorcerers and actors!).

During the reigns of Taejo, Taejong and Sejong, Korea expanded northwards until all the area south of the Yalu and Tuman rivers was theirs, and was populated by southern migrants. The population increased as fast as new land was brought under cultivation and reclaimed.

Foreign policy was *sadae*, or 'serving the great' as in continuing to pay tribute to the Ming Emperor of China. With the Mongol shackles thrown off, and no distracting Ming-Mongol warring, the Ri could deal with the pirates by sending boats to destroy their ships and settlements. By 1420 the threat was curtailed. Then the forts and outposts of the northern frontier could be bolstered.

The capital was fortified and built up. With peace came greater scholarship and the *sowon* schools of Confucianism, needed for the examination system, flourished about the country. The hangul alphabet was completed in the mid-1440s, along with movable print-type. Korean and Chinese influences led to a rebirth of the arts and sciences, with advancements from arms to poetry.

Although Buddhism again had a hand in the arts, the power of the monasteries was curbed. Over the centuries the monasteries had acquired huge tracts of land and through tax exemption had the wealth to defend them, depriving others to their inevitable discontent. The monks were perceived to have become too powerful, too corrupt and were too collusive with suspicious elements, so they were evicted from the court and cities and stripped of their wealth, albeit slowly, so as not to provoke insurrection. King Taejo finished their tax exemption; King Taejong limited their ownership of land and slaves, which his successor King Sejong reduced further. King Sejo (1455–68) was a practising Buddhist and he supported a brief revival, but his successors were mainly Confucianist.

Copper-type cast printing allowed Confucian texts to be spread amongst the new Confucian schools set up in the prefectures and counties, and the schools achieved a similar build-up of power and privileges that the Buddhists were stripped of. The schools' alumni formed groups for mutual advancement and further ensnaring of the youth. They competed, of course, at court for power and offices, as did the members of the royal families, so all Ri dynasty officials were Confucian scholars.

But their professed veneration of learning and authority was not manifest from the late 1400s, and departments of differing Confucian doctrine stifled their monarchs' wishes so they could concentrate on settling their own scores. The zealous reformers of the Sallim school, a puritan lot, incurred much resentment. To be fired was to get off lightly. Four bloody purges of the 'literati' occurred from 1498 to 1545, so bitter that the bones of dead scholars were dug up and scattered. The ruler Yonsangun was deposed by his own officials in the first purges and the battles became aristocratic feuds, which would mar the functioning of the court thereafter.

These feuds did not affect society as a whole. The comprehensive genealogical records founded under the Koryo were continued. There was a degree of social fluidity, slaves did become tenant farmers as Yangban fell earthwards. Some records were lost, some burnt, some doctored as fallen Yangban sold their status, but the class system remained largely intact, and Korea had slaves until the 19th century. The real threat instead came from beyond Korea's shores.

Japan and the Imjin war

The anti-pirate war and the success in holding off the Mongols made for about two centuries of peace for Korea. Trade routes were established with the Ming and Japan, whose people were allowed to set up trading settlements in the south of the peninsula.

Feudal infighting in Japan in the 15th century meant piracy resumed as Japan's worst export. The Ashikaga military government curtailed piracy and peaceful trade was set up in the late 1400s. But from the mid-1500s the Wako resumed piracy as the Ashikaga declined, now in greater force and sacking whole cities. A new leader, Hideyoshi Toyotomi, brought order and restored peaceful trade with Korea, but this wasn't all he had in mind, for Hideyoshi's imperial plans stretched to India. Korea, of course, was the most convenient land route into China, and Hideyoshi set about persuading the Ri from 1587 to join him against Ming China before taking on all Asia. But the only coherent response from the Ri court, torn between tribute-loyalty to the Ming, profiting from Hideyoshi's scheme and aversion to any involvement, was 'probably not'. Hideyoshi's responded by invading Korea in the fourth month of 1592. Within a month, his 158,000-strong force had taken the capital.

Unfortunately, the good years had allowed the Ri military to stagnate. The court fled to the Yalu and tremulously persuaded the Ming that these invaders were dangerous. A Ming army attacked down to Pyongyang but was repelled, only for another force to charge Kaesong in early 1593. Meanwhile, however much face the Ri had lost on land they won back at sea under the brilliant admiral Ri Sunsin, with his cannon-firing, iron-decked 'turtle boats' that sunk Hideyoshi's supply ships. Hideyoshi's debilitated land forces were then kept pinned down by Korean guerrilla attacks. Hideyoshi sued for peace.

It was a lull. Many Japanese stayed on in Korea, eking a living amid the post-battle chaos until Hideyoshi attacked again with 140,000 troops in 1597. Toughened Chinese and Korean forces were ready, and, aided by winter, held up Hideyoshi's forces until he declared on his deathbed in 1598 that this time enough really was enough.

Japan's forces returned home reasonably unscathed with the priceless booty of many skilled artisans. The Toyotomi family were replaced by the Tokugawam, who resumed simple trade as before, after a few thousand captives were negotiated back to the Koreans. On the peninsula, the wars' taxation and devastation compounded the peninsula's material exhaustion. Local rebellions during the conflict preceded passionate factional fighting at court in a series of coups in the 1600s, including the Injo faction of 1624 that briefly installed a new royal family.

Further north, the war had emptied the Ming's coffers, who faced growing threats from the Manchus in northeast Asia. Ming-Manchu fights stumbled into Korea until the Manchus stood victorious on Korea's borders with Ming China shoved westwards. Now the Manchus demanded suzerainty: the Koreans were to be the Manchus' 'younger brother'. Refusal was met with a punitive invasion in 1627. Still, Korea conspired to have the Ming return, until the Manchus, styling themselves as the Qing, rumbled the plan and invaded Korea again in late 1637. Korea's misery would only cease, seethed the Manchus, upon payment of food, troops and the handing over of 'hostage' envoys. They did, and relative peace was Korea's prize for 200 years.

Not in the court. The literati purges had opened a can of worms. Ancestor worship, the importance of filial piety, familial and old clan ties, sowon alumni and regional relationships meant that the fights of the forebears were carried on by their successors. From the 1550s until the late 1700s, factions fought and splintered into 'westerners', 'northerners', 'greater' and 'lesser northerners', 'southerners', and so on and on, in a maelstrom of fights, coups and burning buildings.

So no-one really saw the real aliens turn up in the 1700s. There had been some bitty contacts with Europeans. Jesuits reached Japan in the late 1500s. Some Dutch washed ashore in 1627, and one became prominent in the Korean army for his cannon-casting skills. Yet in practical terms, Korea's foreign relations had only ever involved jostling between China and Japan.

Meanwhile, European missionaries had been spreading the Gospel across Asia, and Catholic missionaries had had great success in China by the 1790s. From the late 18th century the Catholic Church was spying Korea as the next great congregation. A Chinese priest smuggled himself into Seoul and began converting peasants by the thousand. Bad enough, but Catholicism forbade ancestral worship and therefore threatened the ruling family's legitimacy. News filtered to the court of the Peking government's sufferance of Christian subterfuge, and Korea's Christians were thus pre-emptively persecuted. In 1801 court official Hwang Sa Yong appealed to Peking's French bishop to send in armies to purge the Korean government of its anti-Catholicism, but the message was intercepted. The court's suspicions were proved, and they were mightily alarmed by the extent of these Catholics' reach and conspiring. The mass 'martyring' of Catholics ensued.

The great powers come...

The Western nations in the 19th century, mainly the French, Russians, British and Americans, wanted the locals converted to Christ because Christians were easier to trade with than the average Oriental. Lone trade ships began arriving, with an English merchant ship anchoring off the Chongchung province coast in 1832. More and more came and prospected but more often than not returned empty-handed, having been (usually) politely turned away by the Koreans.

These foreign powers were not used to being rebuffed, however politely. China's ports were jemmied for trade following the Opium War in 1842, and Japan's doors were blown open in 1854. Korea had no right not to trade with the West, and if it couldn't be reasoned with, then it would be forced. The occasional trading ships off Korea's coast started sporting more arms. Solitary French, Russian and British warships began hailing more frequently off the coasts.

By the 1860s, King Kojong was a minor and the country was under the regent Taewongun, who concentrated on rebuilding the country's fortifications and reformed the military. The Ri worried that these increasingly aggressive Western traders were the external force of destruction, while western religion would destroy Korea from within. The country wasn't doing well. A ruinous drought from 1812 had apparently killed millions. Rice riots occurred in Seoul in 1833. The Tonghak 'religion' fused Eastern and Western religions, yet promoted the interests of the poor and not the usual deference to the rich. Its creator Choe Cheu was executed for 'confusing society' in 1862, but his death apparently sparked uprisings by destitute farmers of all classes in the southern provinces. Many merchants and officials were killed before this burgeoning insurrection was put down. More unrest followed in 1864, so all in all the Ri were in less genial mood to receive anyone.

Russian pressure to trade was aggressive, but the French priests' offers to mediate with them in 1866 made the Taewongun suspect a broader foreign plot, and so interrogated and executed nine priests before a bloody purge of tens of thousands of converts. The French took great exception to their priests falling to the sword, and their navy invaded Kanghwa Island in retaliation, but were routed by Korean forces. That year, the armed American missionary trader General Sherman arrived in Pyongyang, but was beached and burned in the shallow waters of the Taedong River. A punitive occupation by American forces of Kanghwa Island in 1871 was as successful as the French occupation. American Admiral Rogers was dispatched to organise the protection of US vessels from Korea 'tiger hunters' along Korea's shores, but Taewongun took heart: his reforms had enabled his country to repel all boarders.

There were other tacky incursions. In 1867, a priest, a German and an American adventurer, bent on raiding royal tombs, sailed from Shanghai to extort concessions from the king for trade and missionary work. Another rumour that circulated Beijing's diplomatic circle was that Korea was volunteering to help expel all foreigners from China. Bolstered by military success, the Taewongun kept Korea closed and belligerent. He believed battle to be the only language these barbarians understood and had stelae erected round the country to remind the people how awful foreigners were and the fate of collaborators.

The Japanese

But since the 1860s' Meiji restoration, the imperial Japanese government had reformed itself and the economy along Western lines. Convinced that these Western ideas Korea could learn from, Japanese emissaries were repeatedly sent to persuade Korea to open up and expand their trade links along more Western lines. King Kojong, enthroned since coming of age in 1873, was as suspicious of outsiders as his father Taewongun. Nor were his courtiers interested in reforms that would put them out of work. They were convinced that these Japanese were simply Eastern conveyors of Western subversion, using trickery to smokescreen more base motives. In 1875, the Japanese warship Unyo sailing off Kanghwa island was shelled by Korean land-batteries. The incident proved to the Koreans they were right, as did subsequent events. The Japanese retaliated to this ill-mannered action with an armed expedition to Korea, demanding unprecedented trade concessions. These included residence rights in three Korean ports and a Legation in Seoul, in the 1876 Treaty of Kanghwa. The treaty also secured 'independence' for

Korea from China. This gun-muzzle diplomacy secured a major foothold in what was a long, profitable relationship for Japan, with Korean rice poured out to Japan as Japanese goods and ideas poured in.

It only led to more factionalism in the court. Queen Min and her family favoured Japanese-style reform, but Taewongun still skulked in the court's shadows and, as some feared, reforms disposed and made malcontents of government and army men alike, who flocked to Taewongun's conspiring. In 1882, they rebelled against the queen, killing her, her family and ministers, burnt down the Japanese legation and caused its minister and staff to flee to sea in a junk. Only the intervention of the Qing (also called the Manchus), seeing a way to reassert themselves over Korea, saved the day for King Kojong, sending 2,000 troops to Seoul, suppressing the rebellion, and restoring the Min. Even more joyously, the slain queen was actually alive and well for an impersonator had taken the blade for her.

Brilliantly, the Qing intervention protected Japanese subjects in China's empire, as agreed by the two countries in 1871; so Korea was back under Chinese suzerainty. Nevertheless, the Chinese pressed for greater Korean relations with the outside, arguing this was inevitable and a mix of competing influences would prevent any one foreign nation from dominating, ie: Japan. Commercial treaties quickly ensued with the US, Germany, UK, France, Russia and Italy, with investment inflows (into mining, railways, universities and hospitals) and Western-style banking, customs and communications in post and telegraph being set up.

At the court, the arguments over how to secure Korea's future became more twisted and no less cloak-and-dagger. It divided into the pro-Chinese conservatives and pro-Japanese modernisers. The latter advocated ending Korea's vassal status to China, for how could Korea be the equal of any outside power otherwise, and to this end wanted the country to industrialise. Distracted Chinese military forces led to the modernisers attempting a Japanese-supported coup in 1884, similar in reach and domestic bloodiness as the 1882 incident, and as successful. Again, the Japanese legation burnt; again, Japanese nationals were killed.

Perhaps now Japan's ambitions had finally been thwarted, the Chinese could prevail in this ding-dong battle for control. Yet into the power vacuum came the Russians, their empire heading south from Siberia and their envoys busy in Korea laying diplomatic and commercial foundations. The only imperial power to stop them was the British, by blocking a Russian sea-route. The British were less interested in taking the region but determined to check Russia's empire. Korea was saved, except for the obviousness of how little control Korea had over its own destiny.

Korea's diplomatic strategy involved many foreign powers cancelling out each others' aims, but economic forces were undermining this power-balance trick. Taxation for the court's expenditure increased to help sustain the unwieldy bureaucracy, procure foreign arms and establish diplomatic missions in those countries whose cheap goods flooded the country and destroyed the local cottage industries. This trade demanded money, not barter, and farmers became tied into exporting their grain to where most of the imports originated: Japan.

Peasants lost their subsistence living to usury and penury as the state's taxes escalated. Uprisings and banditry grew. Yangban joined forces with peasants and in the southwest the Tonghak resurrected, beginning a serious rebellion in February 1894. Japan ignored Korean claims about dealing with the crisis and, with the Taewongun in tow, sent troops in July 1894, sinking the Chinese fleet on the way to driving the Chinese army from Korea altogether.

The Japanese brought reform. Amongst many points they made the Yangban and commoners equal before the law; abolished slavery; abolished the practice of whole families being punished for the crimes of one member; and standardised the currency.

Russia, France and Germany became concerned about anyone except themselves controlling the region. Their 'Three Powers Intervention' demanded from Japan swingeing concessions in Korea (and further north saw China smashed open for the last time). Not outdone, the pro-Japanese faction in the Korean court launched their own coup against the now pro-Russian Queen Min, killing her and sending the king to hide in the Russian legation for a year, before the coup collapsed and the Japanese found themselves being driven out yet again in early 1895.

In a flamboyant, fanciful assertion of Korean sovereignty, King Kojong then pronounced himself the emperor of Taehan Cheguk, Empire of the Han, with envoys sent out from the nation with its own flag and anthem and now the equal of China and Japan. But Kojong's confidence in his empire was demonstrated by his move into the Kyongun palace with its escape doors into each of the surrounding foreign legations.

A more realistic attempt to galvanise independence for Korea came with So Chaep Il, (also called Philip Jaisohn), a Korean educated in the US who founded the Independence Club, believing that Korea's structure and fate should be decided by Koreans, with a new covenant of civil rights and independence. Students, intellectuals, workers, urban dwellers and government officials of all ranks rallied to the cause. The court aligned with those profiting from the unbalanced trade regime to form the Imperial Association, and following pitched battles with the Independence Club, had the latter outlawed. The only reform was the modernising of the army.

The last gasps of Korea for Koreans were drowned out as the century turned, for Russia, the UK, Japan and others around whipped up a tornado of treaties, diplomatic and military manoeuvres, checking, bluffing, suspecting, and counter-checking each others' imperial plans into east Asia. China's implosion changed it from player to prey. Finally, tiring of the frenetic hoo-ha, Russia and Japan decided all-out war would reach a conclusion of sorts. Japan set troops in Incheon in February 1904 that lead to a Korean-Japanese Protocol, with the Japanese guaranteed real powers. They then launched off to fight Russia and won. The Russians left Korea, and the Japanese were back, minus the Chinese, minus the Russians, in force, in charge, with the papers to prove it. It was conclusive indeed.

Shortly after, Japan and Korea signed a treaty of protection. A Japanese Resident-General was installed in Seoul to direct the country's foreign affairs as an *in situ* extension of the Tokyo Foreign Office, directing Korea for Japan's ends, to 'protect' Korea against further foreign interference. The diplomatic agencies of those other countries that battled to be in Korea were abolished along with 'Korea's' foreign policy. Indeed, to all geopolitical purposes, Korea, having lost its autonomous national entity, no longer existed at all. Reforms, laws, appointment of officials all required the Resident-General's approval. The king was forced to abdicate; the army was disbanded; the administration of justice and prisons came unto Japanese hands, as did the police. Ownership of the land, particularly by the peasants, was difficult to prove to the Japanese authorities taking it over en masse, and resistance was met with execution.

Resistance groups, poorly armed and poorly led, sprung up across the country, carrying out guerrilla attacks on Japanese positions, but the guerrillas' dispersal and the randomness of their attacks achieved nothing but the accelerated drafting in of more Japanese forces of repression. There were, though, thousands of recorded disturbances by individuals and crowds demanding independence. Two of the most spectacular included two Koreans assassinating the Resident-General Ito Hirobumi at Harbin railway station in October 1909, and in December, the pro-Japanese Prime Minister Ri Wanyong was stabbed. But these only served to convince the Japanese that total domination was necessary. In August 1910 the protectorate was formalised in a treaty of annexation, with the Korean government dissolved two months later, all political organisations banned, and all foreign intervention finished. Korea was gone.

Korea under the Japanese

The Japanese were the masters of the region. They'd taken Manchuria, flattened the Chinese, ousted the Russians from the region in presence and power, and booted all Western interests from Korea, with the exception of Christian churches and hospitals. Korea was to be Japanese by all measures, so they banned Korean-language newspapers and any 'large' meetings of Koreans.

The Resident-General was replaced by a Governor-General, a retired Japanese admiral or general appointed by the emperor, to whom the Governor-General answered and no-one else. With this autonomy the Governor-General could appoint the provincial governors, senior judicial members and high civil-service positions, ostensibly to be shared between Koreans and Japanese. But in practice all those jobs with any seniority went to the Japanese. Grass-roots control came through the ever-increasing police force that had numerous summary powers from flogging and fining to imprisonment. The fact that educators and non-military officials wore Japanese-style uniforms and swords proved beyond doubt the nature of Japan's rule.

Now that the Koreans and their culture mattered little beyond how they could best serve Japan, the colonisers set about reforming the country's economy. From 1912, a comprehensive land registration programme was carried out over six years, establishing nationwide the rights (and restrictions) of the nation's farmers. Many Yangban peasants lost their pre-existent claims, were ruined or made de facto registered tenant farmers on enlarged estates that were therefore taxable by the authorities, and regularly were.

Japan's own industrialisation needed increased Korean rice production to allow its cities to swell with factory workers (Japan suffered rice riots in 1918). Investment from the landlords and Japan's ministries poured into agriculture to increase rice output, and rice exports to Japan indeed went up significantly. However, the exports outweighed actual production gains, and the Koreans were forced to import millet.

Investment went into new planting techniques, irrigation and crop varieties but mainly into the use of chemical fertilisers, the production of which underpinned Korea's own industrialisation. Chemical plants for fertilisers were powered by Japanese-built hydroelectric systems. Mining was another industry that benefited from Japanese investment, producing the raw ores for Japan's manufacturing industries and steel mills, and manufacturing plants came on stream, connected by a vast road and rail network. Most of the industrial growth, operated by the cheap labour of former farmers, was concentrated in the peninsula's north as the south held more and better quality farming land.

In 1931, a bomb of unknown origin blew up the Japanese railway near China's Shenyang in the 'Manchurian Incident' (otherwise known as the 'Mukden Incident' as Shenyang had been renamed by Japan), that pre-texted the Japanese military occupation of southern Manchuria. Hence Japan's political economy was galvanised from the pit of the global depression for more vigorous imperial adventures in China and the Pacific. Investment poured into Korea. Chemicals and food-processing became the major industries, accounting for over half of the Yen value of Korea's output, with their own spin-offs in affiliated industries. Iron and steel output increased dramatically, as did ceramics and light-industries, like machine tools. The peninsula was being built as a great staging-post for Japan's Asian empire, and road and rail links were built to the Korean coast closest to Japan and out into the Asian mainland. Well designed, well-plumbed cities housed Korea's burgeoning industrial workforce, some of whose children received schooling in the practical disciplines of maths, basic sciences and engineering.

But the best schools were for the children of the Japanese plant owners, managers and the imperial administrators who inhabited the best-built parts of town. Proportionally, three times as many Japanese as Korean children and youth went to school (and with no higher education for the latter). Korean students were taught a history that emphasised how Korea and Japan were historically joined at the hip. Anyway, all schooling was in Japanese, as was usually the press; colonial attitudes to Korean newspapers never quite reached tolerance.

In February 1936, those in the Tokyo government advocating a more moderate foreign policy were literally cut down and killed by fanatical army officers. By early 1937, it wasn't enough for Koreans to serve in Japan's war factories (although by 1945 two million Korean men were working in mainland Japan); they were to be needed for the front-lines too. Korean women were rounded up and forced into work for the Japanese armed forces as 'comfort women', an outrageously effete euphemism for enslaved prostitution. The population was imbued with Japanese culture under the 'Transformation into Imperial Subjects' policy, from swearing the oath of loyalty to Japan's emperor to saluting the flag. Korean names were replaced with Japanese ones. Shinto shrines and ceremonies were brought to all Korean communities and families. Korea was the front-line state for Japan's imperial plans, not just a route into the Asian mainland but a supplier of food, workers, war materials, and (subservient) spiritual brethren.

Resistance and war

Soon after the Western powers' eviction from the region as the century had turned, they were diverted away from Korea's annexation by their upcoming (First) World War. Hundreds of thousands of Koreans took flight into Russia, America, and China. But those that stayed hadn't trusted those fickle foreigners anyway, and the idea of a Korean nation, itself only realised through contact with the outside world, wasn't to be buried by any colonialists.

In the 1910s, the Japanese authorities so keenly sensed any whiff of rebellion that many Koreans were imprisoned, tortured and killed on suspicion of crimes they hadn't even considered. Incidents were just that, isolated expression of malcontent while no coherent resistance formed, although Japan's land and administrative reforms dispossessed, displaced and ruined Koreans from every social strata.

All the Koreans needed was a rallying call, which came in early 1919. Intellectuals, Yangban, professionals and students joined together in signing a 'Declaration of Independence'. They were hoping to catch the eye of the Western powers emerging from war and use US President Woodrow Wilson's spirit of independence, but the Korean delegation to Versailles was ignored. Still the declaration was proclaimed in Seoul on March 1, two days before the funeral of former King Kojong. Japanese police arrested the leaders, but a crowd gathered, grew restless and shouted Manse! (10,000 years, so Long Live Korea!). They were fired upon by military police, the army and the navy, but Korean turnout reached the thousands. Two months of demonstrations followed and a million people joined the Samil or 'March 1 Movement' on the streets, demanding independence, wrecking colonial buildings and fighting the army hand-to-hand.

The international attention this gained focussed less on Korea's independence movement and more on the savagery used in suppressing it, and the only concessions were a few Korean-language newspapers and limited opportunities in education.

Nevertheless, March 1 had demonstrated the huge, latent sense of Korean nationalism, there to be tapped. The anti-Japanese guerrillas, beaten into the Manchurian hinterland (where future leader Kim Il Sung's forebears had fled to), were invigorated in their struggle. In Shanghai, a self-declared Provisional government was set up by Syngman Rhee, a Korean imprisoned by the Japanese before escaping to study in the US. Shanghai was also home to a Korean Communist Party, set up in opposition to the Provisional Government-in-exile, but it was not the only political party to take that name. Socialist societies were founded in Seoul and Tokyo, and in 1925 the Korean Communist Party was founded in Korea, using the anniversary of Emperor Sunjong's death to attempt another 'March 1-style' movement. Russia was by then a fully fledged communist empire, the Soviet Union, and would later be central to Korea's development and division.

For now, however, the Sunjong rally illustrates that Korean political resistance, full of vigour, was confused. Factions across the political spectrum reached for any symbol of Korean nationalism. The Japanese were, in contrast, eerily singular in their purpose of suppressing insurrection. However, despite mass arrests, imprisonment (with some leaders emerging from prison only in 1945) torture and executions, resistance movements regrouped, reformed, and reorganised. In the 1920s, farm and factory disputes and strikes racked up from dozens to hundreds and thousands. Wonsan and Seoul went on general strike in 1929 and 1930 respectively, and that year 54,000 Korean high-school students were involved in disturbances across Korea.

Resistance groups were already operating from Manchuria, and following Japan's annexing of the area in 1931, Chinese and Korean guerrillas cooperated in carrying out merciless attacks on Japanese troops. By the mid-'30s, three anti-Japanese armies were operating in the Manchurian area, called the North Eastern Anti-Japanese United Army (NEAJUA) that had Chinese and Soviet support. Many partisans fled into the Soviet Union and there they were armed, trained and filled with political thought. Japanese forces were harried, pinned down and cut up in the region's cold, harsh terrain, and it was from this frozen hell that a future leader, Kim Il Sung, would be forged. Although later DPRK historians would shroud his early years in myth, what's not in doubt is that this charismatic young leader (born in 1912) wreaked enough havoc to warrant the Japanese assigning a crack unit to track him down.

Japan's imperial plans led to full-scale war with China in 1937 and the US in 1941. Imperial overstretch required Koreans to take the higher jobs they'd always been denied, and enter the Japanese army. All this achieved was to create a stock of Koreans that would later be branded collaborators and compound post-war misery.

By late 1945, Japan was on the brink of defeat. As he had promised the Americans months earlier, Soviet Premier Josef Stalin prepared to launch war against the collapsing Japanese forces in East Asia. To hasten Japan's surrender and draw an awesome close to the East Asian war, US President Truman dropped two atom bombs on Japan, days before the Soviets were due to attack. The Soviets carried on, routing and taking prisoner Japanese forces in the east and landing their own forces in northern Korea.

The US proposed a joint occupation to 'share the burden' of rebuilding the country, dividing the country into North and South by the latitude line of 38°

across Korea's midriff. The Soviets agreed, and in early September US forces arrived at Incheon to take their zone of control.

The Soviets wanted a friendly communist nation on their borders, and the Americans wanted anything but another communist nation slap next to their new Asian base, Japan. With the two worlds of communism and capitalism about to collide on a global scale in the Cold War, the Americans and Soviets set about looking for suitable leaders in their halves of the country. Neither side paid much attention to the wishes of the Koreans, and with French and British agreement, the Soviets and US agreed a five-year trusteeship of Korea in which time they would instigate elections for one national government.

Although they disagreed on many things, none of Korea's indigenous political groups took well to the trusteeship, but the trustees considered them too incoherent and politically immature to run the country, as in fact it had been run by the Japanese for the last 35 years. There was already a government-in-waiting in Korea, the Korean People's Republic (KPR), formed by political leader and former political prisoner You Un-hyong and presided over by Syngman Rhee, president of the self-proclaimed Korean government-in-exile. But US forces' commander General Hodge regarded the KPR as crypto-communists, mainly for its popular policy of land reform, and, governing the South with remnants of the Japanese colonials' assistance, set about closing down all 'communist' activities. In the South, left-wing groups, labour unions and advocates of land reform were banned and imprisoned, and communist newspapers closed. Korean Communist Party leader Pak Hon-yong fled north. In the north, the Soviets had reluctantly cobbled together a coalition of communists, nationalists and Christians as well as considering the KPR, but their trusteeship would be pointless without installing a good communist in charge. In that they already had the youthful but toughened officer Colonel Kim Il Sung, freshly arrived in October 1945.

Kim Il Sung and the Korean Workers' Party

Only 34 years old, Kim had spent most of his life outside Korea, with years in Stalin's Soviet Union, leading his own reconnaissance brigade into Manchuria for the Red Army. Tough, straight-talking and respected by his Soviet supporters, he had a loyal core of fellow guerrilla-fighters. His military background and impressive record of nationalist resistance was key to his ability to organise and get the forming People's Army on side. He was placed to lead the provisional government of the communist party set up in 1946. In August 1946, the communists merged with their political opponents, the more social-democrat New People's Party, a group led by Koreans formerly based with the Chinese communists in Yanan during the war years and which appealed to the educated middle-class. The merged party was the North Korea Workers Party, thus a politically broad church with mass appeal. Cadres toured the country, appealing to the peasants to join the Party and break their bonds with their suppressive landlords in the new Korea. A rural groundswell signed up for the Party that swiftly dominated all politics, and they were rewarded with a revolutionary land reform that dispossessed landlords and distributed the land among the peasants, while the Japanese-owned industries were nationalised as a Soviet-style two-year economic plan for industry was put in train. To be sure, soon enough, the Christian and nationalist politicians would be made redundant, if not arrested. Meantime, the Yanan faction were more useful than obstructive to the functioning of government.

In the South, Syngman Rhee, now in Seoul, survived the KPR's demise and agreed to the trusteeship if the Americans helped crack down on any political protest against Rhee, which, being usually from left-wingers, the US command did so approvingly. With US provision of financial incentives for Rhee's supporters, and some local military arm-twisting for Rhee's detractors, Rhee became South Korea's dominant political leader. Not dissimilar tactics allowed the Soviets to establish Kim Il Sung as the key political leader and he set up a military-based administration in Pyongyang.

By 1947, either side of the parallel had its own government, with Kim Il Sung's communist, Soviet-backed regime in Pyongyang and Rhee's right-wing, US-supported regime in Seoul. These provisional governments were necessarily authoritarian to quell sporadically violent unrest and factional fighting, and get the economy going again. But Korea's unification was a fading vision. Nationalist efforts to negotiate a unification treaty floundered because the two domestic governments' temporary set-up gave them questionable political and legal power. Their leaders were getting along as badly as their Soviet and American supporters, without whose backing no meaningful deal was possible.

Realising its increasingly heated relationship with the Soviets was obstructing unification, and that the Soviets were too stubborn to agree on anything, the US decided that a unitary government should be decided by the Koreans themselves. In late 1947, the US requested the United Nations to organise a general election for all Korea. The Soviets suspected foul play, justifiably as both powers had helped ban, incarcerate and assassinate (including Yo Un Hyong) the more radical opponents to their favoured leaders. Fearing their man Kim Il Sung wouldn't win, the Soviets refused elections for their half, but elections in the South were held in May 1948. This election established, under President Syngman Rhee, the Republic of Korea (ROK), recognised as Korea's legitimate government by the Western powers. The Soviets then organised their own northern election in August, delivering Kim Il Sung as president of the new Democratic People's Republic of Korea (DPRK) which was recognised as Korea's legitimate government by the Soviets and their communist allies.

Korea had stable governance, if under two groups and not one. Resistance now to Rhee's government continued but was pushed underground and into the hinterlands. The farms and factories were producing, although the idiocies of a divided economy were immediately manifest, with most of the factories and power in the north and the farms in the south. The North-South border was closed and there were regular, large skirmishes across it by opposing militia. But the situation was stable enough for US forces to withdraw in June 1949, leaving a few military advisors and promises of military aid. The Soviets departed the North, leaving weapons and weapons' factories for the North's 'defence'.

Independent at last, Rhee and Kim immediately began to whip up their halves about the urgent need for unification, and persuading their populace that only military force could achieve this. Barely five years after Japan's hated rule had collapsed, Korea was heading to war with itself. Pre-empting Rhee's plans for unification, Kim Il Sung and Pak Hon Yong visited Stalin in April 1950, assuring him that they had enough supporters in the South to ensure a swift, decisive victory. On June 25 1950, 70,000 North Korean troops smashed southwards across the 38th parallel. The Korean War had begun.

Korean War

Northern forces hammered southwards with the lightly armed, poorly trained southern forces retreating in such panic they destroyed bridges that their own troops couldn't retreat across. Within a week, the North had taken Seoul, but as swiftly, the US and United Nations had voted to intervene on the South side. Fifteen countries' forces were combined into one UN command under US General Douglas MacArthur. The decisive move came in early September, as the DPRK army compressed the South around Pusan, a US Marine division landed at Incheon and cut the DPRK supply and reinforcement routes. The UN force heartily battered the DPRK army back over the 38th parallel, then pressed on to unite Korea under UN auspices. However, China's newly established communist government grew very wary that, besides their North Korean brothers losing, Korea under the Americans could only serve to harass communist China. China's premier and foreign minister Zhou Enlai threatened direct military intervention if American forces crossed the parallel and didn't leave the liberation to southern troops. Nonetheless, MacArthur was eager to finish the job, and by October's end, UN forces had reached the Yalu, taking Pyongyang by land and Wonsan by sea and pounding every city from the air. The Chinese, as they'd threatened, counter-attacked in late November with hundreds of thousands of troops. The UN Command was unprepared for the attack and the evil winter weather, and within two months they had been pushed 30 miles south of Seoul. There they dug in, and the Chinese suffered their own staggering losses in April and May. Herein the war ground into stalemate as both sides toed and froed around the 38th parallel.

Armistice talks were proposed in June 1951, to which the UN commander General Ridgeway (who replaced the too-hawkish MacArthur) agreed. Two years of negotiations followed while scores died in futile battles every day. Along the way, US President Eisenhower, elected on a promise to end the war, threatened the DPRK with atomic attack.

On 27th July 1953, the US, China and the DPRK signed an armistice at the small village of Panmun'jom, south of Kaesong, ending the fighting but not the war: peace has never been officially declared. The cost of the war has been estimated at around three million Korean civilians and 700,000 soldiers, a million Chinese troops, 54,000 American soldiers and 3,200 from the other allied countries. Many of the northern civilians were killed in air-raids, in which a greater tonnage of bombs were dropped on Korea's cities by the US air force than either Nazi Germany or Imperial Japan ever received. And as for a unified Korea...

The reign of Kim Il Sung to today's DPRK
The DPRK domestic set-up

The war hadn't achieved a unified Korea, nor dislodged or de-stabilised either government. So now we will look at the set up of the DPRK government and its development.

Notwithstanding minor constitutional changes, the balance of power (at least in theory) rests between three main branches of government: the State, the Party (Korean Workers' Party, KWP), and the Military. All are made up of various agencies and committees with varying levels of interdependence and autonomy. Each branch of government has its own agencies and supporting bureaucracy, and also ownership and control of different elements of the economy.

From the DPRK's founding, the top state post was that of premier, a post that with a cabinet known as the Administration Council ran the country through numerous ministries. Kim Il Sung held that job until 1972 when the more senior post of president was created. The president and the council are elected by the Supreme People's Assembly, that consists of 674 representatives, voted in by popular election every five years. This body appoints the judiciary, passes laws and calculates the annual budget.

The KWP is not the only political party. There's also the Tonghak-derived Chondoist Chongu Party and the Korean Social Democratic Party, concerned with peace, reunification and the imposition of a social democracy for one Korea. In practice, the assembly is dominated by KWP representatives and the assembly ratifies policies already decided by the KWP leadership. The top KWP leadership post is the General Secretary, who works with a small advisory group known as the Politburo, and both consult with the Central Committee, a several-hundred-member group that discusses state and ideological policy. The General Secretary, Politburo and Central Committee run the party between party congresses that until the '80s used to happen (very) approximately every four years. Congress involves a few hundred party officials from across the country debating policies put to it by the leadership. Congress elects the Central Committee and Politburo. A Central People's Committee was created in 1972 that would supersede the Politburo, but isn't considered much more than symbolic.

The final branch of power is the military, the Korean People's Army (KPA), whose top posts are Supreme Commander and the Chairman of the National Defence Commission, ultimately commanding millions in service and industry.

As said above, each branch has its own sector of the economy under its governance. What these sectors produce, the people they employ in what conditions, income generated and to what end the goods and income are put, all have a bearing on the relative balance of power of the three power branches. Nor is any one branch totally independent of the other. If the KWP dominate the agencies of the state, then the KWP is *de facto* the state, then the General Secretary of the KWP wields great power. The army, however, has a firm monopoly on employing the nation's fit young men who themselves have a firm interest in joining up and working in the army's own economy sectors and networks. Commanding the army is critical, and when the Korean People's Army (KPA) was founded in early 1948, its leader Choe Yng-gn and its tens of thousands of troops were the hardy stock of guerrilla-fighters in Manchuria; Kim Il Sung's kind of people, and he was their kind of leader.

The different branches of government indeed have their own newspapers. While the subject matter may obviously differ, the unquestioning support and veneration of the Kims does not. Dissenters are noted and their opinions discounted; if they persist, they're publicly named, denounced, and demoted (they used to disappear). This is largely the result of the extremely personalised rule of the country that Kim Il Sung inculcated from the immediate post-Korean War period, for the top posts mentioned would soon all be staffed by one man: Kim Il Sung.

Kim takes charge

Before the Korean War was over, Kim Il Sung took action to consolidate his position as leader. Across every echelon of the DPRK government were Koreans with a variety of backgrounds in terms of class, education, and their roots in the country with life-long ties of friends and family. Aside from these loyalties, their individual political opinions, and the factions thus created, were influenced by where they had served their political apprenticeships during the anti-Japanese war, as in the Soviet Union, China, in Korean guerrilla activities or from outside Asia altogether. Kim was not one to wait for any disagreements with his policies to snowball into opposition and challenge to his leadership. Purges of the KWP began in 1952 when he indicated that some cadres were infected with sloth and other vices. He upped the ante in his expurgation of potential opponents and, by the end of 1955, a dozen senior figures had been imprisoned or executed on charges of spying for the US, including the former Korean Communist Party leader, Pak Hon Yong.

Thus emboldened, Kim set out his own vision for Korea, to set up the country's political-economy along the same lines as Stalin had done in the Soviet Union from the 1930s and '40s where Kim Il Sung had been trained and based for years. Kim Il Sung committed the DPRK's economic growth to heavy industry, a very centralised form of governmental control and unquestioned, highly personalised leadership, which has drawn many parallels with Stalinism. But simply transposing the 1930s' Soviet model on to Korea wouldn't take into account Korea's unique circumstances and history, certainly not for Kim. His Juche philosophy, Marxism infused with Korean nationalism, was soon to become the governing philosophy of the DPRK.

Kim consolidates

However, the Soviet Union's Premier Nikita Khruschev denounced all things Stalin in 1956, and a few Soviet-Koreans in the KWP criticised the leadership

JUCHE

Juche is a Korean word of two syllables, *Ju* meaning 'master' and *Che* meaning 'oneself', so literally translated it means 'Master of one's self'. Although the term first became widely used in 1955, most DPRK histories trace its origin back to June 1930 when the young Kim Il Sung outlined a new path for the Korean revolution at meeting of revolutionaries in Kalun. Kim Il Sung's father Kim Hyong Jik, when president of the Korean National Association, advocated the idea of Chiwon – 'Aim High' – to achieve Korean independence. This idea and the tenets of Marxism were important sources for Juche ideas. Juche (ju-chay) also known as Kimilsungism, is the socio-political philosophy developed by Kim Il Sung and expounded upon by Kim Jong Il that is the governing philosophy of the DPRK, as stipulated in Article 3 of the 1998 DPRK Constitution, towards realising the ultimate socialist state. Juche is celebrated by its followers for its 'scientific' answers to questions of man's destiny and, as the plaques at the base of Pyongyang's Juche Tower show, Juche has (small) followings worldwide. This is a brief outline of the Juche idea and what it means for the country and its people.

Juche states that man is the master of everything, and decides everything. Man is distinguished from the other countless physical and organic entities surrounding him by possessing the three attributes of creativity, consciousness and Chajusong, which means 'independence' in a broad and more profound sense. Chajusong is man's innate will to live, to develop independently, and master his own destiny and world.

Chajusong involves man overcoming and subordinating the will of nature to his own ends. Man adapts the environment to suit him, distinguishing man from other organisms like plants and animals that adapt themselves to their environment.

Animals can mould the environment for themselves, but their endeavours are purely instinctive, whereas man has developed and learnt (eg: building shelters, developing from caves to mud-huts to brick houses to tower-blocks) and is improved by his creativity. Man's consciousness allows him to observe and understand the properties of his environment and manipulate it thus.

Chajusong and creativity are related as recreating the world can only be done in order to master it, and consciousness realises that Chajusong requires creativity to achieve mastery, recognising Chajusong's needs and directing man's energies into moulding his surroundings accordingly. Therefore, all subjugation is to be resisted, and Juche strongly denounces dogmatism and flunkeyism.

There's also man's social and political life, critical because the three attributes are only realisable in social contexts, through linear education and thought development. Man can only progress beyond his instincts through education, discussion and practice to realise his Chajusong, consciousness and creativity.

There's no plan to the universe. The existent physical, spontaneous relationships between physical entities are due to their particular properties that have fallen into being. Man is the only pro-active transformer of the world. In the Juche world, nothing has value beyond its potential use or harm to man. In capitalism, value and worth are given monetary form, and greed prevents serious scientific advancements from benefiting society (consumer durables do not endure but are designed to break). This value system is also subjective and therefore unscientific and irrational and no way to run a society. Juche insists it must be in the interests of the individual to be engaged, but engagement comes through exciting and channelling his energies towards societal ends. Machines and materials can never be valued over man, for they are useless without men and exist only to serve him and society.

Marxism espouses that socio-historical progress comes from developments in the production of material wealth. Transformations in social-history have come about through changes in the productive forces, production relations and production of material wealth.

Juche argues that history is the process of the masses enhancing their position and role to realise Chajusong. The masses struggle for Chajusong; when society's structure denies or constrains Chajusong, then society is changed. In international diplomacy, Juche demands each nation stand its own ground and defend its collective Chajusong. The DPRK put this into practice by maintaining a steadfast independence and neutrality during the difficult years of the Sino-Soviet split. The DPRK refused to join COMECON (the Soviet bloc economic union). In the mid 1970s the DPRK became a member of the Non-Aligned Movement and established good relations with many Third World countries. In recent years the DPRK has stood up to pressure from the US. Their life and soul is independence, and they must act as sovereign nations, pursuing paths to further their independence without buckling to outside interference or pressures. This means also that a nation's true Chajusong can only be achieved through economic self-sufficiency, for any reliance on others shifts power into their hands. Similarly, to prevent the wrong class from controlling and abusing the power of the state, the masses must seize control of the state and its economic means of production. Society's structure is underpinned by its forms of economic production, so seizing them is the first means to change society into more advanced states as the masses need. History is a series of struggles, from primitive society through feudalism to industrialisation, involving the struggle to subdue nature, wherein the creative processes are fostered, practised and developed.

To realise Chajusong the masses must be brought up to be the masters of society, and be free of all exploitation and oppression. Old ideas die hard while imperialists continue to infiltrate and spread reactionary ideas, so

continued overleaf

JUCHE *continued*

even the liberated need remoulding. Ideological remoulding eliminates old ideas incompatible with man's Chajusong and equips him with the progressive ideas needed for independence and creativity, but it's hard work. People need to be remoulded like nature.

In 1975 the line of the Three Revolutions was put forward – the ideological revolution, technical revolution and cultural revolution. Basically the ideological revolution was to be complemented by the technical revolution to free people from the shackles of outdated technology and liberate people from backbreaking work. The cultural revolution would bring everyone up to the standard of an intellectual. Progressive ideas mean a high level of scientific and technical knowledge, with a strong physique. Thought determines men's worth and quality. Knowledge doesn't mean respectability, because much knowledge and bad ideology is disastrous. Only sound ideology, via good ideological remoulding, can direct knowledge to society's benefit.

Juche has the interests of the masses at its centre, so the masses must learn Juche. Study requires organisation, which the masses must accept to be successfully imbued with the philosophy of revolutionary struggle. Revolution means the struggle of the masses to defend their Chajusong, their life and soul.

for the direction in which they were taking the country. Beating his detractors with the stick of nationalism, by late 1956 most of the Soviet-Koreans and the Yanan Koreans from the former New People's Party had been purged from the KWP for their 'foreign influences'. Up through the ranks of the party and the state bodies, Kim promoted his anti-Japanese guerrillas, rough, tough, hardy folk, of common stock and educated as such, promoted more for their ties to Kim than for their technical or political talents. Meanwhile, Party membership was growing into millions across the country, taking in a groundswell of farmers and peasants, the people whose origins paralleled those of Kim's senior appointees in the Party and agencies of government. By the end of 1958, through purges and promotions, Kim's grip on the KWP was iron-tight. Over the next decade he consolidated his personalised rule through fewer party congresses, more purges and a developing personality cult with a heavy military flavour (see *Cult of the Kims*, pages 34–5).

Foreign policy

It's a misnomer to write of the two Korean regimes' relations to each other as 'foreign relations'. The DPRK and ROK have always been the two halves of the Korean whole, yet undeniably their want and efforts for reunification have dominated their political environments. However, as both regimes and their backers only recognised themselves as Korea's legitimate government, reunification only ever looked possible through one regime removing the other, and, as no formal peace was ever declared, the peninsula has spent the

For successful revolutionary tasks, political work must be aimed at educating and rousing the people into action. Creative and revolutionary zeal should be prioritised over all other work, whatever it is. People cannot simply be ordered towards a particular goal; they must have their hearts set to it first, whereupon no challenge is too great. Political work entails persuasion and education, but this must be pitched to cater to the workers' different backgrounds, trades, ages, etc. One persuader per ten workers is a good ratio for instilling revolutionary fervour.

More than anything, harnessing this zeal needs good leadership by the leader and the party. The leader is the brain to the body of the masses and is the supreme representative and embodiment of their interests; his acts represent their will. He leads them to victory and so devotion to the leader is the highest expression of revolutionary zeal.

With many thanks to Dermot Boyd-Hudson for his help here. The above is sourced from *The Immortal Juche Idea* by Kim Chang Ha, Pyongang Foreign Languages Publishing House, Pyongyang Korea, 1984. For further information visit Juche Idea Study Group of England, web: www.language-museum.com/jisge/, or Study of the Juche Idea, web: www.cnet-ta.ne.jp/juche/defaulte.htm.

years since 1953 on a war-footing. Tensions between the three sides (for the US has long had a permanent, well-armed, military force in the ROK) oscillate to this day, and the last half-century of relations have been a cycle of negotiations and brinksmanship interspersed by bizarre feats of violence.

For the DPRK, the creator and perpetuator of Korea's division have always been the United States and its puppet ROK government. For the United States and ROK, peaceful reunification has been impossible with an uncompromising communist regime. To the West, the DPRK has been a warmongering pariah as a Soviet puppet or, worse, on its own initiative. If the DPRK regime was determined to be free of all outside pressures or coercion, as Juche aspired, then the country would be assisted into isolationism by throttling US economic sanctions. The continuity of the situation partly stems from the vehemence of Washington's anti-communist policy, and on the DPRK side from the longevity of the Kim dynasty. The issues over which the DPRK and ROK have disagreed have remained the same, with some fluctuations in relations through the changing regimes in the south (the ROK has been the democracy it is today since 1989).

The DPRK and ROK made stuttering attempts at reconciliation almost immediately after the armistice. At the 1954 Geneva Conference, Kim Il Sung proposed an all-Korean commission to discuss reunification without any foreign interference or forces on the peninsula. A confederation of the two Koreas would be empowered to oversee their own foreign and defence policies, but that died a death. Tentative moves for rapprochement were made

THE CULT OF THE KIMS

Everywhere, everywhere, everywhere in the DPRK there are images of the 'Great Leader' Kim Il Sung and his son the 'Dear Leader' Kim Jong Il. The leaders' portraits hang side-by-side high on the walls of the largest public halls to the commonest private rooms, and are cleaned with dustcloths assigned only to that task. Their faces peer out from the paintings and mosaics emblazoning buildings, walls, junctions, and the badges on people's lapels. Bronze statues of the Great and Dear Leaders front buildings, top hills, dominate town squares across the country, and the leaders' philosophical treatises and teachings, carved in stone, flank public squares and highways or are enscribed on to Korea's holiest mountains and boulders.

During his leadership, Kim Il Sung managed to visit nearly every city, town, village and farm, factory, military base, construction site, port, nursery and hospital, dispensing 'on-the-spot guidance', every occasion being marked on a map in Pyongyang's Korean Revolution Museum. His every word was noted and filmed by accompanying officials and journalists, to be looped in print and film. His birthplace at Mangyongdae is a shrine, visited daily by throngs of pilgrims. All that he touched or commented on has become hallowed grounds: the seat he took on the metro; a tree he remarked upon in Wonsan; rooms he visited in rural schools have plaques detailing the time, day, comment and the same is happening for Kim Jong Il.

Buildings are named by the date that the leaders visited them, or have meaning built into their grouting. The number of stone slabs on Pyongyang's Juche Tower, built for Kim Il Sung's 70th birthday, equals the days that he had been alive. The lowly cabin where Kim Jong Il was reportedly born in 1942 is exactly 216 metres from a mountain behind it, a distance that miraculously mirrors Kim Jong Il's birthdate of 2/16, a day marked by a double rainbow and a bright star in the sky, and the news spread fast (born in a lowly building, mid-winter, bright star, the news spread far and wide ...are all Messiahs born this way?).

DPRK history is not completely soaked in such colourful myths (although the mythologising of Kim's forebears has seen his great-grandfather accredited with the sinking of the *General Sherman*), but every subject taught from nursery to university is infused with the wisdom of the Kims and Juche. Departments at Kim Il Sung university are devoted to studying

by the DPRK in 1960 following the removal of Rhee from office, but Seoul's new military regime would have none of it.

Kim was not disconsolate by this rebuff, however. Socialism was working. By 1960, the DPRK GNP was US$140 per capita, hammering the US$100 of the ROK, an impressive recovery that was partly explicable by Soviet and Chinese aid. The DPRK jostled between the two powers for aid, playing one off against the other and thereby being the pawn of neither, but Khruschev's favouring of coexistence with the capitalist West was unacceptable to Kim who considered their writings that cover everything from economics to art to opera. Films and plays exist to propagate the greatness of DPRK socialism and its ultimate victory over imperialism, and the Kims' role in this.

Kim Il Sung has affected time itself. His birthday is a national holiday and the DPRK's years are counted since Kim Il Sung's year of birth. And he's still in charge. In 1998, four years after his death, Kim Il Sung was made 'Eternal President' of the DPRK by the Supreme People's Assembly.

As Kim Il Sung's rule became sharply more personalised and authoritarian from the 1950s, so his deification commenced, and his leadership was based on an expanding personality cult derived from Stalinism, with himself commanding a mass party and centralised command economy. He was feted as a military hero, a philosopher, a father of the nation figure, a genius who intervened in the most personal way with on-the-spot guidance, whose comments were canonised and whose critics disappeared. Many if not most people would have seen him in the flesh at some time in their lives, as he spent more time touring the country than in the capital in the fifty tumultuous, traumatic and spectacular years in which he dominated the country's public life. From the late 1960s, the monumentalism of his character was being matched in massive architectural works, and from thereon, the DPRK's history was his story.

From then on his son Kim Jong Il was promoted in government and print as the only man with the cojones to succeed his father. In a drawn out succession, Kim Jong Il took over the significant post of General Secretary in July 1997, after three years of official mourning for Kim Il Sung had elapsed. In 1998, Kim Jong Il became Chairman of the National Defence Commission, *de facto* president – but the latter title went to Kim Il Sung, herein the 'Eternal President'.

Transferring power from father to son reflects Korea's history of dynastical rule, and the country's authoritarianism has parallels with Korea's preceding Confucian-based regimes, based on deference without question from subordinates to superiors. That Kim Il Sung is still venerated and worshipped as the country's 'Eternal President' is a modern extension of ancient ancestral worship, something that continues at all societal levels in today's ROK, and as alluded to above, the cult has distinct Christian tinges (why else would Billy Graham and Kim Il Sung get along so famously?).

coexistence tantamount to defeat. Deteriorating Sino-Soviet relations in the 1960s led the DPRK to back China at the cost of its Soviet aid but Kim was worried that the two would fall out to the detriment of their shared beliefs. He was scathing about China's evident failures to publicly lambaste America's engagement in Vietnam. However, China's Communist Party was lurching into extremes, soon to culminate in the Cultural Revolution, and returned fire that Kim was too pro-Soviet. Sino-DPRK relations soured, just as a spate of violent incidents marked US, ROK and DPRK relations in the late 1960s. In January

BLUE HOUSE RAID

On January 21 1968, a DPRK special-forces unit of 31 men set off with a mission to assassinate ROK President Park Chung Hee. Issued with ROK uniforms, the men crossed through the DMZ undetected, their ultimate target being Hee's Blue House residence in Seoul. A lone woodcutter reportedly discovered the men encamped and somehow rumbled their plan, but was allowed to live to alert the ROK security forces. The unit was stopped not far from Park's house by ROK troops, and in the ensuing gun-fight, 28 of the raiders were killed. Only one raider was caught and under interrogation confessed that the unit were to also attack the US embassy. The other two commandos were never caught.

1968, a team of DPRK commandos were caught and killed on a raid on the ROK president's house. Two days later, an American spy-ship, the USS *Pueblo*, was captured by the DPRK navy and the crew held captive for a year. All 31 crew-members of an American EC-121 spy-plane were killed when it was shot down by a DPRK MiG fighter in April 1969, and in August a US helicopter was downed as it strayed across the DMZ into the DPRK.

In the early 1970s, thawing Sino-US relations and reduced US forces in the ROK goaded more inter-Korean talks. High-level talks alternated between the two capitals and a crucial joint communiqué was issued in July 1972, which was a milestone for ROK-DPRK relations (another milestone that year was the creation of the post of president of the DPRK, which Prime Minister Kim Il Sung was elevated into). Work towards reunifying the country would be without foreign interference and without force, and with reduced slanging matches (the media attacks on one another had descended from acerbic through vitriol to scraping for insults). A Pyongyang-Seoul hot line was set up, as was a South-North Coordinating Committee (SNCC) for further negotiations and implementing the agreement. But it was a false dawn. The SNCC met only three times. The DPRK stressed that reducing inter-Korean armed confrontation was a prerequisite to all else, demanding in particular that US aid to the ROK must stop. Seoul preferred both Koreas' political systems be recognised, with mutual non-interference and economic cooperation preceding arms reductions.

Pyongyang proposed replacing the armistice with a peace agreement. The ROK side was worried by a reduced US presence and the communist victory in Vietnam. A call from the DPRK for South Koreans to overthrow President Park's government wasn't conducive to successful negotiations. Tensions escalated along the DMZ and the Pyongyang-Seoul hotline was cut. At the beginning of the decade, the Korean People's Army had some 400,000 frontline troops; by the end, this figure had topped a million. Evidently the two sides weren't getting along so well and arming themselves to the teeth was one way to deal with relations.

Previous page A misty Pyongyang morning (NB)

Above Cooling fountains in the centre of Pyongyang (RT)

Right Juche Tower, dominating the Taedong River (NB)

Below Kumsusan Memorial Palace, Kim Il Sung's home
in life and death (NB)

Casting further

Jostling for favour between China and the Soviets, and apparent unending aggravation with the ROK and US, the net for friends and funds was cast further in the early 1970s. From 1972 to 1974, the DPRK government procured large loans of foreign capital from countries like Sweden, France and Japan, machinery and funds to create new export industries that would repay the lenders. To further its nuclear power programme, they joined the International Atomic Energy Association in 1974, and the DPRK was accepted into the Non-Aligned Movement (NAM) in 1975. Kim presupposed that this neutral group of developing nations, not really involved in the machinations of the Cold War, would be a good place to promote his anti-imperialism and a supporting crowd for the DPRK, especially in United Nations negotiations. While Kim was to be held in high regard by the non-aligned movement, it wasn't quite the coherent and cohesive freelance political force he had envisaged. Nor were the capital loans from elsewhere being paid off by its exports, and the Ministry of Finance defaulted on the country's foreign debts, which would cost it dearly later (see *Economy*).

By the end of the '70s, the DPRK leadership was somewhat galled by China's warming relations with America and Japan, but this spurred some further discourse between the two Koreas in 1980, with a plethora of meetings over discursive details between them. Ultimately, the talks went nowhere, however, as General Chun Doo Hwan established military rule in the ROK and was not up for negotiating. In October, Kim Il Sung proposed establishing the Democratic Confederal Republic of Koryo, with both sides equally represented in a national assembly and a confederal committee with charge over national defence, foreign affairs and economic coordination. Coexistence was the key feature; both regimes would continue in lesser forms within the confederacy. Chun rejected the idea, much to the annoyance of Kim, who then allegedly took direct intervention in the ROK political realm by ordering the assassination of Chun's cabinet in Rangoon in October 1983.

THE RANGOON MASSACRE

On October 9, 1983, the ROK's leader President Chun Doo Hwan, while on a state visit to Burma, went to lay a wreath at Rangoon's martyrs memorial. Due to traffic problems, Chun's car was delayed in arrival, and just as he did so a bomb exploded at the memorial, killing 21 people and wounding 46. As well as four Burmese dignitaries, Seventeen ROK government officials, advisers and journalists were killed, including the ROK foreign minister and deputy prime minister. Burmese Police managed to arrest their first suspect two days later, despite the man trying to blow himself up with a hand-grenade. Two more suspects alerted to the police by villagers also tried to commit suicide with grenades, but only one succeeded. The two surviving agents were interrogated into revealing their DPRK origins.

DPRK assistance and relief to the flood-stricken south in 1984 led to discussions on humanitarian and economic cooperation. In 1985, performing arts groups and sports teams were exchanged and separated families briefly re-united for the first time. In the party's higher circles, ideas of minor economic reforms similar to those China were taking were banded about as the economy slowed and the last seven-year plan evidently wasn't delivering. Capitalist enterprise zones were considered and a joint-venture law enacted, but there that train of thought was halted. Kim Il Sung visited the Soviet Union in May 1984 and it appeared that everything was forgiven and forgotten for a new phase of rapprochement and new economic, military and diplomatic links resumed. Immediately, the DPRK's fortunes lifted; yet now the fortunes of the DPRK rested with Soviet success.

Talks with the ROK ground to a halt in late 1985, and were suspended in January 1986. As usual, provocative joint US-ROK military exercises, performed annually since 1978, were blamed, but unusually, the DPRK didn't resume dialogue afterwards. The aftermath of the Rangoon bombing had been weathered and the DPRK hadn't changed its bargaining positions.

The ROK makes friends with the DPRK's friends

Except the international situation was changing. By the late 1980s, the ROK economy was soaring, approaching output levels ten times those of the DPRK. The ROK economy's success and the power this bought attracted both the USSR and China as they dallied towards economic reforms of the capitalist kind, and humanitarian and sports exchanges began between China and the ROK. Indeed, the ROK had been wooing communist nations since 1984, and in 1988, the ROK's newly elected president Roh Tae Woo's outreaches to the north cemented ROK relations with the Soviets and China. The world was presented with the ROK's new glories at the glittering 1988 Seoul Olympics, attended for the first time in 12 years by virtually all communist and capitalist invitees, with which the ROK was star ascendant. The DPRK's offer to co-host the games having long gone by the wayside, they accepted ROK financial aid in return for a promise not to disrupt the games.

The DPRK leadership seethed as its rich brother befriended all its old allies. So, unseen, DPRK diplomats in Beijing made contact with their American counterparts just after the Olympics finished, a prescient move as a year later, the DPRK's greatest allies in eastern Europe evaporated with the Soviet bloc. Soviet trade declined in 1989, and in late 1990, the Soviets announced no more aid, no more barter, just hard currency. The DPRK's world of friends was gone almost overnight, and things looked rapidly bleak.

Japan

One route out could be Japanese investment, but that would need better relations. For many Koreans, north and south, Japan is still the great unforgiven for its colonial rule of Korea. Koreans are still aggrieved that it was the victim, Korea, that was divided and not the aggressor, Japan; something that many Japanese also consider an injustice. Worse, Japan's economic revival stemmed from massive US financial and capital investment poured into the country to make it an operational base for fighting the Korean War. Kim Il Sung was brought up mind and soul in fighting the Japanese. Anti-Japanese resistance was infused into Juche and every history book in the country.

The Japanese government only recognised Seoul as Korea's legitimate governing body, so DPRK-Japan relations were largely through informal channels, including trade links via the association of Koreans in Japan, Chochongnyon, that gained several hundred million dollars of investment over the decades. Japan was to be by the 1980s a major trading partner with the DPRK. Officially, DPRK-Japanese relations were generally poor at best, exacerbated by a spate of kidnappings by DPRK special forces of Japanese citizens in the 1970s and '80s and defaults on large loans. In 1990, a Japanese delegation in Pyongyang, trying to have a fishing-boat crew released from spying charges, were presented with the suggestion by DPRK foreign officials of normalising relations. Haggling would continue for the next decade, but it was a start.

Still, destitution loomed. China's economic reforms were glanced at and a Free Trade Zone was set up in December 1991, but substantial economic reforms were an anathema to Kim and everything five decades of socialism had cost. The late 1980s to '90s were not marked by pro-capitalist radicals arriving in the DPRK government. Indeed, the Politburo and Council were staffed more by ageing anti-Japanese guerrillas: Kim buttressed his beliefs by surrounding himself with his oldest cronies. And it was in the late 1980s that Kim's regime showed its old mettle, over the nuclear issue.

Nukes in Korea

By the late 1980s, the international community (mainly the ROK, US and Japan) became concerned that the DPRK was producing weapons-grade uranium and would soon have the nuclear bomb. The DPRK Foreign Ministry was vague on the issue but cited the many threats made to them with US tactical nuclear weapons on the peninsula. Inspections of the DPRK's nuclear facilities by the IAEA were repeatedly refused. Tensions rose and some US senators advocated bombing DPRK facilities at Yongbyon, north of Pyongyang.

In fact, the DPRK had hankered to join the exclusive club of atomic powers practically since the country's founding, and in 1974 the DPRK joined the International Atomic Energy Agency (IAEA) that gives nuclear know-how for peaceful means. For years it seemed that the DPRK's intentions were peaceful enough, which were borne out in 1985 when the DPRK signed the Non-Proliferation Treaty of Nuclear Weapons. Only by 1990 was it obvious that DPRK's nuclear electricity reactors weren't really big enough for serious electricity production but could deliver lots of plutonium and enriched uranium: bomb material. However, Pyongyang did agree to talks at the prime-ministerial level with the ROK, and following rounds of bi-capital talks, in September 1991 the five permanent members of the UN Security Council approved both Koreas' membership of the UN. The following month, US President Bush announced the withdrawal of US tactical nuclear weapons from the peninsula, heralding a breakthrough in inter-Korean relations. In December, both Koreas signed the Agreement on Reconciliation, Non-aggression, Exchanges, and Cooperation between the South and the North. It was a landmark agreement. The DPRK officially recognised the ROK's existence for the first time, and vice versa, and they agreed to negotiate a formal end to the Korean War.

Joint sub-committees were set up to develop economic ties and communications, cultural exchanges, united sports teams representing both Koreas, and familial reunifications, on top of measures to deflate military tensions. They also agreed the joint Declaration on the Denuclearization of the Korean Peninsula that would set up an effective bilateral nuclear inspection regime.

Not that all this brought peace. In 1992 IAEA inspectors found discrepancies between amounts of plutonium produced and how much they found, and complained of restricted access to plants. Tensions roller-coastered with DPRK stick-shaking and America's Congress called for increased sanctions, if not bombing. With the economy stalling through diminishing harvests and no energy supplies, the DPRK threatened to cancel its treaties unless dialogue and aid began. US President Clinton ordered sanctions in mid-1994 and the DPRK withdrew from the IAEA. In desperate diplomacy, former US President Jimmy Carter visited Kim Il Sung in July 1994 and brought some diffusion of tensions with a possible 'aid for atoms' agreement. The octogenarian Kim Il Sung, back to the wall, was still demanding no surrender, not without a good price anyway. In October, the DPRK and the US signed the Agreed Framework, to wit the DPRK would freeze (and partly dismantle) its nuclear programme, stay in the NPT and allow full inspections. The US would provide 500,000 tonnes of fuel oil annually (replacing the lost imports from Russia) and lead a consortium to build two light-water reactors by 2003 (nuclear reactors but less potent) through the Korean Peninsula Energy Development Organisation (KEDO). The DPRK got some guarantee of energy supplies and a nuclear-free peninsula finally looked possible.

Kim Il Sung departs
On 8 July 1994, Kim Il Sung died suddenly of a heart-attack. He was 82. His sudden passing was profoundly traumatic for the DPRK people. He had led them out of the bitter ruins of the Korean War, and placed himself at the helm of the country's reconstruction and development into a providing, fiercely sovereign state.

The succession
Since the early 1970s, the man feted and groomed as the DPRK's next leader, the rightful heir of Kim Il Sung's power and authority, was none other than Kim Jong Il, Kim Il Sung's first son. From 1980, Kim Jong Il was given numerous successively higher positions in the Party, and that year it was announced that he would indeed succeed his father, and his own thoughts on

Juche were published shortly after. Little was known about the man, however. He was rarely seen in public in the way that Kim Il Sung toured the lands, and was rumoured to be a recluse, who spent too much time watching the Western films in his incredible collection, films that if anyone else had been caught with them would have meant a trip to the mines. Favoured actresses and directors of ROK films were apparently kidnapped and brought to him, and much has been written about Kim's preference for film femmes. The difficulty is that whereas DPRK publications about Kim Jong Il venerate him, ROK publications are at the other extreme with the most salacious, scurrilous tales that can't be trusted.

But following Kim Il Sung's death, the West wondered whether Kim Jong Il would indeed take over. Could an entire regime, a system of governance, built around one man in fact and fable actually survive his loss and the handover to a.n.other, even if the successor were his son? Questions arose over who was really in power. The posts of General Secretary of the KWP and president of the DPRK remained empty while the country remained officially in mourning for three years.

During this time, the country, through floods, droughts and the breakdown of energy supplies (see *Economy/Famine*) entered into its first great famine. The trickle of defectors crossing into China was turning into a stream of refugees fleeing over the Yalu. In 1995, United Nations' relief organisations were given unprecedented requests to see the situation. Food and medical aid were forthcoming over the next months and years, from, among others, the US, Japan and ROK, but the politicking going on in the country's leadership was impenetrable at best. An indication of business as normal north of the DMZ came in December 1996 when a DPRK submarine ran aground off the ROK coast. Twenty-six commandos swam ashore and so began a violent manhunt which led to the deaths of all the commandos and 13 ROK soldiers and civilians.

The most serious indication of internal dissent was the defection to the ROK of the ageing International Affairs Secretary, Hwang Jang Yop, in February 1997. Hwang was a senior Party member and committee chair, an interpreter of Juche philosophy and a man of very high standing with bountiful perks of state, had he wished to indulge. But he was an aesthete, a man of principle who would go on to tell his southern hosts that the regime was collapsing from within and couldn't have long to live. The rest of the world looked on, awaiting implosion.

In October 1997, Kim Jong Il indeed took the post of General Secretary of the KWP. Kim has also been confirmed as commander-in-chief of the Korean People's Army, so he is nominally in charge of both halves of the power-duopoly of the KWP and KPA that runs the country today.

There was not a noticeable change in policy in Kim's first months. To the poker-table of the diplomats' casino, the DPRK brought its sophisticated multi-stage missiles. In August 1998 a Taepondong 1 missile sailed over the northern end of Japan, proving to the world that despite all the rumours, the regime was alive and well enough to build and launch that kind of weaponry.

ARE THE NORTH AND SOUTH IRRECONCILABLE?

Dr James Hoare, Chargé d'Affaires of the British Embassy to Pyongyang 2001–2002

The division of Korea in 1945 had little to do with any historic or cultural differences on the peninsula. For about 1000 years, Korea had been a unified political entity, with a remarkable homogeneous population. There were linguistic and other differences among those people, but the 38th parallel, the line chosen in 1945, bore little relation to them. Rather it was selected by the United States since it seemed the very least that the Soviet Union would accept. Just as important, in those opening days of the Cold War, it gave control of Seoul, the country's capital since 1392, to the Americans. But the Korean people never accepted the division.

However, the failure of either side to win an outright victory in the 1950–53 Korean War meant that the division has been perpetuated to this day. The war ended the 38th parallel's formal role. The line of actual military control, which became the Military Demarcation Line with the signing of the Armistice on 27 July 1953, though it ran close to the 38th parallel, did not follow it exactly. Instead, the South Koreans held territory above the parallel to the east of the truce village of Panmunjom that had been in the North before the war. The North, for its part, held Kaesong, capital of the country in the last but one dynasty, and the Ongjin peninsula, both south of the parallel and both in South Korea before June 1950.

After the signing of the Armistice, while both Koreas claimed to work for the reunification of the peninsula, each set about the creation of separate states. They did not deny the essential historic unity of the peninsula, but each side drew on cultural and historical material that could be used to stress its legitimacy, and in the process downplayed the claims of the other side.

In the South, this meant stressing the role of Seoul, the capital of a united Korea from 1392. The speech of Seoul was presented as the 'national language'. At the same time, South Korean propaganda emphasised the tradition of the Silla kingdom. Silla, one of the traditional 'Three Kingdoms' of Korea, with its capital at Kyongju in the southwest of the peninsula, had unified much of the peninsula under its rule from AD668. Silla's role assumed particular importance after Park Chung Hee came to power in

Seriously unimpressed, the Japanese government promptly withheld US$1bn earmarked for the already delayed reactors. The US Congress would also suspend some oil shipments over DPRK missile sales to America's enemies. As a result of the 'Berlin Talks' between the US and DPRK in late 1999, the Clinton administration lifted some sanctions and offered food aid in exchange for the DPRK freezing its missile programme. Was this a breakthrough?

1961, since he came from that part of the country. The tradition of concentrating on Silla continued under his successors, since they too came from the southwest.

Although in North Korea, Seoul was to remain officially the capital until 1972, with Pyongyang listed only as the 'temporary capital', much stress was laid on Pyongyang's much longer history compared to that of Seoul. Indeed, Pyongyang was proclaimed to be the site of the capital of Tangun, the legendary ancestor of the Korean people. The speech of Pyongyang was promoted as the 'standard language', in the North. Historically, North Korea looked to another of the 'Three Kingdoms', Koguryo. Koguryo had been the largest of the kingdoms. At their greatest extent, Koguryo's territories stretched north far into what are now China's northeastern provinces, and south to Han river valley around Seoul. The kingdom's warriors also acquired a reputation for fierceness in battle.

North Korea has placed much emphasis on these themes. There has never been any claim that these are the only strands in Korean history but the stress is on the importance of the Pyongyang region and the superiority of Koguryo over Silla. The role of Pyongyang as an older capital than Seoul has been boosted by the claim that this was the capital city on earth of Korea's mythical founder, Tangun. Even more conclusive evidence, in North Korean eyes, for the sacred nature of Pyongyang and its claim to centrality in Korean history, was the alleged confirmation in the early 1990s that a tomb just outside the city was that of Tangun and his family. Refurbishment of the tomb of King Tongmyong, the supposed founder of the Koguryo dynasty, also just outside the city, reinforced the claimed importance of Pyongyang in the (unified) nation's history. No doubt an additional factor was that Kim Il Sung, ruler of North Korea from late 1945 until his death in 1994, came from the small village of Mangyongdae, just outside Pyongyang.

In addition to these factors, the continued North-South division has enhanced a sense of separateness. In vocabulary, customs, politics and general behaviour, North and South have grown apart. They no longer sing the same words to traditional songs, for example, even though the tunes remain the same. Increasingly, it is unlikely that they would even use the same instruments. None of this is irreversible, but the emphasis on separateness means that eventual reunification will be that bit harder.

Foreign relations

Since 1999, the DPRK has been on a pretty successful diplomatic campaign. By the end of 2001, the DPRK had established full diplomatic ties, or set out on the road to them, with the EU as a body and 13 EU countries (including the UK, France, Italy, Spain, Germany and the Scandinavians), the Philippines (completing the ASEAN nations, except Burma, of course), Canada and Australia.

Relations with Japan

Meetings and negotiations have followed throughout the decade since the 1990 breakthrough, and full diplomatic ties were looking as likely as a few long-standing issues might allow.

The DPRK is demanding recompense for Japan's colonial crimes, including the issue of Korean 'comfort women' in Japan, while the Japanese demand the return of a dozen Japanese abducted in the 1970s and '80s. Today, Japan is concerned over the DPRK's nuclear and missile programmes.

These days, more pragmatic concerns of the DPRK leadership could mean billions in Japanese investment might suffice as 'recompense'. Chochongnyon does most of the DPRK-Japan trade in technology transfers and goods (used cars) that now amount to around US$600 million a year. Communications (phones, flights, ferries) and cultural links are also operating, and Japan has donated considerable funds and foodstuffs to stave off the DPRK famine. Great headway was made in 2002 in re-establishing diplomatic ties between the two countries, but Japanese fears that aid for the reactors may end up in military hands has led them to shelve funding. The DPRK still demands apologies backed up by hard cash.

Relations with the US

DPRK-US relations also improved considerably during the late 1990s, and US President Clinton was poised to be the first US president to visit the country (notwithstanding that they were still technically at war). US Secretary of State Madeleine Albright visited in October 2000. Much of the progress in DPRK-US relations stemmed from the build-up in trust that had been going on since 1994, but the clincher to warming relations was a pro-negotiation Washington which allowed the ROK President Kim Dae Jung to lessen tensions between the two Koreas with his 'Sunshine Policy'. This precipitated a virtuous cycle of US-DPRK relations, and the US and DPRK media began to use substantially less colourful language when describing the other. The peace wasn't confirmed but the propensity for war to break out was reduced far below any other time. However, until a peace treaty is signed by all sides, US and ROK relations with the DPRK can, and do, change with their administrations.

Southern sunshine and a new dawn

The greatest diplomatic advances, those that may have precipitated all others, were with the ROK and their President Kim Dae Jung's 'Sunshine Policy' with the country. The former political prisoner and activist Kim Dae Jung's 'Sunshine Policy' was a more pragmatic acceptance of the north, encouraging permanent economic and diplomatic assistance and cultural exchange, and the DPRK has reciprocated the approach. In late 1999, the ROK basketball team visited Pyongyang and the DPRK team went to Seoul. In June 2000 was the historic summit in Pyongyang between the two sides' heads of state. It began with a hurrah as, stepping from the plane at Pyongyang airport, Kim Dae Jung was surprised to see Kim Jong Il awaiting him at the foot of the stairs. The warmth and cordiality of this moment set the tone for the summit.

More families were reunited on Liberation Day, August 2000. In September, the ROK and DPRK teams marched together at the Sydney Olympics. The ROK held half of the World Cup football games two years later, and although no ROK-team games were shown on DPRK TV, after the tournament the two sides had their own friendly, with one flag and a traditional folk song replacing their respective anthems. It was a fitting 0-0 draw. On the subject of football, the ROK team's performance in the 2002 World Cup was a magnificent surprise; however, they were not setting a precedent:

Other developments were an ROK promise to finance the rehabilitation of the DPRK's infrastructure. Road and rail links between the two sides are being constructed across the DMZ, which involves the partial de-mining of this section. It's hoped that Kim Dae-jung's successor, President Roh Moo Hyun, can extend the diplomatic roads into the north.

And there are changes afoot within the country. In January 2001, three central DPRK newspapers published a joint editorial proposing to develop the economy in a profitability-oriented manner, basically a public declaration from across the country's power structure that the DPRK was not shuffling but stepping towards market liberalisation. In January 2002, the official 'Arduous March' phase of the country's development (or contraction) was declared over. So would begin the 'Construction of the Powerful State'. Two months later, the titular head of state Kim Yong Nam announces adjustment of economic foundations of the country at the Supreme People's Assembly session.

Bombs and rockets

However, nothing moves without energy. KEDO (the Korean Peninsula Energy Development Organisation) was dragging along, and as the century turned it was clear the light-water reactors would not be finished by 2003. With the more confrontational George W Bush administration, in early 2001 the US agreed to an indigenous ROK missile programme. In February 2001, the DPRK expressed its frustration that the Agreed Framework wasn't being implemented by the US and that the DPRK might consider the Framework to be defunct. The Bush administration ignored the warning and called the DPRK the 'road-kill of history', placing the country on the infamous 'Axis of Evil' list, which substantially alarmed the DPRK and irritated the ROK. US aid in food and monetary terms declined sharply, although this may have been due to the DPRK's recovering economy.

In April 2002, the White House posted that the DPRK was in full compliance with the Agreed Framework and that funds for the very late reactors would be released, for which a ground-breaking ceremony was held in August. But in October 2002, US special envoy James Kelly reportedly presented evidence to DPRK Foreign Ministry officials that the DPRK had recommended uranium enrichment that was claimed to be in violation of the Agreed Framework. The US accused the DPRK of having nuclear weapons;

THE NORTH KOREAN WORLD CUP FOOTBALL TEAM OF 1966, 'THE GAME OF THEIR LIVES'
Nicholas Bonner and Daniel Gordon; web: www.thegameoftheirlives.com

> In May we were having a picnic with the players. Ri Chan Myong, the goalkeeper of 1966, turned to us and said, 'We'd love to return to Middlesbrough and thank the town for their support ... and that's how it started ... and we have not stopped working on it since.'
>
> Nick Bonner and Dan Gordon,
> makers of the film *The Game of Their Lives*

On July 19 1966, a group of hitherto unknown footballers from the Democratic People's Republic of Korea defeated the mighty Italy 1–0 in Group Four of the World Cup in England. The result meant a humiliating first round elimination for Italy, who boasted in their ranks some of the finest and wealthiest footballers on the planet. The North Koreans, averaging 5ft 5in (162.5m) in height, and having had a foul committed against them every four minutes of play in the tournament, had produced the greatest shock in World Cup history.

The North Koreans, the first Asian team to appear in the World Cup finals, had qualified for the World Cup by beating Australia 9–2 over two legs, both matches played in the bizarre surroundings of 'neutral' Cambodia due to neither country having diplomatic relations with the other. Indeed, Norodom Sihanouk divided the Phnom Penh stadium in half, with each team having the boisterous backing of 20,000 Cambodians. North Korea, as winners of the Asian qualifiers, should have faced the winners of the African qualifiers for the one place open to Africa, Asia and Oceania, but a mass boycott by the Africans meant North Korea were on their way to England.

This itself produced a diplomatic headache for the British authorities, who at one stage wanted to deny the Koreans a visa as they felt it would imply recognition. For the same reason, the British government also wanted to ban the North Korean national anthem and prevent their flag from flying at matches. In the end, a compromise was reached, the Koreans were allowed in and their flag flew proudly at all venues. However, no anthems were played at any matches, save for the opening game of the tournament (England v Uruguay) and the final itself (England v West Germany).

At the start of the tournament, the Koreans were 1,000–1 outsiders and a 3–0 defeat in their opening game against the Soviet Union did little to suggest that the World Cup was to witness its greatest ever sensation.

However, the local population of Middlesbrough, a working class town in the northeast of England, whose local professional side also played in red, had taken the Koreans to their hearts, and chants of 'Korea, Korea' were heard throughout all their games. Indeed, when Pak Sung Jin equalised seven minutes from the end of their second game, against Chile, the roars and stamps of feet were so great that a strip light in the press box crashed to the floor. Chile, incidentally, had finished third in the previous World Cup, held in 1962.

> Pak Do Ik. He scores. North Korea have taken the lead with five minutes of the first half left. What a sensation. Italy a goal down to North Korea. Who ever would have believed it? They are absolutely overwhelmed.
>
> Frank Bough, BBC commentary, 1966 ©BBC

Such was the fanaticism of the local populace for their newfound heroes that, after the sensational defeat of Italy, over 3,000 Middlesbrough fans travelled across Britain to Goodison Park, Liverpool, for North Korea's next game, the quarter final against Portugal. Remarkably, the Koreans stormed to a 3–0 lead inside just 24 minutes. Again, almost to a man the 50,000-plus crowd were solidly behind the Koreans, remarkable considering that just 13 years earlier, the host nation had been at war with North Korea.

For the Koreans there was to be no fairytale ending. Eusebio, Portugal's greatest ever player, produced a magical display, and his four goals powered Portugal to an unforgettable 5–3 victory. Had the Koreans held on, they would have faced the host nation, England, in the semi-final at Wembley.

Meanwhile, the Italians, who had been the favourites to win the trophy for the third time in their history, had caught the first available flight home, and returned to their homeland to a hail of rotten tomatoes from irate supporters. But what happened to the players from Korea? For years, rumours persisted, particularly in South Korea, that North Korea's World Cup heroes had been sent to labour camps on their return from England and remain in dishonour.

The making of the film

Nicholas Bonner (Koryo Tours) and Dan Gordon (filmmaker) spent five years in North Korea tracking down the players of 1966. 'We were the first Englishmen that Han Bong Jin, No 11, had seen for 35 years. "Is the mayor of Middlesbrough still alive?" was the first question he asked us … and as the players waved us goodbye at Pyongyang train station he shouted, "Send the people of Middlesbrough our very best wishes."'

In 2002 they released the award-winning film, *The Game of their Lives*, about the seven surviving members of the team and their recollection of the event. The film uncovered archive material of the return of the players to Pyongyang and revealed they were alive and well and still revered as heroes. The filmmakers investigated the allegations that the players lost the game against Portugal because of womanising and drinking. They found the

continued overleaf

THE NORTH KOREAN WORLD CUP FOOTBALL TEAM OF 1966, 'THE GAME OF THEIR LIVES' continued

team had been celibate for the training up to and during the World Cup and, though they had drunk the bar dry before the match, it was of soda water only.

The return to Middlesbrough

In October 2002 Bonner and Gordon took the seven players back to Britain and the scene of their triumph at Ayresome Park. The stadium has since been demolished to make way for a housing estate but the fans remember the ground and the victory with such fondness that steel tacks in the gardens of the homes mark the lines where the pitch used to be, with a bronze ball in a garden where the centre spot was and a bronze casting of Pak Do Ik's stud mark where he struck the winning goal against Italy. A crowd of 33,000 gave the players a standing ovation at Middlesbrough's new stadium and the North Korean flag flew over the Town Hall.

> I learned that football is not only about the winning. Wherever we go … playing football can improve diplomatic relations and promote peace.
>
> Pak Do Ik interview, October 2001

> It still remains a riddle to me … the people of Middlesbrough supported us all the way through, I still don't know the reason why.
>
> Rim Jung Son, No 5

> This showed how much the English people loved us … especially those from Middlesbrough.
>
> Interview reply on the support they were given,
> Ri Chan Myong, goalkeeper

the DPRK denied this, then declared it true, which the US and ROK disbelieved. Bush unilaterally suspended oil shipments on November 14, next day presenting the ROK, Japanese and EU delegates sent to discuss the issue with a *fait accompli*. Winter set in and a third famine loomed for the DPRK, as food donations fell short through overstretch and political malice. Less for electricity and more in wilful defiance of the US, the plutonium-producing reactors at Yongbyon recommenced operations in December 2002. If the US is really to strike us for having nuclear weapons, reckoned the regime, we had better make a load of them to put them off.

Rising tensions

Tensions are escalating thick and fast and this section will be out of date by the time it's printed. The year 2003 unfolded with the US continuing to shake sticks by bringing two dozen B-52 bombers to Guam, within striking distance of the DPRK's reactors. The DPRK countered by throwing out IAEA monitors, withdrew from the Non-Proliferation Treaty, cancelled Armistice talks and test-fired missiles, one on the inauguration day of the new ROK President, Roh Moo-hyun. However, Roh has vowed to build upon his predecessor's work of building relations with the DPRK, and is avidly against any kind of attack on the DPRK by the US. Japanese-DPRK relations are souring over the latter's bombs and missiles, and Japan lobbied to support further US-proposed sanctions.

However, an actual US strike on the DPRK reactors is very extreme. Notwithstanding DPRK claims for electricity needs and the rights to self-defence against an aggressive megapower, any such strike would cover the region in radioactive fallout, and following that, refugees, a worrying prospect for China, Russia and the ROK. China is also obligated to defend the DPRK through a 1961 treaty, so any air-strikes could be phenomenally dangerous. By mid-April, sanctions were also looking unlikely as China refused to support them through the Security Council. The situation reached a precarious impasse, until the DPRK dropped its demand for one-to-one talks with the US and agreed in principle to multilateral talks. President Bush took this as a vindication that his pre-emptive policy and success in Iraq had caused Kim Jong Il to blink, although a nuclear DPRK isn't in China's or Russia's interests either and their diplomatic efforts were instrumental in bringing the DPRK round. 'Multilateral' talks between the DPRK, its greatest ally, China, and the US began in late April, in a modern parallel with 1951. Irrespective of the outcome, President Roh promised aid and to accelerate North–South economic and diplomatic initiatives that would hopefully fill the shortfalls of renewed US sanctions.

However the nuclear issue pans out, western commentators will continue to mark the million-man KPA and the high proportion of GDP devoted to military activities as long-standing proof of the DPRK's aggressive tendencies, while defectors and refugees have given diverse and deep testimony over human rights' abuses in the country.

Websites

For more on the nuclear issue, try the Federation of American Scientists, web: www.fas.org. A very good site for current affairs and issues about the DPRK is www.nautilus.org. You can track daily updates at www.nytimes.com, as found at www.kcna.co.jp and www.bbc.co.uk/monitoring. Alternatively, try north-korea.narod.ru/pyongyang_watch.htm, or www.worldperspectives.org/dprk/, which is a general interest site. A whole host of sites focusing on the DPRK perspective can be found at www.kimsoft.com and also at www.koreascope.org/eng/main/index.jsp. See the *Media and Communications* section, pages 84–5, for more DPRK sites.

ECONOMY

The DPRK economy has historically been a command economy. Since the DPRK's inception, the economy was built along a similar system of centralised control as the Soviet Union's economy in the 1930s. In both cases, the ultimate socialist state was to be achieved through mass industrialistation based on huge increases in agricultural output. Thus achieved, the state provides cradle-to-grave jobs, housing, food, medical care, education, goods and clothing.

In command economies, output is not dictated by the laws of price, supply and demand, but according to targets set by the government. Successive multi-year plans (in the DPRK starting with a One-Year Plan in 1946 and getting longer ever since) demand certain economic sectors to produce quantitive targets (usually increasing) by a certain date. For example, the DPRK's 1978 Seven-Year Plan demanded that coal output in 1984 would rise from 80 million tons to 120 million and fertiliser from five to seven million tons. The plans include the inputs and incentives needed to increase production.

There is very little private ownership, the state 'owns' and runs industries, banks, transportation, financial institutions etc as monopolistic enterprises. Workers are assigned to task-oriented work units that compete to (over-) achieve the targets, with rewards or cuts depending on their collective results. Mobilisation and propaganda campaigns exhort the workers onwards and upwards, and the workers can be rewarded from the total of their productivity increases.

Centralised governmental control and direction of each economic sector comes through ministries, committees, and agencies at the national level down through committees and agencies at the provincial, county and city levels. The lower levels provide the statistics and information on developments, bottlenecks and issues their superiors need to plan, decide and overcome problems. Party control, as a distinct influence from solely state directives, comes through Party cadre occupying key managerial and committee posts in these sectors.

Planning has become more complicated as the DPRK economy has developed from being predominantly agricultural to an advanced industrial economy, with increasingly complex sectoral interactions and input needs. Ministries and agencies have varied and developed over time in response to planned (and unplanned) situations, the most dramatic being the collapse of the Soviet Union in the early 1990s, but we shall come to this after the following history.

The division of Korea in 1945 cut off the north from the greater agricultural resources of the south, and the south from the concentrations of heavy industry in the north. The infrastructure of industry, road and rail installed by the Japanese colonialists was all very well except that the Korean economy had been run by Japanese, not Korean, as the Japanese kept Koreans excluded from the higher echelons of education and government of their own country. The majority of the north's population were agricultural and were educated only to that level.

Between 1945 and 1950, the Party prioritised the 'Revolutionising' of the country's agriculture to produce abundance, not famine, and allow its workers to migrate to the cities' industries. A minority of landlords owned most of the land, with the overwhelming majority of peasants living as tenant farmers paying rent in kind (from 50% of crops upwards). Reform came as communist agitators had promised: all land, livestock and buildings held by Japanese, traitors, absentee landlords, religious organisations and Koreans with over five chongbo (2.45 acres) were confiscated and re-distributed among the peasants; theirs but not to sell, rent or mortgage.

Landlords were harassed by police and party cadres, shunned by the peasants and investigated for anti-communist activities. Large and absentee holdings were confiscated first in a seemingly random fashion to avoid inciting any organised backlash by the landlords; lesser landlords either hoped to be spared, or collaborated. At best they received smaller plots, or were run from the province, southwards; otherwise it was hard labour.

The peasants were encouraged into the Party, more land was appropriated, cultivated and funds released for fertilisation and irrigation. Farmers paid tax in kind and sold the rest, although 'patriotic rice' was occasionally appropriated for patriotic ventures, like large building projects.

The Korean War of 1950–53 destroyed the north's cities, their industries and the people that worked in them. War also wrecked the country's agriculture; mass call up for the army and factories left crops unattended, while raging battles destroyed those that grew. The smoking husk of post-war Korea meant that nothing short of complete reconstruction was necessary. Rapid industrialisation was sought and needed a strong agricultural base, so the first priority was to increase agricultural output.

During and after the war, and into the late '50s, the farms were collectivised into co-operatives, ie: individual farms were combined into larger social, work and administrative units called ri, eliminating the final vestige of capitalist ownership in the countryside. Collectivisation was a practical necessity as the land and labour were pooled to make up for the missing men, but it was also a move of emancipation for women, who both achieved collectivisation and ran the farms, as is still the case today. By late 1958, all farms were collectivised into 3,800 cooperatives of around 300 households each, introducing new planting techniques, chemical fertilisers, industrialised and mechanised agriculture, and electrification through generators and hydro-power.

Farming joined the other economic sectors of industry, trade, culture, etc, that were all under state control by the end of the 1950s, and the productivity increases allowed for increased rural-urban migration to the city factories, based on cheap food at fixed prices for the urbanised workers. Government investment (there being no private) from the 1954–56 Three-Year Plan poured into agriculture, housing and education, but half of government investment was in heavy industry, in mining, coal, steel, copper, chemicals, and manufacturing of machine-tools.

These developments were built upon in the 1958 'Chollima Undong' (Flying Horse) movement, the first great mass-mobilisation campaign (and it's never really stopped) where increased output was to be attained through the implementation of the Chongsanri Method and the Taean Work System. In the Chongsanri Method, Party officials were given much greater input in the production process in the farms and factories. Party cadres were placed as hands-on managers empowered to solve any of the problems and use the ideas that workers confronted them with, in a micro-version of Kim Il Sung's own highly interventionist style. Output was also to be increased by whatever means worked, usually increased shares in the output or other material rewards to the group. Group rewards besides, the workers were exhorted to produce ever more with ever less means and time, and were bombarded with slogans like: 'Let us produce more with existing labour and facilities'. This kind of management developed into the Taean system, with more committees between the numerous work levels in a factory from shop-floor to CEO, that remains largely in use today. So the Party's economic and political control infiltrated every level of production, and industrial and agricultural management were of concern to the Party as well as the factory managers.

The fire of the 1950s' economic growth was stoked in the 1960s. At this point the economy of the DPRK was racing ahead in income per capita over that of the ROK, and Kim Il Sung confidently predicted that if the ROK got anywhere under capitalism, it'd collapse soon enough anyway. Nonetheless, the DPRK economy saw high rates of growth in all sectors, and critically for its 'defence' and socialist cause, its economic growth and per capita income outstripped the South's throughout the decade. As Juche proscribed, the DPRK had to propagate revolution by force and defend itself from attack from US and Japanese imperialists. A huge proportion of its manufacturing industries were for arms (defence industries were estimated to be up to 30% of GNP in the late 1960s and 1970s, and as high as 26.7% of GNP in 1995 as a 'military first' principle has taken over). Although Juche advocated the economy develop independently, ie: with minimal trade and capital flows from beyond its borders, the DPRK's Soviet, Chinese and eastern European socialist brethren supplied material aid and trade throughout the mid-1980s.

Nor was the DPRK averse to foreign investment from capitalist countries, only that inflows of capital to diversify the economy's output in the 1970s didn't fit the bureaucratic, insular economy and the DPRK defaulted on its foreign debts, precluding it from Western capital markets. Similarly to the other command economies of the socialist bloc, the DPRK's multi-year plans' over-emphasis on heavy industry and commodity export suffered in the commodity market crashes of the late 1970s, while heavy bureaucratic control stifled technical and productive innovation. Capitalist investment from abroad was encouraged. Joint-ventures were allowed from 1984, tourism was promoted in Kumgangsan and special economic zones were set up in Rajin-Sonbong on the Russian border, around Sinuiju, Kaesong. Foreign interest has fluctuated but steady Chinese and ROK investment has been inflowing since the late 1990s. Aid slowed as the other socialist economies spluttered, while minimal foreign trade meant the DPRK hadn't the foreign currency to buy what it couldn't produce itself. Because a quarter of the country's output and technical investment was monopolised by arms industries producing for domestic use, what the economy couldn't produce was a lot. The balance of diverting resources into a nuclear power-cum-weapons programme and development of intercontinental rockets was to use them to bargain, but would bombs and rockets earn more in bargaining than they could lose in sanctions and diplomatic reproach? Well, at least the rockets can always be sold for hard currency.

The DPRK's trade deficit with the USSR became unaffordable. Barter-trading with the USSR was curtailed by the latter for hard currency in 1991, as the Soviet economy staggered towards free-market economics. China followed suit. Soviet trade fell from 55% of the DPRK's 1990 total to 14% in 1991, worsening as the Soviet economy crashed. Soviet fuel imports, principally oil, collapsed by 85%, throttling the DPRK's transport and industries' ability to operate. The ensuing energy crises, compounded by failing hydro-electric power output, affected industrial output of goods (and food, see *Famine*, below) with which to trade and earn foreign currency, as flagship state industries' output fell to 20% of the norm.

Simultaneously, aid and trade with the DPRK's eastern European allies died with their socialism, and the DPRK hadn't any significant manufacturing capacity for quality consumer goods to sell elsewhere. The DPRK's trade with 'imperialist' free-market economies, (mainly Japan) existed but the links were minimal, its credit record poor, debts accumulating and US sanctions kept the DPRK from markets that the pro-independence spirit of Juche might yet have allowed. The DPRK's industries were worn and decades of insulation meant they were comparatively out-dated. In late 1993, it was announced that the Third Seven-Year plan had failed, a staggering admission in itself. The worsening energy crises then began to break down the country's agricultural basis that had made the DPRK's industrialisation possible, and the DPRK tipped towards famine.

Famine comes to the DPRK

Korea's agriculture has historically been prone to calamity, as the mountainous peninsula has little fertile land in a country prone to flooding and drought. A terrible drought of 1812–13 reportedly led to a million deaths, and during rice-riots in 1833 rioters burned and trashed many parts of Seoul.

The division of Korea left the South with most of the country's arable land, and with the quality, fertile land at that. Regardless of tremendous output increases achieved since the Korean War, food has been rationed for Koreans for many years, with rations based on occupation, age and region, averaging around 220kg per capita annually as a solid supply. Factors that had proved critical to increasing agricultural output included the mechanisation of farming in output and transportation, (tractors and trucks replacing men and oxen) and the vast expansion of land under pumped irrigation. Chemical fertilisers and pesticides were also produced and employed in increasing amounts. The DPRK was more than self-sufficient, or self-reliant, in food output. The DPRK's Juche was grown from the fields.

FLOODS AND DROUGHTS

Floods don't just destroy growing and stored crops. Soil, tended and fertilised over years is washed away with irrigation systems, agricultural landscaping, equipment, farms and people's lives. Silt and debris give the floods more physical clout to damage other areas, blocking, damaging and demolishing channels, roads and structures, and the best land is left under a thick scum of sand and silt, that the petrol-less bulldozers cannot shift.

People escaping direct death and injury have to deal with the loss of land and livelihood, and the immediate problem of lost food stores and sanitary water supplies. Damaged and destroyed communications hinder the ability to deliver aid; conversely, people are unable simply to flee to unaffected areas. The DPRK Ministry of Foreign Affairs announced flood damage to be some US$15 billion in 1995.

Either it rains, or it doesn't. Drought also blights Korea's crops, and in 2001 the worst spring drought in 80 years followed the coldest winter in 50 years. Spring's wheat, barley and potatoes were affected, then the drought prolonged to scuttle autumn's rice and maize. Droughts reduce Korea's hydro-power, causing power cuts: refrigerators for vaccines and pumps for sanitary water turn off. Adding insult to injury, the major food-producing areas in the southwest also suffered severe floods that year. Deforestation in the country is one local explanation, the treeless hills drying the micro-climate while rainwater rages down the hillsides with nothing to soak it up. Plots and clumps of new trees are bedecking the fringes of farms and barren hillsides as the government vigorously afforests the country.

Nevertheless, the country's increasingly unstable climate is also on the sharp end of severe droughts affecting Mongolia and northern China as the Gobi desert expands east.

But by the early 1980s, food shortages were being reported as the economy stagnated, and by the 1990s, the situation became disastrous as rations for farmers were reduced, causing upset, and Chinese and Soviet subsidies ended. The DPRK's contracting economy reduced fertiliser and pesticide output, as well as production of new tractors and pumps and spare parts for those already in use. Broken machines couldn't be fixed, and harvests couldn't be reaped or sown. But the critical issue was energy; oil imports from the Soviet Union died with it, and the DPRK literally ran out of fuel. Two-thirds of the DPRK's electricity comes from hydro-power, in irregular supply due to droughts and flood damage, and so irrigation systems didn't work when needed – aside from the mass destruction caused by drought and floods on the crops and farms (see box). Much of the land was exhausted from overuse or fertiliser saturation. Unfortunately, depleted foreign earnings prevented the importing of fertilisers, pesticides, parts and oil; they hadn't the money, and this applied to importing food. Workers, soldiers, women and children went from the factories to the fields to supplant the shortfalls in mechanical power, but output slipped then plumbed below minimum subsistence levels. In 1995 and again in 1997 international aid was requested as rumours ripped through the international community of a calamity in the making. The United Nations Food and Agriculture Organisation and World Food Programme (WFP) found in late 1995 that the 220kg average was closer to 170kg, below that needed for minimum nutritional requirements. In summer 1995 WFP estimates for 1995 showed that Korea needed some 4,740,000 tonnes to meet minimum calorific intake, but was deficient in 1,250,000 tonnes, a quarter of a billion dollars' worth in rice alone.

The human cost has been appalling. Estimates of mortality from starvation from 1995 have reached over 3 million, or over 10% of the total population. UNICEF states mortality rates in the 1990s for children under five rose from 27 to 48 per 1,000, while over 45% of under-fives are still suffering chronic malnourishment and/or stunted growth. Malnutrition compounds people's susceptibility to flood-borne gastro-intestinal diseases, like diarrhoea.

The WFP amongst other international organisations has worked to rehabilitate the country's agriculture through variations in crop and fertiliser use, but restricted access to information and parts of the country has been frustrating. The deficit in domestic food production has fluctuated by up to 1.8 million tonnes in 2001, but international aid in oil and food has been forthcoming, particularly from China. Nevertheless, aid from the South, Japan and the US has sometimes been delayed by wrangling over Korea's nuclear programme on top of long-standing bad relations, and accusations that aid goes to the army first. Aid funding targets have also frequently not been met on programmes for food relief, vital drugs, immunisation, nutrition, water and sanitation, and education.

In early 2002, the WFP and UNICEF could access more of the remaining provinces and counties. But the floods and droughts continue, and restructuring projects perennially seek funding as the international organisations continue to work in the country.

Rehabilitation

As the DPRK's agricultural system is renovated, other initiatives are under way. Kim Jong Il has personally led delegations to Russia and China to observe the process of their development from command to fully-fledged free-market economies.

Aid and foreign investment are most forthcoming if diplomatic relations are good, for business follows the flag, and the late 1990s and early 2000s saw hugely accelerated diplomatic initiatives with the European Union, Japan, the United States and the ROK. The US had relaxed a broad range of trade sanctions in 1998 but the Bush administration has sought to re-impose them from early 2003, notwithstanding constraints on public bodies like the World Bank from loaning funds that came from listing the DPRK as part of the 'Axis of Evil'. Nevertheless, the ROK has made promises to fund the rehabilitation of the DPRK's infrastructure and foreign investment is being encouraged in all industries – from mining to steel and manufacturing – and in new areas like IT and even animation as DPRK restrictions are being lifted. ROK joint-ventures in the DPRK are now worth US$110m export dollars a year, and the economy's long contraction in the 1990s finished in 2000 when 1.3% GDP growth was recorded, followed in 2001 by 3.1%. The Pyongyang Chamber of Commerce was accredited by the International Chamber of Commerce in Paris in May 2000. Many well-known foreign firms are investing in the country, restoring its infrastructure and capitalising on the country's highly educated but low-wage workforce. The capacity to produce and the will to renovate are still very much in evidence among the Korean people. Only the building of success breeding success based on solid, trusting relationships with the world beyond takes time. Free-flows of information are critical to this.

In March 2002, the government announced that the rationing and therefore the government provision of some goods would cease, ie: be subject to market forces and pricing, which was becoming increasingly the case in some economic sectors anyway. Markets had always existed in some form and clandestine suppliers of goods from China, Russia and Japan had supplemented more usual goods' flows into the country for years. However, the state still provides all shelter. For accommodation, people used to pay a nominal maintenance fee for an apartment which was theirs for life, and a single-digit percentage of wages on utility bills. Bills and rents have gone up significantly to levels (or wage percentages) more akin to capitalist economies. Most significant was the abolition of rationing for basic foodstuffs: money, not coupons, now gets food. Private initiatives in shops and trade are appearing. The 'foreigners' won' was abolished in favour of hard currency trading while the local won was dramatically revalued (from 2.12 won to the dollar to over 200 won to the dollar), although this was establishing nationwide what had been the case in the Rajin-Sonbong Free Enterprise Zone for years. From factories and power-plants to restaurants and stalls, the principles of supply and demand are being set in place, while firms seek their own profits and not state help and workers seek monetary bonuses for their labour.

Energy remains the most fundamental issue that the DPRK must solve. Droughts create a problem as two-thirds of the DPRK's electricity comes from hydro-electric power. In addition, completion of the light-water reactors is dependent on the US, Japan and ROK. Finally, in order to secure steady supplies of oil, the DPRK must be able to both access and pay for these supplies. Stabilising relations with these countries will be critical to the future success of the DPRK reforms.

Websites for further information

Prospective investors should consult:

Roger Barrett at the Korean Business Consultants www.kbc-global.com, or www.fbda.net

www.tradepartners.gov.uk/north_korea

European Union Chamber of Commerce Korea www.eucck.org

World Food Program www.wfp.org/index2.html
Food and Agriculture Organisation of the United Nations www.fao.org/
UNICEF www.unicef.org/emerg/DPRK.htm

PEOPLE

Koreans are an ethnically and culturally homogenous people, as seen in terms of their racial heritage, facial features, language and history. No wars or feuds are as longstanding and bitter as those between two brothers, which describes Korea's division perfectly. The people of both states want unification, but cannot yet agree as to how this will come about. The most obvious difference is in the ROK exists with a significant Western influence, visibly present in capitalist pop culture, that has flowed in through the development of the ROK economy and the presence of American forces there. In the ROK are also some minorities of other Asian nationalities and ex-pats.

The number of minorities in the DPRK is restricted to Chinese and some Japanese, and a minute ex-pat community, whose presence will never undo the country's decades of hermetic existence.

Meeting the people

Beyond your guides, you may not meet that many Koreans, and Koreans themselves might seem cold or indifferent if they acknowledge you at all. This is not a country where a whole village will pile out to see a foreigner. Historically, foreigners have often not been of great service to Korea and this point is often put to the people.

Consider also the strains afflicting this country. No family can have escaped unaffected by Korea's division, the war and the recent famines. The DPRK's reconstruction has taken decades of back-breaking work with scant resources, against reciprocated aggression from other countries and based on insecure flows of trade and aid. As the country's allies were lost in the 1990s, so all the health and nutritional gains evaporated as the economy ground to a halt, a time referred to with some understatement as an 'arduous march'. These people have had a time of it.

So it's not surprising that here more than anywhere, friendships take time to build and a lot of trust. That said, those friends made are friends for life and are notably generous and warm. All Koreans, like anyone else, like a drink and a dance and to picnic in the woods. Be sure to wave and smile while passing through the country.

Social set up

The old Confucian-based order of royal Korea demanded respect for age, learning, filial piety and authority, the latter justifying a society based on hierarchy and class. Providing for the individual was secondary to serving the collective. Confucianism is no longer officially practised in the DPRK (and scarcely in the ROK), and the DPRK order has been overturned by a half-century of communist revolutionary rule, but the underlying influence of Confucianism is discernible. Age is still revered (see who gets served first at a

EDUCATION

Children in the DPRK attend state nurseries or crèches so that their parents can work normally, and from age four receive a universal, compulsory 11 years of education, beginning with a year in kindergarten. Hence the DPRK has a very high literacy rate. School uniform is universally blue bottoms, white shirts and a red neckerchief. Pupils may have on their arms small badges with horizontal stripes and little asterisks, the number of both patterns indicating a position of responsibility (asterisks determine job) in the school, class or class-group (shown by the stripes).

Education has three strong themes of practical knowledge (maths, sciences) and political knowledge (Juche). The third involves 'social education', which Juche prescribes in detail. Children join the Pioneer Corps and the Socialist Working Youth League where they learn the workings of collective life, and children can engage in many extra-curricular skills and activities at the children's palaces around the country. Older children are drafted in at the right times of year to help with harvests and other labour tasks that introduce them to the workers and their world. Pupils progress to high-school, then the forces, college or into specialist work units.

table), and so is education. A great success for the DPRK has been the implementation of universal, compulsory education for all. Education is one route to escaping the poverty of one's origins and theoretically makes the basis for a classless society, as communism suggests.

Familial devotion and filial piety are Confucian social currents that the Party puts great emphasis on. Still, the revolution's social impact has been the erosion of old ties of family and broader networks based on kin in the countryside. These ties took a great shock from Korea's division (affecting one in seven Koreans) and the losses of the Korean War. In the DPRK, small villages were merged into large cooperative farms, family and kin moved to the cities as the country industrialised (60% of the DPRK's population is urban) and travel restrictions were introduced, all further eroding the links. However, the family is officially the most venerated, virtuous social unit (if not the kin network) and the above strains have for many people accentuated the importance of their own families.

In the past, one's position in society was inherited as much as earned, and due respect and reward for one's social position underpinned social stability. Today, whether in the Party, the Army or just a normal civilian, like anywhere else, people of different livelihoods in the DPRK earn different amounts of money a month. However, two distinctions with the West are that it's the state and not the market that decides levels of pay, because the state owns everything, and second, pay is (or has been until very recently) of secondary importance to the other lifestyle elements provided by the state, namely

INTO THE MILITARY

From 17 to 25 years of age, Koreans are eligible for conscription into the Korean People's Army (KPA), Navy or Air Force for at least three years. Unless they fail the physical checks, college or reserved occupations (and the training for which) can defer if not rule out serving in the forces. Servicemen and women are not just for defence but are engaged in construction projects and farming, providing supplements to their own rations, or work in one of the KPA's many sub-industries, and one in five people's work relates to the KPA in some way.

accommodation, food and some clothing. Apartment size and food rationing have been graded by job and affiliations, and location. The distinction between town and country isn't just a matter of city-limits and checkpoints; the material supply and support for the cities is notably better than for rural areas, and Pyongyang outstrips all cities.

Aside from the distinction of military and Party members, people are categorised according to their general field (workers, farmers, officials, cooperative units) and then graded by specific job, and paid according to scale. There are three main classes, subdivided into 51 sub-grades, into which you are born and can rise and fall.

Regarding social stratification, your starting point in life, your job and location depends on your Songbun, your gauge or 'karma' of political reliability and commitment to the Great Leaders and the Party. Your Songbon weighs heavily on your career prospects, where you will live (town, country, apartment), who you might marry or befriend.

Songbon isn't determined solely by what your achievements, but sources from familial backgrounds as well, for Songbun is recorded by the security

INTO THE PARTY

Joining the Korean Workers' Party (KWP) is a good idea, and it has over three million members today, mostly industrial workers, bureaucrats and intellectuals. Weekly meetings on political thought and 'behavioural' issues are compulsory. The most diligent members, exemplary in their knowledge and understanding of Juche, economics and sociology (so very likely well educated) and selflessness in Party work may become Party cadres. Cadres are posted into every element of life here, and the extra hours of study a week are outweighed by enhanced career prospects and raised social status.

In addition to the KWP, there are other mass organisations for people to join, although it seems most are variations on a theme of collective work in the name of the country and the Leaders.

WHO'S WHO: HOW TO TELL

Of the people in uniforms, their colours are approximately thus:

- khaki-green, thick cloth, boots, Korean People's Army, although the detail's in the hatbands – red for army, blue for intelligence
- khaki-green, lighter cloth and red stars on the beret, Workers and Peasants Red Guard Paramilitaries (or Union)
- dark blue, air force
- blue and white, bell-bottoms, navy
- black, civilian police
- azure blue, traffic police and railway police (so, are you in the road or at the station?)
- light grey, construction brigade

'Shock brigades' have their own uniforms for the tasks to which they are detailed.

Civilian clothing provides clues about people's positions or contacts. I've no idea what makes a Japanese suit stand out from any others, but it's a show of money and knowing the right people, in the right shops. Virtually everyone in civilian clothing wears a Kim Il Sung or Kim Jong Il lapel pin. This indicates first that you are indeed a citizen of the DPRK; it's also thought that the size, metal and colouring of the pin indicates a wearer's union affiliations, department and possible seniority. But the quality and style of the pins also vary according to income and age, suggesting the societal hierarchal positioning denoted are more generational than deliberate.

Vehicles also say a lot about who is driving them, where they're from, possible connections, etc. Vehicle registration plates indicate their origins and sometimes purpose. The most common plate colour is white, for 'public', vehicles from particular government or local departments. On 'public' plates, first is written the vehicle's home city or province, then the vehicle's department's number (eg: 88 is tourism, 30 is Ministry of Foreign Affairs, 50 for taxi) then the vehicle's number in that department fleet. Black plates are army, yellow are privately owned (probably donated from Japan), dark blue is diplomat, white with a red star is VIP. There's also red, thought to be for high ranking party officials. You might get the spectacle of a VIP visit; the roads are closed as a fleet of black limousines flash and wail past, all flags waving.

services and updated continuously. Your ancestors' victories and crimes provide the social context of your birth and your future.

As Kim Il Sung has explained in his tomes on Juche, control of the state and its economy was seized from the controlling class and given over to the masses in a remarkably comprehensive overturning of society. Korea's pre-1950 rulers are now ruled by those who are (descendants) of good 'revolutionary' stock, and Songbon sustains that changeover. If your forebears were anti-Japanese fighters, then you probably rule today. Top Songbun gets good military posts, college, careers, apartments and families, and the privileges start young. Children of the elite attend the Mangyongdae Revolutionary Institute near Kim Il Sung's birthplace.

If you descended from factory-workers or peasants, your Songbun has a good grounding. Middling Songbun means hard work (revolutionary fervour as Juche demands) can get a work or military posting proximate to party cadres who might look kindly on you, and higher education is not impossible. If your forebears were Yangban or some form of middle-class professional, well, the odds are stacked. Kim Il Sung stated that 'after liberation we did not reject the old intellectuals because they came from rich families', and intellectuals as an educated class were essential for Korea's rebuilding. But that didn't mean they, or their descendants, were innately trustworthy. Good jobs of choice are attainable through party membership, not possible for someone with bad Songbon, as is higher education and the military; they go where the farms, factories and mines need them, and the only way up is to demonstrate exemplary 'right-thinking' through your work and life. Juche, as every person learns, emphasises self-sacrifice and hard work; dedication and revolutionary spirit can achieve everything, including good Songbon. As the Koreans put it, the best are considered 'tomatoes', red all the way through; 'apples' for the superficially committed, and 'grapes' are nearly irredeemable.

These indicators have deep roots. The use of familial records and professions in Songbon takes precedent from the aged genealogies and land registers used through much of Korea's history to determine people's social class and their entitlements. Today, uniforms are one obvious distinction between the services and the civilians, but the more subtle distinctions in people's apparel, ie: suits and the lapel-pins with different styling and colours, could be said to have origins right back in the Sillan bone-clan system that required visual indications of one's social position. Also, how one person's crimes implicated their whole family existed up until the Japanese took over in the 1900s, but has been revived.

For further information try the websites: www.amnesty.org or www.pyongyangsquare.com. Alternatively visit the Academy of Korea Studies, www.aks.ac.kr/EngHome.

Women

In olden Korea, women were lesser beings, for as Confucius said, wives are subservient to husbands, as the yin-yang symbolises. Women were not allowed to be seen in the streets, effectively under social-arrest in their walled homes during daylight, where they tended to their duties as homemakers and mothers. Women had to be veiled to leave the house. The traditional game of see-sawing (jumping up and down on either end of a see-saw) was devised so women could glimpse village life over the garden wall.

Women in modern Korea are emancipated and educated, and in the DPRK their equal status and social rights are enshrined in the constitution. At work, the gender balance is just about 50:50, while professional women have made their careers in the Democratic Korean Women's League Party and the judiciary, and many co-op farms are still run by women in an overhang from the depleted male reserves around the time of the Korean War. Nevertheless, not even the DPRK's social engineering could eradicate traditional male chauvinism that still half expects little more of women than to smile and file.

Language

The origins of Korean language go back to the earliest invasions of the peninsula by ancient Asian tribes, and Korean is considered to be part of the Altaic family of languages. Modern Korean is derived from the language of the Silla, with some influence from China's mandarin language. Another similarity is with Japanese, in that both languages have different grammar and vocabulary according to the level of politeness with which a person of a particular age, gender and social status addresses another. Many Chinese and Japanese words have been borrowed over the centuries, their meanings and pronunciation changed with time.

Historically, imported Chinese texts for Buddhism and Confucianism meant that Korean scholars had to read Chinese, and so used Chinese characters for writing, as can be seen on ancient (and recreated) sites around Korea. Various attempts were made to create an indigenous script over the centuries, until King Sejong's initiative led to a brilliantly simple phonetic script being developed by the mid-1440s. Called *hangul*, the new written language had 17 consonants and 11 vowel sounds represented in very simple characters, from which all the syllables could be constructed (since then the number of characters has dropped to 24).

Korea's educated elite damned *hangul* as an idiot's or commoner's means to communicate. The simplicity of *hangul* meant it did spread with relative ease among the non-elite. The literati argued that this proved their point, while the dual use of Chinese characters and *hangul* would be a written indication of education and class. Conversely, the literati's opposition solidified *hangul*'s suitability for Kim Il Sung, as a language for commoners was more revolutionary.

The attempts by Japanese colonialists to expunge the Korean language didn't succeed. From 1948 in the DPRK, all foreign influences, from borrowed words (especially Japanese and English-derived ones) to Chinese characters, were expurgated. All DPRK texts are completely in *hangul*. The DPRK 'dialect' uses Pyongyang as its standard, and northerners think the Seoul accent is nasal. Northern dialect also differs from the South in the former's complete absence of any modern American or Japanese slang. 'Polite' language has also been reduced in the North, from five noted levels down to three. In the ROK, the original number of polite levels and the use of some Chinese characters in writing continue. For words and phrases, see pages 215–18.

Religion

The most important religions that have historically succeeded across Korea have been Shamanism, then Buddhism, replaced by Confucianism and following that, Christianity. None thrive in today's DPRK. There are four officially-approved religious organisations, one each for Buddhists, Catholics, Protestants and followers of Chundo Kyo (a derivation of the Tonghak, combining elements of Christianity and Buddhism). The Buddhist and Christian organisations represent the DPRK at international conferences, but there are few thousands of followers of either religion, compared with millions before the 1950s. Practitioners who didn't head south during the war ceased their worship for their own good. The DPRK constitution allows for both freedom of religious beliefs and ceremonies within the prescribed religions, and for people to disseminate anti-religious propaganda. There are a great many Buddhist temples in the DPRK that have been rebuilt since the Korean War, and restored and rescued from the ravages of neglect, and are staffed by monks willing to entertain visitors, but the spotlessness of these sites suggests the monks are the only practitioners.

Arguably another religion is dedicated to the late Great Leader Kim Il Sung and his son Kim Jong Il. Their teachings, actions, visits, deeds, achievements, images, writings, are absolutely everywhere the visual presence of which is accentuated by there being nothing else of comparison.

For more information try Human Rights Watch at www.hrw.org or Index on Censorship at www.indexonline.org.

Culture
Cinema
'Like the leading article of the party paper, the cinema should have great appeal and inform the audience of reality. It should play a mobilising role in each stage of the revolutionary struggle,' wrote Kim Il Sung.

Should you get to settle in a cinema seat with a bucket of corn, be aware of the educational value of what you're about to see. Categories for DPRK films include: historical and literary classics like *The Flower Girl* or *The Sea of Blood*, with healthy infusions of revolutionary thought; socialist-realism films, promoting the success and development of socialism, like *Girl Chairman of the Cooperative Farm* or *The Flourishing Village*; themes of revolutionary tradition, with the Party and its ideals at the centre; and war films, fighting imperialism in its Japanese or American forms. Overarching themes are the oneness of the Korean nation, the realisation of Juche's teachings being the only way to live, and a strong spirit of selflessness and sacrifice being essential to achieving any collective goals, from reaching output targets to achieving national reunification.

In historical outings, common motifs include injustices and atrocities being piled upon lowly villages and families. Fathers get killed early on, providing the rage and reason for the remaining unlikely heroes to 'find themselves' and engage in amazing acts of self-sacrifice. Mothers not performing their own selfless feats, like storming a Japanese-held fort in *The Sea of Blood*, give their children to the revolutionary tasks (ultimately Kim Il Sung's guidance, who fills the spiritual void of the deceased fathers and becomes the 'father of the nation'). *The Story of a Nurse* celebrates the bravery and vision of a young nurse who follows the army over 1,000 *ri* behind enemy lines. Just after her efforts

RELIGIONS
Shamanism
The oldest religion in the peninsula that took root particularly in the north, shamanism is devoted to the worship of numerous spirits and gods believed to inhabit the elements and in particular the individual spirits inhabiting animals. The spirit believed to inhabit Mt Paektu is one long-surviving example of shamanism. In the north it came to be supplanted by Buddhism.

Buddhism
Buddhism arrived from India in the 6th century BC. An Indian noble eschewed his wealthy upbringing and through meditation achieved 'enlightenment'. Enlightenment here means to escape the cycle of birth, ageing, sickness and death through the renouncing of worldly desires and living in moderation. The soul enters nirvana, a paradise without want. It was Korea's state religion from the 6th to the 14th centuries AD, and through government patronage, beseeching the Buddha to protect their Korea, grew into a powerful sub-state over the years. This was partly why the religion was swiftly replaced by Confucianism as the state religion from the late 14th century onwards.

Confucianism.
This was originally more a code of morals and conduct than a religion but was given quasi-religious elements in its 2500 years. Although scarcely practised in the ROK, let alone the DPRK, Confucianism is still evident in Korean thinking, shown through their reverance for age, learning and desire for social harmony. Confucius was a Chinese scholar from the 6th century BC, who believed study was the way to the truth and the righteous virtues of benevolence, righteousness, decorum and wisdom. These were the virtues to ensure social harmony and stability. He formulated a detailed behavioural code to govern the relationships of the family, community and state, on the premise that stability would arise from everyone knowing their place in society. He espoused that authority and hierarchy continued from the family to the emperor and that there were five relationships to adhere to: sons showing respect, obedience and filial piety to their fathers; subjects loyalty to their rulers; the young revering the old; wives subservient to their husbands; friendships governed by mutual trust. Confucianism increasingly underpinned the structures of government and administration in Korea.

are rewarded with Party membership, her unit is bombed. 'Breathing her last,' says a throaty voice, 'she asks that her party card and her party fees be forwarded to the Party Central Committee, and dies a heroic death.'

Everyone must watch out for those of aristocratic heritage, inherently unstable people who might try counter-revolutionary activities. In *The First Party Commissioner* a former anti-Japanese revolutionary fighter is sent to the country to form a Party organisation in an iron smeltery. There, workers of

Chinese philosopher Zhu Xi in the 12th century expounded upon Confucianism to form Neo-Confucianism, with more religious undertones and involving ancestral worship, and it was this form that replaced Buddhism as the state religion in the 14th century.

Christianity

Christianity was first brought into Korea by freelance missionaries moving on from China, and then seeped in via traders and explorers. Christian teachings of paradise in the afterlife and an early release from poverty appealed to the poor and thousands converted, but their teachings were an anathema to the ruling classes, for Christianity dismissed ancestral worship (and therefore the legitimacy of the state rulers!) and encouraged individualism. Several purges killed thousands of converts in the 1800s, but by the 1880s, Protestant missionaries were pouring into the country, and as teachers and doctors were more tolerated for their poverty relief. Such works continued under Japanese rule. After 1945, many Christians headed south as the northern government converted churches for secular use. The ROK is today home to 25,000 churches, while Pyongyang has one Catholic and two Protestant churches. Kim Il Sung's parents were Christians, and there are micro-detectable influences in Juche philosophy and the cult surrounding the Kims.

Tonghak

This confluence of Buddhism, Taoism and Christianity was known as 'Eastern Learning' to the Koreans and was propagated by a squire's son, Ch'oe Chu'n. It preached salvation from destitution and placed all men (and women) on an equal footing with heaven, so envisaging a world without any class constraints or barriers. It appealed greatly to the majority of poor farmers, whilst causing panic in the upper classes, and peasants and disaffected Yangban rallied to the cause in their thousands in the early 1860s and throughout the decades to 1894, when the Tonghak mass-peasant uprising came close to destroying the House of Chosun (the Japanese 'rescued' them). The movement morphed into a less spiritual political philosophy that actually survives in some form in today's DPRK as the Chondoist Chongu Party. The proto-Marxist tenets of Tonghak must have saved the movement from the chop of the KWP.

former aristocratic stock conspire to kill him, but he crushes their reactionary subversion and establishes the smeltery's first Party cell.

In *Three Revolutionary Red Flags* and *The 100 Days Battle*, the workers are taught how Juche can make them self-reliant to meet the targets of the country's Chollima speed campaigns, which means films also cover issues of the day. From the 1970s, with Kim Jong Il's promotion as Kim Il Sung's successor, a sub-theme became the son taking over the revolutionary charge, and later revolutionary films touch on the class conflicts of the country's new technocrats.

The future of DPRK cinema is safe with Kim Jong Il. Films are Kim Jong Il's passion; aside from his own reputed private collection of 15,000 films, he's written about and had a hand in many of the DPRK's cinematic products, and secured the success of many silver-screen starlets.

Painting

For depictions of 'ordinary life', the socialist-realism view of the communist world, commited to canvas mostly from the 1930s to the 1960s, is still being exhibited here and produced, albeit on a reduced scale. The rosey-cheeked, flag-flying workers and farmers are depicted gaily hailing each other amid bumper crops, gleaming tractors and glowing blast-furnaces in the rural and urban idyll of the DPRK, while stoic-faced soldiers, chins up and eyes fixed amid blizzard-blinded battle against big-nosed foreigners, are shown defeating imperialism and advancing socialism. A great many paintings are celebrations of the life and achievements of the Kims, who dominate the pictures by the positioning, size and colouring of their figures. Another favoured medium is coloured woodcut prints.

There's little in common with such official art and the traditional painting styles that depict natural scenes of mountainsides, flora and fauna and ancient Korea. These images are shown from a few, deceptively simple brushstrokes of black ink to the wall-sized paintings and murals found in large public buildings. The first great examples of Korean painting are found in the earliest tombs and mausoleums, of scenes from court and portraits of the gods of the day. The **Songhwa Art Studio** in the Pyongyang International House of Culture is where current trends in DPRK fine art are found, and the **Art Gallery** on Kim Il Sung Square has an excellent chronological review of Korean art.

Pottery

The earliest Korean pottery found regularly is earthenware with combed surfaces, but the earthenware took plain surfacing during the Bronze Age. During the 2nd and 3rd centuries BC, a greyish-blue glaze grew prevalent, followed by the short-lived lead-glaze. From China in the ninth century came the green-blue tinge of celadon. Celadon had been imported for centuries from China, where its production was universal, and the techniques and styles were built upon by the Koreans over the next 500 years of Koryo rule, eventually surpassing the wares of China itself and were even exported to Japan. The most sophisticated designs and decoration of Korean ceramics is considered to have occurred in this period, charged by the demand for pottery resulting from the growth of Buddhism in Korea and its prescribed uses of tea and incense. Cranes, willow trees and peony blossom were common motifs, as were the Buddhist-related lotus flowers, carved on to the surfaces and filled with coloured glaze, carved right through the clay or moulded into sophisticated forms.

Meanwhile, the production of white porcelain was being perfected in China and these techniques were mastered in Korea by the late 14th century. Porcelain, being tougher than celadon, gradually supplanted it in common usage. Left plain white or lightly adorned with cobalt-blue designs, the simplified porcelain designs reflected the more frugal, less ostentatious Confucianism that was replacing Buddhism. Such were the skills of Korea's pottery makers that many were kidnapped to Japan by Hideyoshi's forces in 1592 and 1598. Light brown décor on porcelain's white surfaces had by the 18th century taken its place alongside the blue designs, but the most common form of pottery found across the peninsula is still the huge earthenware pickling jars for *kimchi*.

Music

Contemporary 'pop' music has rather formally attired men and women in front of suitably suited bands behind panelled music stands, knocking out crushingly sentimental (and quite sexless) numbers about long-distance relationships of friends and family, hometowns, reunification and landscapes, like *Doves Fly High*, *My Home*, *Sweet Home*, *The Peak of Mt Gumsoo* and *Yearning For My Beloved Mother*. Hits to get down to from the Korean People's Army Choir, which you'll certainly see on TV, include *Soldiers Hear Rice-ears Rustle*, *The Leader Has Come to Our Outpost* and *Warm Feelings Creep Over the Ridge*, with a heavy accent on Russian military music. A pop music industry built on teen hysteria, as has spread to Russia and China, just doesn't exist in the DPRK.

The state actively promotes and supports the teaching and production of dance and music in many forms, as long as the output is healthily infused with politically correct ideals.

Kim Jong Il views opera thus:

> The creators of music must complete revolutionary opera songs as in
> *The Song of Kumgang-san Mountains*: 'For fifteen long years through
> snowstorms, He fought for the rebirth of this beautiful country, The
> towering peaks and crystal-clear streams, Praise Marshal Kim Il
> Sung's kindness in Song.'

Tell the Story, Forest, *A True Daughter of the Party*, and *The Fate of a Self-Defence Corps Man* are all hit operas from the 1970s.

Apart from the mass-spectacles of Arirang and the Mass Gymnastics, and the medley presented at the Mangyondae Schoolchildren's Palace, opera, dance and music recitals can be seen in Pyongyang, mainly at the Mansudae Arts and Moranbang theatres.

Literature

A staggering amount of literature produced is dedicated to the works of Kim Il Sung and Kim Jong Il. Juche, revolution and the needs for the struggle of anti-imperialism underpin all modern philosophical and historical works, which strive to prove the superiority of socialism over all other lesser societal creeds.

Similarly to facets of culture, writers in the DPRK are state-supported and state-subordinate. From poetry to popular novels, literature must serve to 'depict man and life and serve the popular masses truly', wrote Kim Jong Il, 'we need a humanistic literature, which gives prominence to the principle of independence, the development of independent individuals, and which creates the image of the truly typical man of the new era, thereby contributing to the transformation of the whole of society in accordance with the concept of Juche', clarifying how man prizes, glorifies and will die for independence.

Pyongyang riverfront

Practical Information

WHEN TO GO

The rainy season's very humid, cloudy and sticky, and not brilliant for radiant photography as the rain soups up poorer roads and rail lines and curtails access. The best times to go are April to June and September to October, when it is cool, dry and colourful, from spring's heaving tides of white blossoms to autumn's cascades of gold and red. If there are Mass Games on (usually from late April to June) they are an absolute must-see.

DPRK TRAVEL

For tourists, trips to the DPRK take at least two weeks to arrange, for visa applications to be checked out and for the trip's itineraries to be arranged and agreed by both sides. Tourists only visit the DPRK on guided tours, with private transport arranged by the Koreans. Even a solo traveller will have two guides, a driver and a car to zoom about the country, and a guide is with you virtually all the time. The guides have the permits that all Koreans need to travel from city to city, checked at checkpoints surrounding the cities, and which tourists cannot obtain themselves. Access to many parts of the country is completely prohibited, such that even workers for esteemed NGOs like the World Food Programme can't enter large areas. Foreigners' free movement around the country is as proscribed as that of locals, who need good reason to get permits. Combined with the severe shortages of petrol and a very intermittent electricity supply, this means that there is no practical public transport system in the country.

For tourists, the range of places open to visit is limited to the capital, Pyongyang, and a handful of other cities near to national parks that protect mountains deemed significant for their history or wildlife. Pyongyang can be explored freely without guides – most of its bars and restaurants are open to all; but another issue is currency. Until recently, there were three types of currency: the local currency (won), special won for foreigners, and hard currency. The foreigners' won has been abolished, but that doesn't mean that foreigners can use local won. Hence foreigners are limited to the 'approved' restaurants, shops and exhibitions that accept hard currency.

All these limits mean that foreigners are effectively kept to the best parts of the cities and countryside, the well-tended, well-fed areas, where the needs of the locals are being met, so exposure for the average visitor to deprivation doesn't happen. Against the great diplomatic strides achieved in the last five years, a very deep, historical distrust of foreigners is continually worked up by the state-owned DPRK media, but to that end the locals keep their distance and are ultimately very warm rather than hostile. As long as visitors behave themselves within the paramteters laid out, the risks to them are very, very few.

TOUR OPERATORS
In the DPRK

Korean International Travel Company runs numerous **specialist tours**, such as mud treatment, spa treatment, golf, steam locomotives (in Kaesong and a new one in Nampo), mountaineering in Kumgang and around Paektu, Taekwondo (Korean martial arts), Korean language learning, Juche learning, plant tours for medicinal herbs and specialist wildlife expeditions.

Korea International Travel Company (KITC) Central District, Pyongyang; tel: +850-2-3818901, 381 8574; fax: +850-2-381 7607. There's one office in the basement of the Yanggakdo Hotel.

China, Beijing Yanxiang Hotel, 3rd floor, Qianghuating A2, Jangtai Rd, Chaoyang District; tel: +86 10 6437 6224; fax: +86 10 6436 9089

China, Dandong KITC, Xian Qian Rd, Yuan Bao District Dandong, China; tel: +86 (0) 415 281 2542, 2810457; fax: +86 (0) 415 281 8438

China, Yanji Tel/fax: +86 433 2529689

Thailand Tel: +66-2-321 5797 Korea International Travel Company Bangkok Office 867139 Moodansilintheb Patanakan Road Soi 46 Soun Luang, Bangkok 10250; tel: (66-2) 321-5797 or 653-4083; fax: (66-2) 322-1109

In the UK

Chollima Group 86 Ralph Court, Queenway, London W2 5HU; tel/fax: 020 7243 3829; email: info@chollima-group.com; web: www.chollima-group.com

Explore Worldwide Ltd 1 Frederick St, Aldershot, Hants, GU11 1LQ; tel: 01252 760200; fax: 01252 760201; email: ops@exploreworldwide.com; web: www.exploreworldwide.com

Koryo Tours Call Nick Bonner, +86 1362 109927, tel/fax: +86 10 64167544, email: info@koryogroup.com, web: www.koryogroup.com (and visit www.thegameoftheirlives.com)

Regent Holidays (UK) Ltd 15 John St, Bristol BS1 2HR; tel: 0117 921 1711; fax: 0117 925 4866; email: regent@regent-holidays.co.uk; web: www.regent-holidays.co.uk

Elsewhere

Bestway Tours & Safaris Suite #206, 8678 Greenall Av, Burnaby, British Columbia, Canada V5J 3M6; tel: +1 604 264 7378; toll free: +1 800 6630844 (Canada and US residents only); fax: +1 604 264 7774; web: www.bestway.com

Classic Oriental Tours Travel House Level 3/35, Grafton St, Woollahra NSW 2025; tel: +61 02 9657 2020; fax: +61 02 9657 2029; web: travel@classicoriental.com.au

Tin Bo Travel Service 2nd Floor, 725 Somerset St W, Ottawa, Ontario K1R 6P7; tel: +1 613 238 7093; fax: +1 613 238 8179 / +1 800 267 6668; email: tinbo@on.aibn.com; web: www.tinboholidays.com

VNC Travel Catharijnesingel 70, PO Box 79, 3500 AB Utrecht, Netherlands; tel: +31 30 231 1500; fax: +31 30 231 0232; email: info@vnc.nl Homepage (in Dutch); web: www.vnc.nl

Tour costs

On a tour, the cost is determined by numerous factors, including hotels, meals, guides, transportation, tickets to shows and areas of the country to be visited. It's difficult to obtain a comprehensive breakdown of the costs per element as tours are usually presented as 'costs per day, all inclusive'. To that end, tours are not spontaneous but are long-standing arrangements brokered between the agencies inside and outside the country. That may be one reason that getting a cheaper hotel may not be so easy. Aside from different prices for different hotel bands, and taking it as read that more days means more money, another variable affecting cost is group size and the single-person supplement.

For example, a foreign tour operator can get, say, a rate of around €185/US$200 per person, but going direct gets day rates of €220–257/US$240–280 for a standard tour, which includes the single supplement of €32–36/US$35–40 per night. The cost per person per day goes down as the group size increases, with three to five people at about €147–184/US$160–200, six to nine at €110/US$120 per day and 10+ around €92/US$100 day (maximum group size being around 16).

GETTING THERE AND AWAY
By air
From China

Until very recently there had been for a few years only one carrier to the DPRK, the national **Air Koryo**. Air Koryo operates regular international flights to Beijing, Shenyang, Vladivostok and Khabarovsk, and irregularly to Bangkok and Macau. Air Koryo's domestic schedule flies Pyongyang to Chongjin, Hamhung, Kaesong, Kilju, Kanggye, Sinuiju and Wonsan, but times, prices and availability for foreigners is not known and not revealed by Air Koryo. Prices, times and schedule numbers for the international routes are for early 2003.

Pyongyang (P) JS151 Beijing (B) JS152 Pyongyang Tuesdays and Saturdays. P 09.00–09.40 B, B 11.30–14.00 P. This is US$165 o/w, US$310 rtn.

Pyongyang JS155 Shenyang JS156 Pyongyang Wednesdays and Saturdays, P 11.40–11.35 S, S 15.10–17.00 P. US$80 o/w and US$162 rtn, plus 90RMB departure tax from Beijing/Shenyang and €11 from Pyongyang.

Since March 2003, **China Northern** has offered flights Beijing–Pyongyang and Pyongyang–Beijing on Mondays and Fridays.

Dong Ta Airport 3-1 Xiaoheyan Rd, Dadong District, Shenyang City, Liao Ning Province, China 110043; tel: +86 24 829 4446; fax: +86 24 829 44 33. Pyongyang office: 330/329 Bldg No 3, Munsudong Daedonggang District; tel: +850 2 3817351, +850 2 381 7659; fax: +850 2 3817629

China Northern Part of the China Southern group, China Southern Airlines (Nanfan Hangkong Dasha, 2 Dongsanhuan Nan Road. Beijing: +86 10 65672230/31, 6567 2190/04/05/06/07/08/94Lst/F; web: www.cs-air.com/en).

Flights are as follows:

Beijing CZ655 Pyongyang, Pyongyang CZ656 Beijing, B-P 0810-1040, P-B 1130-1210. China Northern announced in mid-2002 that it would reopen twice-weekly routes Beijing–Dalian–Pyongyang, and that this route would run during the summer months. Routes from Shenyang are also reportedly imminent.

From Russia
Pyongyang JS162 Vladivostok JS163 Pyongyang Thursdays. P 09.40–12.00 V, V 19.30–20.00 P. US$150 o/w, US$296 rtn.
Pyongyang JS253 Khabarovsk JS254 Pyongyang Mondays and Fridays. P 09.50–14.00 K, K 16.00–16.10 P. US$303 o/w, US$582 rtn. Moscow's Sheremetevo airport charges economy US$43 and business class US$73 airport tax.

From Thailand*
Pyongyang JS153 Bangkok, Thursdays, **Bangkok JS154 Pyongyang**, Fridays. P 10.30–14.20 B, B 12.20–20.00 P (times and days can vary). US$405 o/w, US$640 rtn. www.airportthai.or.th.

From Macau*
Pyongyang JS187 Macau JS188 Pyongyang Mondays & Fridays. P 08.35–11.35 M, M 13.05–16.45 P (times and days can vary). www.macau-airport.gov.mo/english.

*It is still advertised in Air Koryo literature (and been confirmed by the Bangkok office, but denied by the Beijing office) that they fly from Pyongyang to Bangkok and Macau. These routes are still flown by Air Koryo intermittently (on a charter basis).

Air Koryo offices
China Swissotel, Hong Kong-Macau Center, Dong Si Shi, Tiao Li Jiao Qiao, Beijing 100027; tel: +86 (0)10 6501 1557/1559, airport 6459 1253; fax: +86 (0) 10 6501 2591
Qibaoshan Hotel No 81, Shiywei Road Heping District, Shenyang; tel: +86 24 23251922, 23251937; fax: +86 24 23251936
Thailand 942/135.4 4th floor, Charn Issara Tower Rama 4 Road, Bangrak, Bangkok 10500; tel: +66 (0)2 2342805/6, AP 5353974; fax: +66 (0)2 2675009, AP 5355974
Russia 101000 Mosfilmovskaya 72, Moscow; tel: +7 (0)95 1436307; fax: +7 095 1476300
41 Portovaya St, Artyom Primorski Krai, Vladivostok Airport, 692800; tel/fax: +7 4332 307684
Macau Rua da Praia Grade 55, 20 Andar-C, Centro Commercial 'Hoi Vong'; tel: (town) +853 353 6634/353 6635, (airport) +853 861329/861111 ext 3878; fax: (town) +853 356631, (airport) +853 861329

Air Koryo flights from Pyongyang to Moscow and Berlin are defunct. Aeroflot and Air China may have flown to Pyongyang in the past, but don't at the time of writing. Check www.aeroflot.ru and www.airchina.com.cn for changes in this.

International flights to and from Rajin-Sonbong were investigated in the 1990s and may yet materialise. Direct flights from Seoul to Pyongyang remain the preserve of high-level diplomacy.

By rail

There is a very regular international rail service from Pyongyang to Beijing. The T27 leaves Beijing railway station (just inside the second ring road, south of Jianguomenwai Street) at 17.25 on Mondays, Wednesdays, Thursdays and Saturdays, arriving in Pyongyang next day. The Pyongyang service T28 to Beijing leaves at 10.10 on the same days, and the Saturday train carries a carriage ultimately bound for Moscow. At Dandong and Sinuijiu, the two cities straddling the Yalu River border between China and DPRK, the international carriages (Chinese, Korean and a Russian) get detached from the long local trains and pushed across the bridge, from the arms of one side's customs officers into the clutches of the other. Both groups take two hours to sift through your papers and possibly bags. Snack pedlars trawl the train corridors and platforms on the Chinese side, selling noodles to be cooked from each carriage's scalding hot-water urn. If possible, bring lots of savoury picnic foods with a mind to share them with your Korean co-passengers, who'll likely share theirs with you. This writer's experience of the buffet car was that its hand-written menu had ten small dishes for €5.

Beijing to Pyongyang o/w fares in summer 2002 were US$95 (deluxe sleeper), US$79 (soft), US$46 (hard) with a minor variation depending on the carriage nationality. Pyongyang to Beijing were similarly priced. Boarding points en route are Tianjin, Shenyang, Dandong and Sinuijiu and prices vary accordingly. Return tickets aren't available from either end. In China, either buy the tickets from the station or go to the informative, English-speaking BTG Ticketing Co Ltd, Tourism Tower, 28 Jianguomenwai Beijing 100022, China tel: +86 10 65150093/24, 65158844/2111; fax: +86 10 65158564, 65155292.

There is also the rail route direct from Pyongyang into Russia to Vladivostok, as used by Kim Jong Il himself to visit Russia in 2001 and 2002. However, the route is irregularly plied (US$80 o/w, class unknown), being set by date and not by days, if foreigners can get on at all. But it's worth asking about: every question becomes a suggestion.

A freight route from North to South is being built across the DMZ. One day it will take passengers.

By sea

The only direct connection from the **ROK to the DPRK** is by the Hyundai corporation ferry that sails from Hyundai Sokcho Ferry Terminal, taking short tours (three or four days) to the Mt Kumgang area on North Korea's southeast coast. The route is the only way ordinary South Koreans can 'easily' visit the north, and makes for an interesting diversionary tour for foreigners in the ROK. A single ticket costs around US$400. Apply to: Hyundai Asian Corporation, 12th Floor Hyundai Building, 140-2, Gye-dong, Jongno-gu, Seoul 110-793, Korea; tel: 82 2 3669 3916, 82 2 3669 3897; fax: 82 2 3669 3690; email: asan3669@hanmail.net; web: htpp://english.tour2korea.com/01culture/Application_Form_1.doc, or ask through KNTO's (South Korean National Tourist Office) overseas branch offices.

The firm now run a route by road. A hundred ROK officials crossed the DMZ by bus to Mt Kumgang, accessing the DPRK for the first time by land through this border, on February 5 2003. This road running near the east coast has been kept open and 30,000 have applied for tickets to cross.

From **China**, there's the *Orient Pearl* ferry from Dandong that runs to the South Korean port of Incheon three nights a week. See *Dandong* section, page 207, for details.

There is also a passenger ferry link to the DPRK from Niigata in **Japan**, serving as a vital cultural and economic link for hundreds of thousands of Korean residents in Japan loyal to the North. The North Korea Service runs around three times a month from Niigata Port, (West Harbour Area) to Wonsan, from where the Mangyongbong 92 goes weekly (one-day journey) to Niigata. A lack of diplomatic ties between the North and Japan (under negotiation) preclude non-Korean-Japanese from using this service, but ...

By road

The only road links used to cross into the RASON zone, but this has changed in the last two years. Roads are being built across the DMZ. Indeed, 80 ROK officials crossed the DMZ by bus to Mt Kumgang along a 40km stretch of road, accessing the DPRK for the first time by land through this border, on February 5 2003, followed by 500 more ten days later. This occurred at the height of the nuclear stand-off and there have been tens of thousands of applications to do this trip since, so it's a measure of the kind of invasion both sides really want. Applications can be made through Asan Hyundai (see above for details) and a guestimate price is US$270 per person.

Since 2001 there's been a **motorcycle rally** starting from the south. The International South–North Korea Motorcycle Touring takes the Hyundai ferry, then drives around Kumgang to Pyongyang, taking in some spas and a circus before trundling back. Contact the International Motorcycle Federation (FIM), KMF (Korea Motorcycle Federation) or AMTA (Asian Motorcycle Touring Association). The August 2002 mission cost US$1,000 per driver.

Korea Motorcycle Federation (Se Woong Jung); tel: +82 02 596 6886; fax: +82 02 533 7953; email: garlicmania@daum.net.

RED TAPE

Visas, usually single-entry, are given for set arrival and departure dates and are designated for exit/entry for Pyongyang, Sinuiju and Tuman. Visas must be obtained before going, and require letters of invitation, whether the visit is for business or pleasure, and your passport should be valid for a year after the travel dates. Because tourists must go on tours, they will either let their travel operator deal with KITC or do that themselves but applications take at least ten days because of how much needs arranging. Along with the application forms of the respective tour company and two (or more) passport photos, travellers must submit a CV and a letter from their current employer verifying the applicant's details. The CV and letter details have to be updated up to the day they are checked: a wrong number or date can scupper the keenest tourist. Journalists need special visas, they are not allowed in on tourist visas, and any caught sneaking in are thrown out at their own expense. More importantly, they endanger everyone associated with them, the other tourists, the external tour firm and particularly the Korean guides. It is tantamount to spying. Sneaking into any country without a visa is a bad idea, and the authorities are not amenable. Don't do it. Most people need visas to visit another country; North Koreans need visas to leave theirs.

If you're staying in the DPRK for more than 24 hours you must register with the Foreign Ministry, something the hotel should do, but they will need your passport for an hour.

South Koreans and US citizens cannot get tourist visas, except if the former go to Kumgang by Hyundai ferry. Americans were banned from 1995 although a few were allowed in for the 2002 Arirang Festival, but that was a one-off. Check with the tour operators for the situation.

Remember that you'll need double-entry visas certainly for China or Russia if you're coming through them, which is likely.

Embassies and consulates

Since 1998, the DPRK has more than doubled its cache of fully established diplomatic relations with other countries, with the number of Western countries growing. Still, many don't have an actual embassy in Pyongyang but cover the DPRK from their Beijing embassies.

China Kin Mal Dong, Mao Lang Bong district, Pyongyang; tel: +850 2 3813133, +850 2 3813116; fax: +850 2 3813425. This stands out as the biggest embassy and the most efficient. It is very good for getting visas back to China – it can get you business visas in a day for US$100.

Germany Munsudong District, Pyongyang; tel: +850 2 381 73 85; fax: +850 2 381 73 97

India 6 Munsudong, District Daedonggang, Pyongyang; tel: +850 2 3817277, 3817274, 3817215; fax: +850 2 3817619; telex: 35035 IND KP

Mongolia Mansu-dong, Pyongyang; tel: +850 2 3817322; fax: +850 2 3817616

People's Republic of Korea Tel: +850 2 3817908; fax: +850 2 3817258; email: ambassaden.pyongyang@foreign.ministry.se

Sweden Munsodong, Daedonggang District, Pyongyang

UK Munsu Dong District; tel: +850 2 381 7980/4 (5 lines), international dialling: +850 2 382 7980/2 (3 lines), local dialling. +850 2 381 2228; fax: +850 2 381 7985, international dialling: +850 2 382 7983, local dialling. +850 2 381 4482 out of hours. Open: Mon–Fri 00.00–08.30.

The most convenient locations for New Zealanders to apply for visas are likely to be North Korea's embassy in Jakarta, which is cross-accredited to New Zealand, or its embassy in Beijing.

DPRK missions

Australia & New Zealand Further advice may also be obtained from the Australian Embassy in Beijing, 21 Dongzhimenwai Dajie, Sanlitun, Beijing 100600; tel: +86 (10) 6532 2331; fax: +86 (10) 6532 4605. Contact the Department of Foreign Affairs and Trade in Canberra (02) 6 261 3305. The DPRK Missions nearest to Australia and New Zealand are located in Bangkok, Beijing, Hong Kong, Jakarta and Singapore.

Austria Beckmanngasse 10–12, A-1140 Vienna; tel: +43 1 894 23 11; fax: +43 1 894 31 74

Canada (mission) 151 Slater St, 6th floor, Ottawa K1P5H3; tel: +1 613 232 1715

China Ritan Bei Lu, Jianguomenwai, Beijing, 100600; tel: +86 (10) 6532 1186, 6532 1154 (protocol); fax: +86 (10) 6532 4862. The biggest DPRK embassy (and one of Beijing's biggest).

Denmark Skelvej 2, Dk-2900 Hellerup, Copenhagen; tel: +45 39 62 50 70; fax: +45 39 62 50 70. Hours: Mon–Fri 09.00–16.00

Finland Kulosaaren puistotie 32, 00570 Helsinki; tel: +358 9 684 8195; fax: +35 8 9 684 8995

France 47 rue Chaveau, 92200 Neuilly-sur-Seine; tel: +33 (0)1 47 47 53 85; fax: +33 (0)1 47 47 61 41

Germany The Interest Section of the DPR Korea at the Embassy of the People's Republic of China is now the DPRK Embassy, Glinkastrasse 7, D-10117, Berlin; tel: +49 (0) 30   229 31 91 and 229 31 89. Contact Mr Ri Sang Yu (former GDR-Embassy official).

Hong Kong DPRK Consulate Chinachem Century Tower, 20th Floor, 178 Gloucester Rd, Wanchai, Hong Kong; tel: +852 28034447; fax: +852 25773644

Indonesia PO Box 5003, JKTM Jakarta 12050; tel: +62 21 521 0131; fax: +62 21 526 0066

Lebanon Mousaitbeh, PO Box 9636; tel: +961 (1) 311490, 868722

Russia (and Ukraine) 72 Mosfilmovskaya St, Moscow; tel: (+7 095) 143 62 49, 143 62 31; fax: (+7 095) 938 21 95. Hours: 09.00–12.00, 14.00–18.00

Singapore 7500A Beach Rd, #09-320, The Plaza, Singapore 199591; tel: +65 6440 3498; fax: +65 6348 2026. Hours: Mon–Fri 9.00–12.30; 13.30–17.00

Sweden Norra Kungsvaegan 39, 181 31 Lindingoe; tel: 767 3836; fax: 767 3836

Switzerland Pourtalesstrasse 43, 3074 Muri bei Bern; tel: +41 (0) 31 951 66 21

Thailand 14 Muban Suanlaemthong 2 (soi 28), Phattanakan Rd, Suan Luang, Bangkok 10250; tel: +66 319 2686 7

UK 73 Gunnersbury Av, London, W5 4LP; tel: +44 020 8992 4965; fax: +44 020 8992 2053

US The DPRK Mission in the US is really the Permanent Mission to the United Nations, 820 Second Av, 13th Floor, New York, NY 10017; tel: +1 212 972 3105/3106; fax: +1 212 972 3154. DPRK officials are restricted to within a 25-mile perimeter of the building.

HEALTH
with Dr Felicity Nicholson
Before you go
Vaccinations

There is no absolute requirement for vaccinations, but the following are strongly recommended. Be up to date with **diphtheria/tetanus** (ten-yearly), **polio** (ten-yearly), hepatitis A and typhoid.

Hepatitis A vaccine (eg: Havrix Monodose or Avaxim) should be taken ideally at least two weeks before travel but can be given the day before if time is short. One dose lasts for a year and a booster dose given six to 12 months later will protect for at least ten years. The vaccine costs about £50 per dose but is well worth the money as hepatitis A is a debilitating disease that is easily prevented by the vaccine.

The newer **typhoid** vaccines (eg: Typhim Vi) are more effective than the older ones and have few risks of side effects. It is worth taking unless you are unable to get to a doctor or travel clinic until a few days before travel and are only going for a week or less. Otherwise it is recommended.

For trips of four weeks or more to rural areas between July and October, **Japanese encephalitis** vaccine is advised unless there are contra indications. The course comprises three doses of vaccine taken over a four-week period. The last dose cannot be given less than ten days before flying out of the UK. If time is short then two doses given no less than a week apart will suffice, but the same time restriction applies.

For trips of six weeks or more, **hepatitis B** vaccine should also be considered. If Engerix B vaccine is used, the course comprises three doses given at 0, 7, and 21 to 28 days. It should also be taken if you are working in a hospital or with children, irrespective of the duration of your trip.

Ideally, then, you should go to a doctor or travel clinic at least four weeks before your trip.

Travel clinics and health information

A list of current travel clinic websites worldwide is available on www.istm.org/. For other journey preparation information, consult ftp://ftp.shoreland.com/pub/shorecg.rtf or www.tripprep.com. Information about various medications may be found on www.emedicine.com/wild/topiclist.htm.

UK

Berkeley Travel Clinic 32 Berkeley St, London W1J 8EL (near Green Park tube station); tel: 020 7629 5710

British Airways Travel Clinic and Immunisation Service There are two BA clinics in London, both on tel: 0845 600 2236. Appointments only at 111 Cheapside ; or walk-in service Mon–Sat at 156 Regent St. For changes, look on the internet (www.britishairways.com/travelclinics). Apart from providing inoculations and malaria prevention, they sell a variety of health-related goods.

Fleet Street Travel Clinic 29 Fleet St, London EC4Y 1AA; tel: 020 7353 5678; web: www.fleetstreet.com. Injections, travel products and latest advice.

Hospital for Tropical Diseases Travel Clinic Mortimer Market Centre, 2nd Floor, Capper St (off Tottenham Ct Rd), London WC1E 6AU; tel: 020 7388 9600; web: www.thhtd.org. Offers consultations and advice, and is able to provide all necessary drugs and vaccines for travellers. Runs a healthline (09061 337733) for country-specific information and health hazards. Also stocks nets, water purification equipment and personal protection measures.

MASTA (Medical Advisory Service for Travellers Abroad), at the London School of Hygiene and Tropical Medicine, Keppel St, London WC1 7HT; tel: 09068 224100. This is a premium-line number, charged at 60p per minute. For a fee, they will provide an individually tailored health brief, with up-to-date information on how to stay healthy, inoculations and what to bring.

MASTA pre-travel clinics Tel: 01276 685040. Call for the nearest; there are currently 30 in Britain. Also sell malaria prophylaxis memory cards, treatment kits, bednets, net treatment kits.

NHS travel website, www.fitfortravel.scot.nhs.uk, provides country-by-country advice on immunisation and malaria, plus details of recent developments, and a list of relevant health organisations.

Nomad Travel Store 3–4 Wellington Terrace, Turnpike Lane, London N8 0PX; tel: 020 8889 7014; fax: 020 8889 9528; email: sales@nomadtravel.co.uk; web: www.nomadtravel.co.uk. As well as dispensing health advice, Nomad stocks mosquito nets and other anti-bug devices, and an excellent range of adventure travel gear.

Thames Medical 157 Waterloo Rd, London SE1 8US; tel: 020 7902 9000. Competitively priced, one-stop travel health service. All profits go to their affiliated company, InterHealth, which provides health care for overseas workers on Christian projects.

Trailfinders Immunisation Centre 194 Kensington High St, London W8 7RG; tel: 020 7938 3999.

Travelpharm The Travelpharm website, www.travelpharm.com, offers up-to-date guidance on travel-related health and has a range of medications available through their online mini-pharmacy.

Irish Republic
Tropical Medical Bureau Grafton Street Medical Centre, Grafton Buildings, 34 Grafton St, Dublin 2; tel: 1 671 9200. Has a useful website specific to tropical destinations: www.tmb.ie.

USA
Centers for Disease Control 1600 Clifton Rd, Atlanta, GA 30333; tel: 877 FYI TRIP; 800 311 3435; web: www.cdc.gov/travel. The central source of travel information in the USA. Each summer they publish the invaluable Health Information for International Travel, available from the Division of Quarantine at the above address.

Connaught Laboratories PO Box 187, Swiftwater, PA 18370; tel: 800 822 2463. They will send a free list of specialist tropical-medicine physicians in your state.

IAMAT (International Association for Medical Assistance to Travelers) 736 Center St, Lewiston, NY 14092; tel: 716 754 4883; web: www.iamat.org. A non-profit organisation that provides lists of English-speaking doctors abroad.

Canada

IAMAT (International Association for Medical Assistance to Travellers) Suite 1, 1287 St Clair Av W, Toronto, Ontario M6E 1B8; tel: 416 652 0137; web: www.sentex.net/~iamat

TMVC (Travel Doctors Group) Sulphur Springs Rd, Ancaster, Ontario; tel: 905 648 1112; web: www.tmvc.com.au

Australia, New Zealand, Thailand

TMVC Tel: 1300 65 88 44; web: www.tmvc.com.au. Twenty clinics in Australia, New Zealand and Thailand, including:

Auckland Canterbury Arcade, 170 Queen Street, Auckland City; tel: 373 3531
Brisbane Dr Deborah Mills, Qantas Domestic Building, 6th floor, 247 Adelaide St, Brisbane, QLD 4000; tel: 7 3221 9066; fax: 7 3321 7076
Melbourne Dr Sonny Lau, 393 Little Bourke St, 2nd floor, Melbourne, VIC 3000; tel: 3 9602 5788; fax: 3 9670 8394
Sydney Dr Mandy Hu, Dymocks Building, 7th Floor, 428 George St, Sydney, NSW2000; tel: 2 221 7133; fax: 2 221 8401

South Africa

SAA-Netcare Travel Clinics PO Box 786692, Sandton 2146; fax: 011 883 6152; web: www.travelclinic.co.za or www.malaria.co.za. Clinics throughout South Africa.
TMVC (Travel Doctor Group) 113 DF Malan Drive, Roosevelt Park, Johannesburg; tel: 011 888 7488; web: www.tmvc.com.au. Consult the website for details of clinics in South Africa.

Switzerland

IAMAT (International Association for Medical Assistance to Travellers) 57 Voirets, 1212 Grand Lancy, Geneva; web: www.sentex.net/~iamat

In North Korea

Medical facilities in North Korea as a whole are basic, particularly in the rural areas. Hospitals and clinics in the latter are usually able to offer only the very minimum medical care. Clinical hygiene is poor, anaesthetics are frequently unavailable, and the electricity supply to the hospitals (even in the capital) can be intermittent. You should try to avoid serious surgery if you can. Take with you any medication you think you are likely to require because supplies are limited and very difficult to buy. Tourist sites may offer medical facilities.

Use bottled water for drinking and brushing teeth. Avoid dairy products, which are likely to have been made with unpasteurised milk, and boil milk (or use powdered or tinned milk, using pure water in the reconstitution process). Ensure meat and fish is well cooked, and served hot. Be wary of pork, salad and mayonnaise, and always cook vegetables and peel fruit. If in doubt:

PEEL IT, BOIL IT, COOK IT OR FORGET IT

LONG-HAUL FLIGHTS
Felicity Nicholson

There is growing evidence, albeit circumstantial, that long-haul air travel increases the risk of developing deep vein thrombosis. This condition is potentially life threatening, but it should be stressed that the danger to the average traveller is slight.

Certain risk factors specific to air travel have been identified. These include immobility, compression of the veins at the back of the knee by the edge of the seat, the decreased air pressure and slightly reduced oxygen in the cabin, and dehydration. Consuming alcohol may exacerbate the situation by increasing fluid loss and encouraging immobility.

In theory everyone is at risk, but those at highest risk are shown below:

* Passengers on journeys of longer than eight hours duration
* People over 40
* People with heart disease
* People with cancer
* People with clotting disorders
* People who have had recent surgery, especially on the legs
* Women on the pill or other oestrogen therapy
* Pregnancy
* People who are very tall (over 6ft/1.8m) or short (under 5ft/1.5m)

A deep vein thrombosis (DVT) is a clot of blood that forms in the leg veins. Symptoms include swelling and pain in the calf or thigh. The skin may feel

Malaria

There are pockets of malaria in the form of *Plasmodium vivax* in the northern territory. At the time of writing, no prophylaxis is advised (in the form of tablets) but you should always use insect repellents from dusk until dawn (the mosquitoes that carry the disease emerge at this time). It is also wise to wear clothing to cover arms and legs and to make your sleeping accommodation as mosquito proof as possible.

Dengue fever

This mosquito-borne disease may mimic malaria; there is no prophylactic medication available to deal with it. The mosquitoes that carry this virus bite during the daytime, so it is worth applying repellent if you see any mosquitoes around. Symptoms include strong headaches, rashes, excruciating joint and muscle pains, and high fever. Dengue fever lasts only for a week or so and is not usually fatal. Complete rest and paracetamol are the usual treatment; plenty of fluids also help. Some patients are given an intravenous drip to prevent dehydration. It is especially important to protect yourself if you have had dengue fever before, since a second infection with a different strain can result in the potentially fatal dengue haemorrhagic fever.

hot to touch and becomes discoloured (light blue-red). A DVT is not dangerous in itself, but if a clot breaks down then it may travel to the lungs (pulmonary embolus). Symptoms of a pulmonary embolus (PE) include chest pain, shortness of breath and coughing up small amounts of blood.

Symptoms of a DVT rarely occur during the flight, and typically occur within three days of arrival, although symptoms of a DVT or PE have been reported up to two weeks later.

Anyone who suspects that they have these symptoms should see a doctor immediately as anticoagulation (blood thinning) treatment can be given.

Prevention of DVT
General measures to reduce the risk of thrombosis are shown below. This advice also applies to long train or bus journeys.

- Whilst waiting to board the plane, try to walk around rather than sit.
- During the flight drink plenty of water (at least two small glasses every hour).
- Avoid excessive tea, coffee and alcohol.
- Perform leg-stretching exercises, such as pointing the toes up and down.
- Move around the cabin when practicable.

If you fit into the high-risk category (see above) ask your doctor if it is safe to travel. Additional protective measures such as graded compression stockings, aspirin or low molecular weight heparin can be given. No matter how tall you are, where possible request a seat with extra legroom.

SAFETY
Petty theft has happened from hotels and other accommodation, so be sure to keep your valuables and passport in safe keeping at all times. Incidents of other crimes against foreigners are very infrequently heard of. Take out full insurance coverage for health, belongings and flights, and cash to cover the trip because the ability to get hold of emergency funds is negligible. Bring all medication that you need and don't expect to get hold of any with any ease in the country. Some form of ID is needed at all times. Visit www.fco.gov.uk for up-to-date advice.

WHAT TO TAKE
- insect repellent
- a small first-aid kit, with headache pills, contact lens solutions and enough of your own medication (do not rely on getting it in the DPRK, see *Health*, page 79)
- a powerful torch (and batteries!) for the lack of street-lighting and evening power-cuts, preferably one that doubles as a lamp for night reading to supplement the low-watt lighting (when it's on)
- quality cigarettes (not American brands) and chocolate are appreciated as gifts for the guides

- instant coffee and any snacks you can't live without
- good reading matter, including this book and any worthy tomes you can donate to the Diplomatic Club to please the fledgling ex-pat community, (for whom tonic water is worth its weight in gold!)

MONEY

It used to be that foreign visitors (principally tourists) were barely allowed to see, let alone use, the local currency of won. Instead they exchanged US dollars for 'foreigners' won' (at a fixed rate of 2.12 won/US dollar), often presented as the kosher currency but its simple designs and very low serial numbers were suspicious. This currency was only usable in special shops, bars and hotels; it controlled the level of exchange, what foreigners could buy, where they could go and what they could do (a 'local' 10 chon piece being needed for public phones and transport), nor could it be converted back into hard currency.

DPRK won of any kind is impossible to obtain outside the country and it is illegal to take it out of the DPRK. Foreigners' won was phased out in 2002 and now local won comes in 1, 5, 10, 50, 100 and up to 10,000 denominations at the rate of around 200 to the US dollar, but in December 2002 the US dollar was dumped for the euro. Nevertheless, local won is not necessarily available any more, so foreigners are largely restricted to shops and restaurants accepting hard currency.

The accepted hard currency is now the euro. Some exchange facilities in Pyongyang will convert US$ into euros for local usage, but obviously it's better to bring euros first of all. Convertible currencies are euros, Japanese yen (JPY), GB pound sterling (GBP), Hong Kong dollars (HKD), Canadian dollars (CAD), Australian dollars (AUD), New Zealand dollars (NZD). To a lesser extent, these currencies, and occeasionally even the Chinese renminbi (RMB), are also directly usable for transactions; again, however, the euro is far preferable and more likely to succeed. Foreign exchange is available at the Trade Bank or its agents, and at hotels and some restaurants. The Trade Bank opens from 09.00 to 12.00 and from 14.00 to 17.00 except Sundays. It's best to take euros in low denominations – it's an effort to spend money in the country.

The tour company you use will specify the currency in which they need payment.

Major credit cards (mostly Visa, less often Mastercard, and never American Express) are in theory accepted at the highest-class hotels and a very few of the large shops, but don't expect to use them. Travellers' cheques issued in euros are usable in the bank but not in hotels or shops; those issued in US dollars will not be accepted.

GETTING AROUND

DPRK transportation is limited, because to travel from town to town and province to province everyone needs a permit, locals and foreign visitors alike (you see the checkpoints around the cities). Locals need good reason to get one from the authorities, which also means the demand, and the need, for inter-conurbation transport isn't there. Foreign visitors' hosts arrange permits in accord with the visitors' itineraries. **Buses** going beyond Pyongyang are for all practical purposes non-existent. **Trains** (except for the international routes to Beijing and Moscow) are difficult to get (suffering from power cuts and floods) and may require arranging an extra coach for you. Timetables are not readily available and tickets must be bought through agents before the day of departure, so train-travel needs planning. For **air travel**, there is no domestic air-service usable by foreigners except charter flights to Mt Paektu. As everywhere, reconfirm international flight tickets some days before travel, although this is likely to be done by the visitors' receiving party. **Bicycles** are scarce, are not available for hire and nor are **cars** except taxis. **International driving permits** are not valid but foreign nationals resident in DPRK can obtain local driving licences after taking a driving test. Locals walk short distances or hitchhike long distances in army trucks. It's unlikely you'll need to hold aloft your magic cigarettes. You and your group will be ferried about right from the airport in an official bus or car, which is clean and comfortable – and traffic jams are unheard of. Beyond the cities, the roads stretch away as straight as runways, empty of cars, road markings, cats-eyes and lights but with beautifully tended verges and central reservations.

ACCOMMODATION

Hotels come in deluxe, first, second and third class, and there are also guesthouses. The local press often reports that the top hotels are 'full' with foreign guests and delegates. It's preferred that you stay in the deluxe hotels, and you'll be informed that's not because they need hard currency more but that that's the regulation, or the other hotels are too inferior for honoured guests, maybe their electricity and hot-water supplies are too unreliable (and yet they're all always full). Point being, you can go cheaper if you want, but co-ordinating this in a group tour might be tricky. Single tourists pay an extra supplement for their rooms. There are some hotels no foreigner can stay at, and it has been the case that certain nationalities go to certain hotels, those from richer countries stay at the pricier gaffs. The greater costs of the top-band abodes is reflected thus: secure hot water and power supplies; more restaurants with longer menus; more entertainment, from billiards to massage and sauna; and greater communications facilities.

The top-end of the Yanggakdo Hotel's prices (being Pyongyang's most modern and deluxe hotel) were, in April 2003, as follows: €220 for a VIP double-room and €164 double deluxe, €104 standard double floors 25+, €94 standard double floors 24. Take off €20 per grade for a single. The following hotel band prices for double standards are approximate:

1st class	€75–95 for a standard double
2nd class	€55–75 for a standard double.
3rd class	€35–50 for a standard double. Guesthouses fall into this category and price band.

EATING AND DRINKING

You will always be well fed. Apart from the handful of foreign restaurants in Pyongyang, DPRK fare is pretty basic stuff with many simple sops of eggs and bread for Westerners. The ubiquitous foods are pickled cabbage (*kim'chi*), bread (*bang*) that comes as white-slice doorsteps, and white rice (*bab*) with vegetables and meat, and may contain remnants of husk; watch your teeth. Other regular dishes are potato (*gamja*) and egg (*dalgya*)-based, soups (*gug*), stews (*jjigae*), casseroles (*jeon-gul*) and salads (*saengchae*). Chicken and fish (*saengson*) are the most frequent meats (mullet and fish-head soups!) Neither pork nor beef are very commonly found, the latter is because it's always been a 'controlled substance', rationed by the state, but it appears in Korean BBQs (beef is *pulgogi*, pork is *kalgi*) where a tray of coals are put centre-table and you fry away – great fun. Usually, set dinners are multi-coursed by separate, simple dishes that keep coming. A set of numerous small dishes for one is called *pansanggi*, and there's a version with spicier dishes of octopus (*nakji*), crab and salted fish like anchovies (*jeotgal*). For a feast on the coast, order steamed crab (*tang*) and a heaving great crab, intact and dead (hopefully) will be hurled on to the table. *Sinsollo* is a Korean version of hot-pot, with sliced meats, vegetables and egg stewed and broiled together in a doughnut-shaped 'chaffing' pot. Pyongyang cold buckwheat noodles (*naeng myun*) are another speciality actually found all over the country: very chewy pre-cooked noodles garnished in ice-cubed water. Very tasty and very heavy, a bowl of cold noodles is a meal in itself.

Mineral water is everywhere at three bottles to the dollar/euro. Soft drinks are strictly local, with lightly fizzy, sweet lemon juice (*remonadu*), lovely pear juice (*baeju*) and an apple juice (*saguaju*) in bottles, along with a bitter cranberry-type juice. Coke and Pepsi appear and part like ghosts. The most common beer (*maegju*) is the blue-label RyongSong brand, a light, lagery brew, and in some places draught beer is available, as a hoppy ale or a dark, malty flagon filler. Does this come from the brewery bought and imported brick by brick from the west of England to Pyongyang? Certainly in Pyongyang now there is the Taedonggang brewery that seems to be supplying many venues with wholesome draught. Heineken and Tiger are becoming more available. There's very little grape-wine (*podoju*), but there's the more potent rice-wine (*cheongju* and *makgeoli*) in various fruit flavours, and imported are the ubiquitous Johnnie Walker and Remy Cognac, as well as other brands of spirits no-one's heard of, like Finest Coventry Gin and Loch Inverness Scotch.

NIGHTLIFE

Nightlife is restricted to a handful (but increasing number) of joints in Pyongyang, but the real charm of the cities after dark comes with their quietness, which is notable by day but deafening at night. Pyongyang is mostly as dark and quiet as Korea's other cities and towns, and if you get the chance, try a night walk in the city. It is spectacularly beautiful, and, I found, romantic to behold such a black, eerie calm in a capital city.

Above Korean Workers' Party monument, with a view towards
Mansu Hill, Pyongyang (RT)

Right On every corner is a tribute to the Great and Dear Leaders (RT)

Below right Korean People's Army poster (NB)

Below Close-up of Kim Il Sung and his brethren on the Grand
Monument on Mansu Hill (NB)

Above May Day Stadium, Rungna Island, Pyongyang (RT)

Right Mother and daughter in traditional dress during Arirang, Pyongyang (RT)

Below Finale of the 2002 Arirang Festival (RT)

MEDIA AND COMMUNICATIONS

One source for English-language publications from the DPRK is The Korean Publications Exchange Association, PO Box 222, Pyongyang; fax: +850 2 381 4632.

The DPRK's indigenous newswire is the Korean Central News Agency (www.kcna.co.jp) and the Pyongyang Times site (www.times.dprkorea.com) but more comprehensive coverage of DPRK leading articles and commentaries can be found through BBC Monitoring (www.monitor.bbc.co.uk). ROK news in English is at www.koreaherald.co.kr.

An all-encompassing site for Korean studies is at www.skas.org/, and for that also see the Korean Studies Review (web: www.koreaweb.ws/ks/ksr/), Institute for Far Eastern Studies (web: www.ifes.kyungnam.ac.kr/ifes) and Korea Progressive Network (web: www.english.jinbo.net).

Television and radio

There are three TV stations: Korean Central Television broadcasting daily and Kaesong and Mansudae stations at the weekends. Their content follows two main themes, the greatness of the DPRK with focus on the Great Leaders' current and past deeds, and how appalling the southern puppet regime/Japanese/Americans are, all with a strong military accent. There are 11 radio stations on AM and FM.

Post and telecommunications

The **telephone** system is divided three ways (and so are the conversations). First are local calls, for which you dial 18111/222/333 … 999 for the central switchboard, then you need a four-digit extension number.   Numbers beginning with 5 are all local and should be seven digits. Please note that the area code for Pyongyang is 02, which must be dialled from elsewhere in the country. Then there are domestic lines for foreign firms, organisations and embassies and a very few select Korean firms with the numbers 382xxxx; they don't need an operator. International lines used by these organisations are 381xxx or 382xxx. It's impossible to dial 381 numbers from a 382 line, and vice versa. Some hotels have IDD connections, which can also be used for in-country 381 calls and hotels can provide international calling service. Prices per minute are approximately: to Asia, € 1.5–3.5, Europe € 4, Africa, America, Australia € $6. Telephone, fax and telex calls can be made at the International Communications Centre in Pyongyang in the Ryugyong-dong, Pothonggang District, Pyongyang. For local calls from phone boxes, 10 chon coins are needed. Local calls can also be made from hotels and post offices.

There's no mobile network yet fully in place, but one is being planned and built! Until then, mobile phones may still be confiscated at the airport to be picked up later (check your entry and exit routes for retrieval if this is still so). Check the situation with the tour operators.

Many firms have email, but the **internet** is not widespread. At the time of writing there is reportedly one internet café in Pyongyang, operating from the Jangsaeng General Trading company office, and its charges are high, but there are plans to extend internet access (albeit censored) to some of the bigger hotels.

Post can be sent through the main post offices and those in the larger hotels. What you write on cards and in letters can and will be read by the authorities, so write lovely things to maximise the chances of delivery. Postcards cost ∈1 to send and take ten days. Any philatelists must visit the stamp shop next to the Koryo, although they might never leave. **DHL** has an officeon : Sungri Street, Jungsongdong Central District, Pyongyang; tel: +850 2 381 6147, 8805, 5501, 322 8560. Open: Mon–Fri 09.30–17.30.

SHOPPING

> The Mayor had, at my request, notified to all the shopkeepers that I was anxious to buy any curios in porcelain or bronze, but nothing of any kind was brought to me, and the shops and stalls seemed quite bare of anything of the kind. Even silk and cotton goods were hidden away in shops of a very humble appearance, and such things as were exposed for sale were of the very commonest description. Sandals, tobaccos, pipes, and basket hats, were the most prominent articles for sale. There was besides a considerable sprinkling of Japanese goods … [and those] from Manchuria – Everything in fact here, as at Soul, testified to the extreme simplicity of the life of the people, and to the absence of anything but a retail trade.
>
> W R Calres, HM Vice-Consul Shanghai
> (and formerly Corea), 1887

Korean shop titles are simply by function, 'Electrical Parts', 'Groceries', 'Children's Clothes' etc, not by the brands carried or the proprietor's name. Many offer services, like barber shops, watch or electrical repairs. They serve the surrounding blocks, an administrative unit having about 5,000 inhabitants and called a *dong*. Each *dong* has a public bath-house, post office, and other services which the locals are ascribed to use there and nowhere else.

Your chances for shopping are limited to the hotel shops and few department stores in the large cities, if you can get the shop assistants there to serve you. Unless they accept hard currency directly over the counter, buying in the department stores involves getting a chit from the first assistant, taking the chit to an exchange booth where hard currency is converted into local won (exact money, no room for change), then taking the chit and the won back to the first assistant, who then hands over the goods. You're as able to use local won as you are in getting hold of any. Rationed goods need ration coupons. Credit cards are accepted in a very few places.

Available for purchase are some beautiful paintings, excellent embroideries and sometimes the spectacular hand-painted social-realist posters, along with Korea's own fruit-powered rice wines and herbal remedies (mainly ginseng).

CUSTOMS
The usual restrictions apply regarding narcotics, firearms, live organisms, biochem and hazardous products. Pornographic literature is banned. Don't bring in any texts critical or derisory of the regime. The amount of foreign currency you're able to bring in and out is subject to restriction and local currency can't be taken out.

TOURIST INFORMATION
Rapid changes domestically (especially regarding power, transport and food) and internationally, the control of information, a reluctance to reprint, no internet, all mean that published information is bitty and usually out of date. In the country the most innocuous questions aren't answered if the questionee doesn't feel empowered to tell you. Try www.fco.gov.uk.

Tour operators and Ryohaengsa (KITC) should be contacted (see above section). The glossy publications *Korea Today* and *Democratic People's Republic of Korea* are available on the Air Koryo flight in, in most hotel shops and online at www.magazine.dprkorea.com, and there's also www.travel.dprkorea.com/English. Many people have written about their DPRK experiences on the web: www.theargonauts.com/index.shtml, www.yunkai.de/stories/northkorea/northkorea.html, www.geocities.com/dprk02/index.htm (an excellently compiled site of text and good photos).

A shoal of websites about DPRK travel is at www.budgettravel.com/nkorea.htm, so trawl through them (no responsibility for the red herrings). The CIA factbook at www.cia.gov/cia/publications/factbook is good for an overall look at the DPRK through CIA eyes.

Photography
You can photograph fairly freely, but your guide might suggest (read, insist) you don't, so don't. Don't take any photos of any military subjects and **ask** before snapping locals; it may lose the spontaneity of a shot but it will avoid genuine ire, and if they say no, respect that. Many indoor exhibitions forbid photography. Do not sneak photos, especially at the beginning. Going along with the guides' requests builds trust and it's when they trust you that things loosen up.

There is a photography shop that can develop films and does passport photos on the 2nd floor of Pyongyang's Koryo Hotel, while 35mm camera film (usually 200) is available from hotel shops and main department stores. However, parts, batteries and other film essentials are far more likely found in Beijing, although Beijing's dust gets into cameras and developing machines. Restrictions for bringing into the country optical equipment are camera lenses over 160 mm or video cameras with higher than 24x optical zoom and for binoculars or telescopes over 10x power. For the last three, check again with the operator before departing.

Public holidays
1 January	New Year's Day
February 16	Kim Jong Il's birthday

MAKING THE BEST OF YOUR TRAVEL PHOTOGRAPHS
Subject, composition and lighting
If it doesn't look good through the viewfinder, it will never look good as a picture. Don't take photographs for the sake of taking them; film is far too expensive. Be patient and wait until the image looks right.

People
There's nothing like a wonderful face to stimulate interest. Travelling to remote corners of the world provides the opportunity for exotic photographs of colourful people and intriguing lifestyles which capture the very essence of a culture. A superb photograph should be capable of saying more than a thousand words.

Photographing people is never easy and more often than not it requires a fair share of luck plus sharp instinct, a conditioned photographic eye and the ability to handle light both aesthetically and technically.
* If you want to take a portrait shot, always ask first. Often the offer to send a copy of the photograph to the subject will break the ice – but do remember to send it!
* Focus on the eyes of your subject.
* The best portraits are obtained in early morning and late evening light. In harsh light, photograph without flash in the shadows.
* Respect people's wishes and customs. Remember that, in some countries, infringement can lead to serious trouble.
* Never photograph military subjects unless you have definite permission.
* Be prepared for the unexpected.

Wildlife
There is no mystique to good wildlife photography. The secret is getting into the right place at the right time and then knowing what to do when you are there. Look for striking poses, aspects of behaviour and distinctive features. Try to illustrate the species within the context of its environment. Alternatively, focus in close on a characteristic which can be emphasised.
* The eyes are all-important. Make sure they are sharp and try to ensure they contain a highlight.
* Get the surroundings right – there is nothing worse than a distracting twig or highlighted leaf lurking in the background.
* A powerful flashgun can transform a dreary picture by lifting the subject out of its surroundings and putting the all-important highlights into the eyes. Artificial light is no substitute for natural light, so use judiciously.
* Getting close to the subject correspondingly reduces the depth of field; for distances of less than a metre, apertures between f16 and f32 are necessary. This means using flash to provide enough light – build your own bracket and use one or two small flashguns to illuminate the subject from the side.

Landscapes
Landscapes are forever changing; good landscape photography is all about light and mood. Generally the first and last two hours of daylight are best, or when peculiar climatic conditions add drama or emphasise distinctive features.
* Never place the horizon in the centre – in your mind's eye divide the frame into thirds and exaggerate either the land or the sky.

Cameras
Keep things simple: light, reliable and simple cameras will reduce hassle. High humidity in tropical places can play havoc with electronics.
* For keen photographers, a single-lens reflex (SLR) camera should be at the heart of your outfit. Look for a model with the option of a range of different lenses and other accessories.
* Totally mechanical cameras which do not rely on batteries work even under extreme conditions. Combined with an exposure meter which doesn't require batteries, you have the perfect match. One of the best and most indestructible cameras available is the FM2 Nikon.

- Compact cameras are generally excellent, but because of restricted focal ranges they have severe limitations for wildlife.
- Automatic cameras are often noisy when winding on, and loading film.
- Flashy camera bags can draw unwelcome attention to your kit.

Lenses

The lens is the most important part of the camera, with the greatest influence on the final result. Choose the best you can afford – the type will be dictated by the subject and type of photograph you wish to take.

For people

- The lens should ideally should have a focal length of 90 or 105mm.
- If you are not intimidated by getting in close, buy one with a macro facility which will allow close focusing. For candid photographs, a 70–210 zoom lens is ideal.
- A fast lens (with a maximum aperture of around f2.8) will allow faster shutter speeds which will mean sharper photographs. Distracting backgrounds will be thrown out of focus, improving the images' aesthetic appeal.

For wildlife

- Choose a lens of at least 300mm for a reasonable image size.
- For birds, lenses of 400mm or 500mm may be needed. They should be held on a tripod, or a beanbag if shooting from a vehicle.
- Macro lenses of 55mm and 105mm cover most subjects, creating images up to half life size. To enlarge further, extension tubes are required.
- In low light, lenses with very fast apertures help.

For landscapes

- Wide-angle lenses (35mm or less) are ideal for tight habitat shots (eg: forests) and are an excellent alternative for close ups, as you can shoot the subject within the context of its environment.
- For other landscapes, use a medium telephoto lens (100–300mm) to pick out interesting aspects of a vista and compress the perspective.

Film

Two types of film are available: prints (negatives) and transparencies (colour reversal). Prints are instantly accessible, ideal for showing to friends and putting into albums. However, if you want to share your experiences with a wider audience, through lectures or in publication, then the extra quality offered by transparency film is necessary.

Film speed (ISO number) indicates the sensitivity of the film to light. The lower the number, the less sensitive the film, but the better quality the final image. For general print film and if you are using transparencies just for lectures, ISO 100 or 200 are ideal. However, if you want to get your work published, the superior quality of ISO 25 to 100 film is best.

- Film bought in developing countries may be outdated or badly stored.
- Try to keep your film cool. Never leave it in direct sunlight.
- Do not allow fast film (ISO 800 or more) to pass through X-ray machines.
- Under weak light conditions use a faster film (ISO 200 or 400).
- For accurate people shots use Kodachrome 64 for its warmth, mellowness and gentle gradation of contrast. Reliable skin tones can also be recorded with Fuji Astia 100.
- To jazz up your portraits, use Fuji Velvia (50 ISO) or Provia (100 ISO).
- If cost is your priority, use process-paid Fuji films such as Sensia 11.
- For black-and-white people shots take Kodax T Max or Fuji Neopan.
- For natural subjects, where greens are a feature, use Fujicolour Reala (prints) and Fujichrome Velvia and Provia (transparencies).

Nick Garbutt is a professional photographer, writer, artist and expedition leader, specialising in natural history. He is co-author of 'Madagascar Wildlife' (Bradt Publications), and a winner in the BBC Wildlife Photographer of the Year Competition. John R Jones is a professional travel photographer specialising in minority people, and author of the Bradt guides to 'Vietnam' and 'Laos and Cambodia'.

April 15	Kim Il Sung's birthday
April 25	Army Day
May 1	May Day
July 27	Victory Day
August 15	Independence from Japan day
September 9	Republic Foundation day
October 10	Korean Workers' Party Foundation day
December 27	Constitution Day

The country basically shuts down for winter.

Time zone
GMT plus nine hours, so midday in Pyongyang is 05.00 in London, 15.00 in Wellington and 21.00 in Vancouver the previous day. Years are given in for the Gregorian Calendar *and* the Juche Calendar. The latter marks the years since Juche evolved, ie: 1912, the year Kim Il Sung was born. So, 2000 for example is Juche 88, as 1912 + 88 = 2000, and 2003 is Juche 91, etc.

Electricity
110-220 (dual system) 60Hz, flat or round-pin plugs, but outside Pyongyang's top hotels, power cuts are frequent (even highly regular) and long.

CULTURAL DOS AND DON'TS
First and foremost, disrespecting the Great Leaders is the surest way to cause heinous offence to your hosts, be they guides, businessmen, whoever. This will mar your relations with them in the immediate sense and for the rest of the trip. You'll be asked to 'pay respect' to statues and shrines of Kim Il Sung and Kim Jong Il, usually by standing quietly in front of it and giving a solitary nod of the head. Just do it. Sometimes flowers must be brought. Do not disfigure in any way any image of either leader, and leave them high and dry and not screwed up in the bin; newspapers are specially folded to prevent the photos of the Leaders being creased.

However, your hosts will be knowledgeable on a great many worldly matters, and ranging debates about politics and economics may start up. Prevent causing unwitting offence by avoiding overt criticism in favour of suggestions: how things can 'be improved' or 'made even better'. Koreans are fiercely proud people and there is always the overhanging Asian concept of 'loss of face'. In conversation no-one should be boxed into a corner and made to lose face, ie: be forced to apologise, concede defeat or accept criticism (which no-one enjoys anyway). The Korean variant is *'kibun'*, similar to face, which values keeping personal relations harmonious. You just have to be diplomatic. Watch for the silences or titters. On another note, here's an extreme example of how to get it all wrong:

> At the Myohyang International Friendship Exhibition, one gift to Kim
> Il Sung that stuck out for me was a fanciful corrugated cardboard
> galleon from a Portuguese printers' union. Somehow, inexplicably,

having padded for hours through the incredibly long showrooms in the exhibition's highly sombre atmosphere (the Exhibition is the holiest of holies, enshrining the world's gifts of tribute and homage to the Great Leaders), this little ship cracked me up. The exhibition guide stared at my mirthful writhing in chilled disbelief, while my interpreter haltingly asked, with quiet, incredulous menace, what was funny. I realised I had well and truly pissed in the font, and only another tourist's intervention with a more harmless explanation saved me.

Anon

Your guides are your means to get around, and they need to trust you as you must trust in them. If you're prone to ignore basic manners, antagonising your guides will wreck any chances of more spontaneous endeavours and cloud the trip's atmosphere. Pyongyang is one city where you can wander freely without guides, but do not run off and leave them. They're hardworking civilians and they are totally responsible for you, and any scrapes or misdemeanours you commit will come back on them.

The final point doesn't need writing but I'll put it anyway, so don't take offence. The tours can perhaps feel claustrophobic, you're always on the go from here to there and may tire, you're with your guides and fellow travellers for all the hours you're awake, but you're going to the DPRK because you know it is a truly worthwhile, once-in-a-lifetime experience. So try to get along with your co-travellers and hosts or it will ruin a unique adventure.

Important titbits

Tipping is not expected but obviously appreciated. If you do tip then do so with great discretion.

Wave people towards you with the palm down and fingers batting back and forth. Don't point. Pour drinks by holding the bottle with both hands, serving elders first. Never sit with your soles pointing at anyone, so sit cross-legged with the feet tucked beneath your thighs, or side-saddle. Women and the young used to sit on their heels as a matter of course, and children would stand up when addressed, something still occasionally seen. Receive business cards with both hands and study appreciatively on receipt before placing in a breast pocket.

Public petting isn't appreciated nor do Korean men take well to Korean women being pawed by anyone, especially foreign men, although it's the women who will incur greater repercussions. One traveller put it this way: 'It's certainly not on the *Sex in the City* scale, but they're not quite the Taliban either'. For women's advances on men, I've no idea. Failure to find the middle ground may be costly.

Part Two

The Guide

*Chollima Statue,
Pyongyang*

Pyongyang

39.1° north 125.45° east, Pyongyang City District, capital of the Democratic People's Republic of Korea, Korean peninsula.

Pyongyang, the DPRK capital, is a showcase city, the political, cultural and educational centre of the country, a city built to show and impress the world with the success, progress and fortitude of the DPRK and its people.

The tiled apartment blocks and concrete high-rises strut alongside the city's wide, tree-lined boulevards cutting from Titanic state buildings to monuments striking for their powerful shapes and size. Roads stretch arrow straight into the distance, linking monuments and plazas set in alignment over the horizon, across the river, across the city. In sunlight, the streets and squares, without a fleck of dust, can literally dazzle. In rain, the harsh, grey geometries meld into the sky while vast, sweeping Korean-style eaves hurl the rainwater away. Into all this order and space some 200 parks and open spaces have been carefully slotted. Most fume-producing factories have been banished to the city's outskirts. Pyongyang reputedly has 58m² of green belt per citizen – four times the amount prescribed by the United Nations, and in spring its hills heave with green. It is, as Kim Il Sung meant it to be, a city without parallel in Korea, or Asia.

'The capital of our socialist homeland, Pyongyang is the political centre, the centre for culture and education and a wellspring of our revolution' – and a well-ordered wellspring at that. In few parts of the city can be found the higgledy-piggledy mash of streets that comes from the organic growth of other cities, as individual people, firms and authorities fight over space and time; this form of Pyongyang's layout has been obliterated. Every corner of every block has been approved according to one overall, unitary plan, and there is an extraordinary homogeneity in the buildings' design. For the parts and the whole, one design fits all as a handful of factories produce the designs of even fewer design institutes. The same singularity of purpose is visible in all the pictures, placards, and slogans round the city, for which and only for which all neon gets used. None advertise any material goods or recognisable brands; all promote the ideal and the leader(s) of Socialism. Pyongyang is a mind-set, an ideal, an idea, the city as the manifestation of the state, the state as the manifestation of the man.

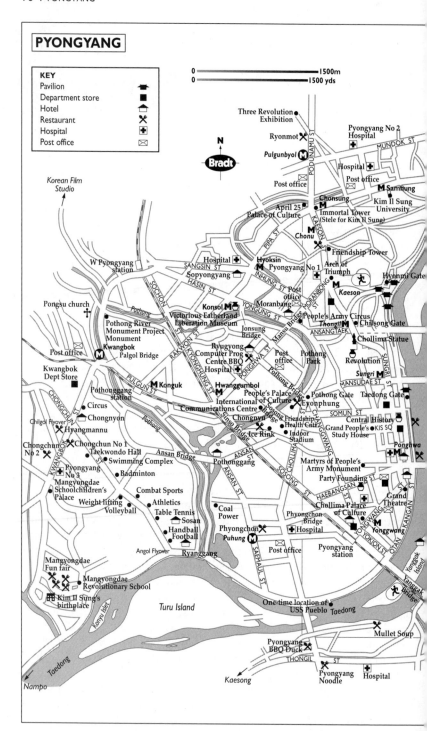

PYONGYANG

KEY
Pavilion
Department store
Hotel
Restaurant
Hospital
Post office

0 ————————————— 1500m
0 ————————————— 1500 yds

Bradt

N

Korean Film Studio

Three Revolution Exhibition

Ryonmot

Pulgunbyol

Pyongyang No 2 Hospital

MUNDOK ST

PODUNAMU ST

Hospital

Post office

Post office

Chonsung

Samtiung

April 25 Palace of Culture

Immortal Tower (Stele for Kim Il Sung)

Kim Il Sung University

Chonu

KAESONG

Friendship Tower

Hospital

Hyoksin

Arch of Triumph

Hyonmi Gate

SANGSIN ST

Pyongyang No 1

Sopyongyang

INHUNG ST

Kaeson

W Pyongyang station

Pongsu church

SOCHON

HASIN ST

Pothong

Konsol

Moranbang

YONGUNG ST

Post office

Victorious Eatherland Liberation Museum

Pothong River Monument Project Monument

Kwangbok

Palgol Bridge

Jonsung Bridge

Mansu Bridge

Chollima Statue

People's Army Circus

Chilsong Gate

Thongil

ANSANGTAEK

Ryugyong Computer Prog Centre BBQ Hospital

Post office

Pothong Park

Revolution

Sungri

MANSUDAE ST

Kwangbok Dept Store

Pothonggang station

PULGUN ST

Konguk

Hwanggumbol

People's Palace

International of Culture

Pothong Bridge

Pothong Gate

Taedong Gate

Circus

Chongnyon

Communications Centre

Singo Bridge

Eyonphung

Chongnyn

Central History

KIS SQ

Chilgol Flyover

Hyangmannu

Pothong

Ice Rink

Chongchun No 1

Friendship Health Centr

Grand People's Study House

SOMUN ST

Chongchun No 2

Taekwondo Hall

Ansan Bridge

Indoor Stadium

Ponghwa

Swimming Complex

Pyongyang No 3

Badminton

ANSAN ST

Pothonggang

SOJONG ST

Martyrs of People's Army Monument

Party Founding

Grand Theatre

Mangyongdae Schoolchildren's Palace

Weight lifting

Volleyball

Combat Sports

Athletics

Table Tennis

Sosan

HAEBANGSAN ST

Chollima Palace of Culture

Phyongchon Bridge

Yonggwang

Coal Power

Mangyongdae Fun fair

Handball

Football

Angol Flyover

Ryanggang

Phyongchon

Puhung

Hospital

SAEMAUL ST

Post office

Pyongyang station

Yangak Island

Kim Il Sung's birthplace

Mangyongdae Revolutionary School

Konyi Islet

Turu Island

One-time location of USS Pueblo

Taedong

Yanggak Bridge

Mullet Soup

Taedong

Nampo

Pyongyang BBQ Duck

THONGIL

Kaesong

Pyongyang Noodle

Hospital

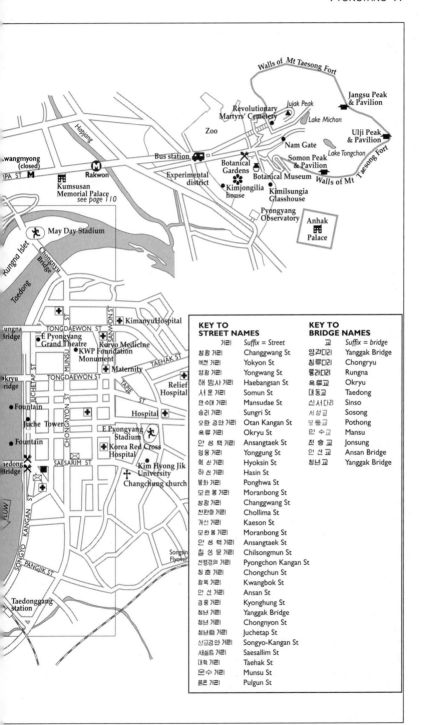

KEY TO STREET NAMES

거리	Suffix = Street
창광 거리	Changgwang St
역전 거리	Yokyon St
영광 거리	Yongwang St
해 방산 거리	Haebangsan St
서운 거리	Somun St
만수대 거리	Mansudae St
승리 거리	Sungri St
오탄 강안 거리	Otan Kangan St
옥류 거리	Okryu St
안 성 택 거리	Ansangtaek St
영웅 거리	Yonggung St
혁 신 거리	Hyoksin St
하 신 거리	Hasin St
봉화 거리	Ponghwa St
모란봉 거리	Moranbong St
창광 거리	Changgwang St
천란마 거리	Chollima St
개선 거리	Kaeson St
모란봉 거리	Moranbong St
안 성 택 거리	Ansangtaek St
칠 성 문 거리	Chilsongmun St
천령경완 거리	Pyongchon Kangan St
청 춘 거리	Chongchun St
광복 거리	Kwangbok St
안 산 거리	Ansan St
경흥 거리	Kyonghung St
청년 거리	Yanggak Bridge
청년 거리	Chongnyon St
청년탑 거리	Juchetap St
상교강안 거리	Songyo-Kangan St
새실림 거리	Saesallim St
대학 거리	Taehak St
온수 거리	Munsu St
붉은 거리	Pulgun St

KEY TO BRIDGE NAMES

교	Suffix = bridge
양각다리	Yanggak Bridge
칭류다리	Chongryu
룽라다리	Rungna
옥류교	Okryu
대동교	Taedong
신서다리	Sinso
서성교	Sosong
모통교	Pothong
만 수교	Mansu
전 승교	Jonsung
안 산 교	Ansan Bridge
청년교	Yanggak Bridge

The city limits drawn on the plans are clearly visible on the ground. The grey cliffs of the perimeter high-rise provide a sharp, vertical barrier to the fields and lowlands lapping round the city. Pyongyang doesn't sprawl like other Asian cities, forever absorbing rural-urban migrants. The city's population is stable at around two million because people do not live and work in Pyongyang without permits, which are as valued as the gold dust mined in the city's outskirts. Koreans cannot in fact leave or enter the city without permits, as the checkpoints on the city's perimeter roads verify, and as a result the lack of inter-urban public transport is deliberate: if no-one needs it, why have it?

The lack of traffic spares the city from pollution and the flying dust brought in and whipped up by vehicles. Incoming rural lorries and buses are hosed down just outside the city perimeters just to make sure, and the regular trams and trolley buses in the city are electric. Everyone mucks in to keep Pyongyang clean, as groups of families are responsible for keeping their immediate locale clean, while brigades of older women tend to the public areas. Water trucks hose the streets. There are very few stalls or vendors and there's little litter because there is nothing to throw away: this is not a consumer society, and what's used gets converted. Watch out for small tools and appliances brilliantly fashioned from drinks' cans and the like.

GEOGRAPHY
'The beauty of its situation well deserves the praises that have been showered upon it by both Korean and European writers,' wrote Jahison. The city straddles the River Taedong, where this major waterway (450km long, 20,000km² catchment area) is joined by the rivers Pothong, Japzang and Sunhwa. The flat plain on which Pyongyang sits is walled in on the northeastern sides by hills, in which coal and gold are mined. Pyongyang, and its manufacturing industries produce mining and construction machinery and products, as well as locomotives, hi-tech electrical goods and IT, textiles and tools, with a burgeoning food processing industry.

HISTORY
Pyongyang has long been a city of importance, being the second or third city for those interludes in history when it wasn't the capital, and always a vital fortress city and trading centre. DPRK historians are adamant that they've nailed the 5,000 years of history myth on to King Tangun who was in fact a real king and who did indeed establish the walled city of Pyongyang 5,000 years ago. It probably wasn't built exactly where Pyongyang is today, but 500 of an estimated 10,000 dolmen tombs have been excavated around today's city that date back some 5,000 years, along with 150 stone coffins, laden with jewelry and ceramics. There's also much from the Bronze Age, predating the Tangun, with slaves and slave-owners' graves identified.

A small town grew around 2,000 years ago south of Yanggak Island on the fertile Taedong plains, and under Koguryo a citadel was built on Mt Taesong in 247, with ancestral shrines, government offices and residences in the adjacent Anhak palace. The building of Pyongyang proper soon followed as it moved from Koguryo's second city to being the capital in 427, on order of King Changsu. Pyongyang was built as a walled city that eventually grew to cover today's Central and Phyongchon districts. The walled city consisted of four parts, inner, central, outer and northern, and its perimeter stretched 16km in length and in parts rose over 10m, with crenellated parapets lacing between up to 16 gates. These walls stood in some form or other until the mid-20th century, protecting the miserable streets inside with varying success from the invaders from the north, south and within.

In 598, a sea borne assault by Chinese forces heading for the city on a punitive venture (not enough tribute was paid from Korea to China) was luckily wiped out by a typhoon. Thirty thousand Tang soldiers marched into the peninsula in spring 661 as their half of the Tang/Silla alliance to defeat the Koguryo, and laid siege to the city. Although the Tang forces gave up the siege, Koguryo was weakened and from its collapse in 668, Pyongyang was abandoned to become a 'city of weeds'. It was not until Wang Kon established Koryo in 918 that the city was reborn.

Wang Kon had Pyongyang reconstructed as a major garrison town to re-establish order in the north, and he contemplated moving the Koryo capital there. The city's administrative and material footprint was reset over the surrounding districts and Pyongyang thrived as second city to Kaesong, both becoming centres of learning from the late 900s with new libraries and academies filled with students from a burgeoning urban population of noble families. But the thriving peace was short-lived. In 1010, the Pyongyang garrison commander General Kang led his troops to Kaesong and deposed the youthful King Mokchong and his nefarious queen dowager mother to install a more suitable monarch. Unfortunately, into the melee from across the Yalu came the Liao, who trashed Pyongyang and burned Kaesong. This led to the building of a great wall of fortified cities north of Pyongyang by 300,000 men from 1033.

A hundred years later, the threat was from within. In 1135, Pyongyang became the base for the bizarre Myochong rebellion. Led by a prophetic Buddhist monk of that name who attained prominence in the Koryo court, Myochong had been persuading the then king, Injong, to move the court from Kaesong to Pyongyang, arguing that the Chinese Chin needed attacking and that Kaesong lacked 'geomancy', something Pyongyang apparently had in spades. Injong was taken in and a palace and several temples with deities were built in Pyongyang before making it the capital. Then another scholar, advocating peace with the Chin, sat Injong down and carefully explained that Myochong's theories weren't quite aligned with reality. Livid, Myochong set up with his followers a siege state in Pyongyang that took a year to crush.

In 1592, it was in Pyongyang that General Konishi of the Japanese army advancing from the south made fleeting contact with the fleeing Ri court, who over their shoulders exclaimed that they would return. After a final abortive night raid by the city's defenders, Konishi entered a Pyongyang empty of people but full of supplies. The Ri however did return that summer, with Chinese and Korean forces encircling Pyongyang, and in February 1593, an army of Buddhist monk soldiers led the city's retaking through the walls

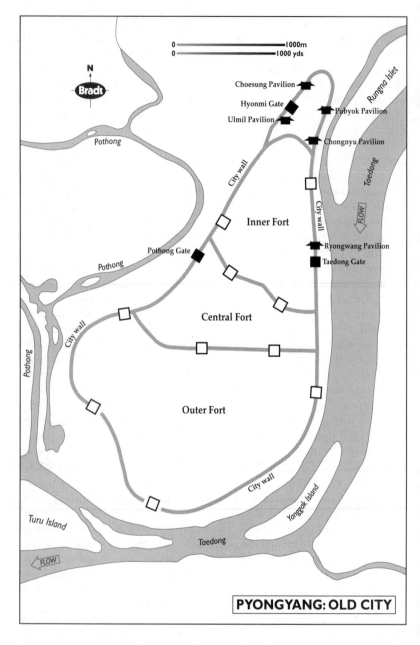

PYONGYANG: OLD CITY

breached by heavy artillery. In 1627 and 1637, the invaders came from the north as the Mongols ravaged Pyongyang on punitive raids, but these were the last significant military attacks for nearly 300 years.

The intervening years saw invaders of a different, Christian kind. 'The Koreans of these northern provinces are, in the opinion of the missionaries, far more satisfactory than their southern compatriots. They are more honest and reliable, as well as more enterprising, diligent, and industrious, a view that is borne out by the foreign merchants who have had dealings with them.' And Pyongyang was 'an excellent centre for evangelistic works'.

The city's military significance didn't wane, however, for by the mid-19th century, Pyongyang had around 295,000 households and 175,000 men listed for military duty, called upon by the Chinese armies waiting in and around Pyongyang as they buttressed the city's forts and walls in the 1894 Sino-Japanese war. Still, three columns of Japanese troops converged on Pyongyang and routed the Chinese after days of heavy fighting, in which a third of the city was burned. In *Fifteen Years Among the Top-knots*, Lillias Underwood reported scenes of carnage with one pile of dead troops and horses stretching 'a quarter of a mile long and several yards wide' that lay rotting for weeks, while bodies in the Taedong polluted the city's only water supply. Cholera broke out the following year.

Pyongyang didn't seem to have benefited much from the decades of Japanese rule that soon followed. Most of the schools and hospitals were built and run by Protestant missionaries who provided desperately needed relief for the city's poor. In 1939, Dr Philip Jahison wrote that Pyongyang had only one notable thoroughfare that led along the riverbank from Taedong Gate. This was the business district, dominated by Japanese traders, particularly rice and bean merchants exporting to Japan and investment banks charging extortionate rates of interest. Jahison wrote that 'the remaining thoroughfares are extremely narrow and dirty. Most of the houses and shops are more or less dilapidated, while there are no buildings of striking importance.' Mud-plastered thatch-shacks were knotted together by dirt tracks flanked by stinking open sewers running into the river, itself jammed with Chinese junks trading legally and illegally.

Pyongyang was liberated in 1945 by Russian forces and became the capital of the 'temporary' state of North Korea, and some impressive buildings, like the Moranbang Theatre, survive from the few peaceful years preceding the Korean War. During the Korean War, Pyongyang was wrested from both sides' hands during the conflict, while hundreds of thousands of civilians here and elsewhere were killed in American bombing raids that had no palpable effect on the war's outcome: 'Bombing could inflict a catastrophe upon a nation without defeating it' (Max Hastings, *The Korean War*). *Pyongyang Review* claims that the 428,000 bombs dropped equalled more than one bomb per citizen there. Except for a handful of buildings, the city was truly wiped flat.

Reconstruction

The capital of the DRPK had to be rebuilt, quickly, simply. The city was planned around the River Taedong as a 'garden city' with over 200 green spaces, tree-lined roads and riverside walks. Buildings shot up using methods and materials stripped down and honed so that the absolute minimum in skills or resources were needed. Industry and manpower resources, recovering from the war, were faced with a colossal demand for materials and workers, and quantity took priority over quality. You don't have to stand very close to buildings to see that balconies, tiling, vertical and horizontal joints often depart from the plumb-line. Interesting concave and convex patterns appear in pre-fabricated, hand-finished concrete walls. Window glass panes have bubbles, bands, fisheye and bottle-glass effects. Spaces exist under doors and their frames.

Still, the buildings of the late 1970s and 1980s are a great qualitative improvement over their predecessors that suffered poor wiring, low water pressure, and uneven heating. Heating in many apartment blocks is of the traditional Korean type, under-floor heating (called *ondol*) with hot water provided from the city's thermal power plants. This does cool over a distance and there's no micro-control facility. *Ondol* is traditionally heated air from a stove piped under the floor, and this form exists so that stovepipes are seen protruding from 18th-floor windows. In the taller buildings, unevenly heightened floors and unaligned lift-shafts prevent operational lifts. By day and night, Pyongyang suffers from power shortages, and the low-energy bulbs and fluorescents flicker by day and emit zingy light at night.

But this is to run one's fingers along the mantelpiece of what is ultimately a stunning achievement, and the march of the high-rise stamps onwards. Pyongyang has many traditional single-story brick and clay huts but are screened from the main thoroughfares by the high-rises out to replace them, so be aware from highpoints and glance through alleys and archways. From the Juche Tower looking east there are many such houses on the fringes of the city, crammed between developments closer in.

Design
For the apartment blocks, the homogenous designs give few architectural clues to indicate a building's age, purpose or occupiers' status, beyond the simple observation that if it's tall and grey it's probably residential, and the taller it is, the newer it is. There are three main types of grand, public buildings. The first is the classically derived grandeurs, all pedestals, pillars and steps like the Moranbang Theatre, or the simplified classicism derived from Soviet-design shops, like Mansudae Assembly Hall and the Kumsusan Memorial Hall. While the floor space was appreciated, the façades changed from the early 1970s when the grand sweep of traditional Korean-style fronts and roofs (examples, Grand People's Study House, Pyongyang International House of Culture, Okryu restaurant) became affordable. Alongside this indigenous design philosophy came arguments advocating how spectacular concrete could be in imaginative hands (Pyongyang International Cinema, Chongryu restaurant, the Ice Rink, Chongchun Street, Ryugyong Hotel, East Pyongyang Grand Theatre, Monument to the Party Founding). The residential developments of Thongil Street, south of Yanggak Islet, and Kwangbok Street in Mangyongdae district, are overwhelming. The May Day Stadium stands alone as a brilliant project in flying steel.

'Let us build our city more beautifully at a faster rate,' the constructors were exhorted. The Pyongyang Maternity Hospital was knocked up in less than nine months to be done before the sixth party congress in 1980. The Grand People's Study House, 600 rooms over 100,000m^2, was built in 21 months.

Whole streets, like Chollima Street in the 1970s and Pipa and Ragwon streets in the 1980s, were built in months, under the so-called 'Pyongyang Speed'. This was also due to the strictures of the multi-year plans.

Interiors

The most ostentatious features of any grand building's interior are their vast chandeliers that bear down through floors and stairwells like almighty drill-bits, and paintings of Korean landscapes that cover entire walls. Plastic 'wood' panelling, fake wood, painted metal slats nailed on to the walls, flock wallpaper – all are common features. There are evidently precious few factories producing the fixtures and furnishings. Try and spot the recurring wallpaper and curtain material from the DPRK's own IKEA.

GETTING THERE AND AWAY

By air, you arrive at Sosan airport, a 30-minute drive from the city, and by train at the Pyongyang railway station, two minutes' walk from the Koryo Hotel.

GETTING AROUND
Metro

The metro's two lines run under the main streets on the west side of the Taedong, the Hyokshin Line going under Ragwon and Pipa streets, and the Chollima Line under Podunamu, Kaeson, Sungni and Yonggwang streets. This is important to know as the seventeen stations aren't always named by location but by good revolutionary terminology, like Hwanggumbol (Golden Fields), Pulgunbyol (Red Star) and Chonu (comrade), even though many Pyongyang sites are similarly named. Nor do any available maps show the precise location of the stations and streets.

Aside from being a swift, smooth link across town, the stunning opulence of Pyongyang metro's architecture and the extraordinarily deep stations with their vertigo-inducing escalators are worth a visit in themselves. The Chollima line opened in September 1973, and the metro resembles Moscow's, though some say Pyongyang's is the more beautiful. The escalators take some leisurely minutes to plumb down 200-odd metres, arriving in marble-clad tunnels that bore away from blast doors to blast doors, for the subway doubles as an air-raid shelter for Pyongyang's citizens. The platforms are underground cathedrals to Socialism, with their marble pillars, vaults and platform-length murals and mosaics of Korean countryside entitled 'Song of a bumper crop' and 'Builders at the construction of a blast furnace'. The chandeliers are themed by station-name, with fireworks at Yonggwang (Glory) and grapes of bumper harvests at Hwanggumbol (Golden Fields). Particularly worthy stations for a look are Puhung, Yonggwang (both of which are firm tour fixtures), Kaeson, Hwanggumbol, Konsol, Konguk and Ragwon. Trains run every five to seven minutes, or every two minutes at peak time, reportedly carting some 300,000 commuters every day. None of this came without a price, however. Korean National Intelligence Service disclosed in 1999 that during the metro's construction in 1971, over 100 lives were lost when part of

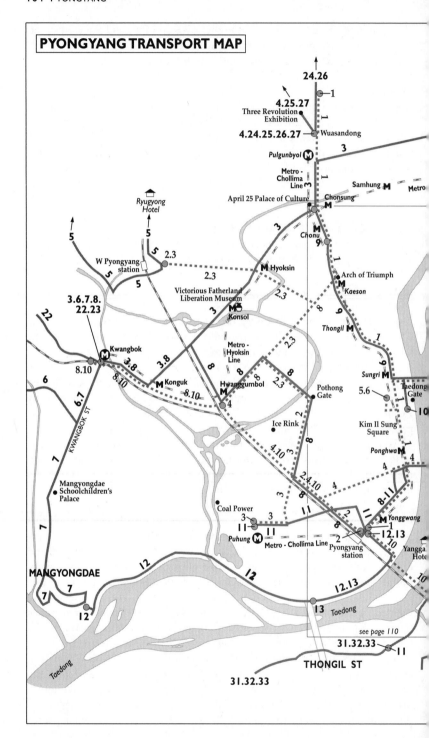

PYONGYANG TRANSPORT MAP

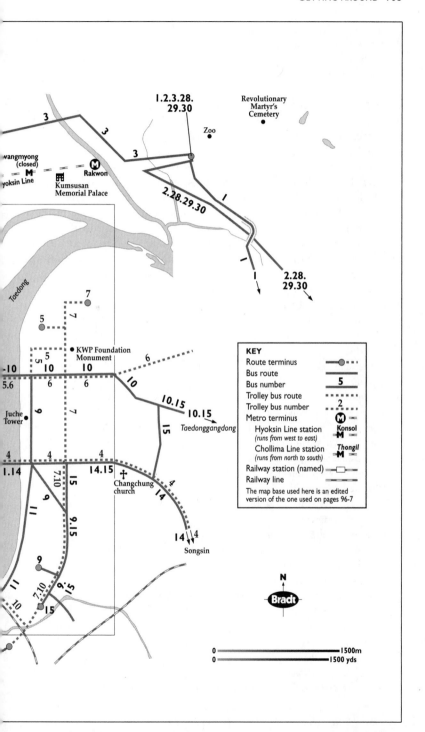

1.2.3.28.
29.30

Revolutionary
Martyr's
Cemetery

Zoo

3

3

3

3

wangmyong
(closed)
yoksin Line

Rakwon

Kumsusan
Memorial Palace

2.28.29.30

1

1

2.28.
29.30

1

Taedong

7

7

5

5

KWP Foundation
Monument

6

5

10

10

10

6

6

10

10.15

10.15

15

Taedonggangdong

-10

5.6

Juche
Tower

9

7

4

4

4

1.14

7.10

15

14.15

Changchung
church

4

14

9

11

9.15

9

7.10

9

15

14

4

Songsin

11

7.10

10

15

KEY

Route terminus

Bus route

Bus number   5

Trolley bus route

Trolley bus number   2

Metro terminus

Hyoksin Line station   **Konsol**
(runs from west to east)   M

Chollima Line station   *Thongil*
(runs from north to south)   M

Railway station (named)

Railway line

The map base used here is an edited
version of the one used on pages 96-7

N

Bradt

0 ————————— 1500m
0 ————————— 1500 yds

an underwater tunnel at Ponghwa station collapsed. Cost had been until late 2002 one 10-chon coin (local). It's now 2W.

For further information try www.metropla.net/as/pyon/pyongyang.htm or www.pyongyang-metro.com

Buses, trolley-buses and trams

There are extensive trolley-bus and tram connections across the city, but these are usually packed out (cost/ticket availability). Women and children have priority on public transport, with conductors in military-style uniform in control and not to be jostled with if they let you on. Trams and trolley-buses are irregular due to power cuts. The trams and most of the trolley- buses are mostly Korean made, now with a few Chinese imports, dodging Russian, Czech and Hungarian petrol buses, and more modern Japanese buses and lorries. For lorries, the situation is a lot of Russian GAZ and KrAZ types, Korean and Chinese copies. On the sides of many vehicles are painted long lines of red stars. Each star shows 50,000km of safe driving, so it appears that some could have cruised safely to the moon and back. More than once.

The following are the trolley-bus and bus routes for Pyongyang with roads and landmarks indicated. Where the vehicles go into unmapped outskirts, their general direction is given (eg: north):

Trolley-bus

1 Pyongyang station – Yonggwang – Sungri – Moranbong – Arch of Triumph – Ryonmotdong
2 Pyongyang station – Sosong – Chollima St – Ryugyong Hotel – Moranbong St – Sangsin – West Pyongyang station
3 Pyongyang Power station – Chollima St – Ryugyong Hotel – Moranbong St – Sangsin – West Pyongyang station
4 Ponghwa – Sosong – Haebangsan – Taedong Bridge – Saesarim – Songsin station
5 Pyongyang Department Store No 1 – Sungri – Okryu Bridge – East Pyongyang Theatre – Munsu
6 Pyongyang Department Store No 1 – Sungri – Okryu Bridge – Tongdaewon – Taehak – Sadong
7 Munsu -Youth St – Rangrang Bridge
8 Friendship Tower – Arch of Triumph – Moranbong St – Ponghwa – Ryogyong Hotel – Pulgun – Kwangbok
9 Ryonmotdong – Ryongsong (north)
10 Kwangbok (Palgol Bridge) Pulgun – Sosong – Yanggak Islet – Rangrang – Taedonggang station

Bus

1 Mt Taesong – Pyongyang Astronomical Observatory – Mirim Bridge (east)
2 Mt Taesong – Samsin (east)
3 Mt Taesong – Mundok – April 25 Palace – Pipa – Hyoksin – Ragwon – Kwangbok
28 Mt Taesong – Samsok (east)

29 Mt Taesong – Kangdong (east)
30 Mt Taesong – Pongwhari (east)
4   Sopo (north) – Three Revolutions Exhibition – Ryonmotdong
5   Sopo (north) – Film Studio
6   Palgol – Kwangbok – Chilgol
7   Palgol – Kwangbok – Mangyongdae
8   Palgol – Pulgun – Ragwon – Kyonghung – Ponghwa – Pothong Gate – Chollima
    – Pyongyang Station – Yongwang – Dept No 2
22 Palgol – Wollori (west)
23 Palgol – Kwangbok – Taepyong (west)
9   Friendship Tower – Moranbong – Sungri – Okryu Bridge – Juche Tower –
    Pangjik – Sanopdong
10 Pyongyang Department Store No 1 – Okryu Bridge – Tongdaewon – Tapje –
    Taedonggangdong
11 Pyongyang Thermal Power Complex – Koryo Hotel – Yongwang – Taedong
    Bridge – Songyo Kangan – Chongbaek
12 Pyongyang Station – Yokjon – Pyongchon Kangan – Angol – Mangyongdae
13 Pyongyang Station – Yokjon – Pyongchon Kangan – Chongsung Bridge
15 Rangrang Bridge – Saesarim – Kim Hyong Jik University – Tapje –
    Taedonggangdong
16 Rangrang Bridge – Pottery Factory (southeast)
34 Rangrang Bridge – Taehyondong (southeast)
35 Rangrang Bridge – Ryokpo (southeast)
14 Songsin – Saesarim – Taedong Bridge – Dept No 2
17 Songsin – Mirim Bridge (east)
18 Songsin – Changchon (south)
37 Songsin – Ripsok (southeast)
38 Songsin – Sangwon (southeast)
39 Songsin – Tokdong (southeast)
40 Songsin – Rihyonri (southeast)
19 Tapje/Taehak – Sadong (south)
20 Tapje/Taehak – Mirim Bridge
21 Sangdangdong – Hyongsanri
24 Three Revolutions Exhibition – Tongbukri (north)
25 Three Revolutions Exhibition – Sunan (north)
26 Three Revolutions Exhibition – Sinmiri (north)
27 Three Revolutions Exhibition – Kanri (north)
31 Chongbaek – Thongil – Wonam (south)
32 Chongbaek – Thongil – Pyokjidori (south)
33 Chongbaek – Thongil – Kangnam (south)

Taxis are usually 1970s' Volvo and 1980s' Mercedes saloons (with 'Taxi' on the
roofs), ostensibly charging ∈ 1.50 per km. They don't ply the streets for trade
but loiter around the big hotels and Pyongyang railway station, and can be
reluctant to go. Phone or get the hotel to call these taxi-centre numbers:
33428, 45615 or 42007.

Other cars include early Russian Moskvichs and Volgas. More and more newish Japanese saloons and 4WDs are appearing, many being right-hand drive (hence not strictly for export from Japan). The absence of a second-hand car market in Japan means these 'old' Japanese cars are ferried out from Niigata to Wonsan and Rajin/Chongjin.

Also look out for the public announcement vehicles, mini-vans with four massive tannoys on the roof, reminding locals of the orders of the day. Otherwise, Pyongyang's wide boulevards remain blissfully clear; 'Pyongyang is exceptional in that the journey times from one part of town to another are the same at any hour, now as ten years ago', commented one businessman. Cars are almost exclusively for 'public' use of some kind. If the very few who could afford a car can actually get one, there's the tight supply of petrol to consider, causing drivers of all vehicles to flick into neutral gear as they coast downhill. Spare a thought for the ingenuity and effort needed to keep the older vehicles roadworthy, after millions of kilometres of driving. Parts supplies are irregular (if available at all, considering the age of some). You might see many sitting by the roadside on jacks and/or with the bonnet up, or rolling round on three incorrectly sized tyres.

There are few bicycles about (they have registration plates), and no hotels as yet hire them out. One firm, Wanshida, is known to import bicycles from China. Women on bicycles is still a mind-bending concept, so Korean women in Pyongyang are reportedly restricted to riding tricycles. Most people just walk, and they do not jaywalk! Use the underpass or the arm of the traffic police will befall you. Public transport beyond the city's immediate limits doesn't exist. You can maybe catch a foreigner's land cruiser, if you've the permits to get somewhere.

WHERE TO STAY
You don't have to stay in the top-class hotels, and indeed the DPRK media are always pointing out that the top hotels are already full with visitors, but you will be given the hard-sell. Note that none of them, even the high-class ones, have heating in the public areas in winter.

Deluxe
These hotels have guaranteed hot water and electricity.

Pyongyang Koryo Hotel Changgwang St; tel: +850 2 18111 ext 7600; fax: +850 2 3814422. Opened in 1985. A little bit south of the city centre and near Pyongyang railway station. 45 floors in twin towers and many restaurants, with two that revolve. The hotel's twin towers are a Pyongyang landmark, with 500 comfortable rooms plus bars, pool, billiards and a bookshop amongst other features.
Yanggakdo Hotel Tel: +850 2 18111 ext 2134; fax: +850 2 381 2930/1. Opened in 1995, this 47-storey glass prism sits on Yanggak Island in the Taedong River, 4km southeast of the city centre. The hotel is second only to the Koryo in the whole country, and has numerous restaurants and amusements, including bowling, an adjacent putting course, the International Friendship Cinema and a football stadium that makes Yanggak Island an Alcatraz of fun.

First-class hotels

Angol Hotel About 7km southwest from the centre, very near Chongchun (Gymnasium) St.

Chongnyon Hotel Chukjondong, Mangyongdae District. Corner of Kwangbok and Chongchun Streets; tel: 72340. Triangular design. Hotel of 30 floors and 520 rooms.

Pothonggang Hotel Ansangdong, Pyongchon District; tel: 48301; fax: +850-2-3814428; telex 38030/38031 BTG KP. About 4km west of Kim Il Sung Square, at the Pothong riverside. Good hotel with 162 rooms.

Ryanggang Hotel Chongchun St, Mangyongdae District; tel: 73825. In the west of the city, where the Taedong and the Pothong rivers meet. Hotel with 330 rooms and a revolving restaurant.

Sosan Hotel Chongchun St; tel: 71197. Opened in 1989. At Kwangbok Street in the west, 4km from the city centre. Big hotel with 30 floors and 474 rooms.

Tourist Hotel About 7km outside the centre.

Youth Hotel Chilgoldong, Mangyongdae District; telex 38047 CHONGNYON KP. Opened in 1989. About 10km west of the centre, near Kwangbok St. Good hotel, 30 floors, 465 rooms.

Second-class hotels

Pyongyang Hotel Sungi St, Kyongrim-dong, Central District; tel: 38161; fax: +850-2-3814426; telex: 38034 POST KP. Opened in 1961. On the west bank of Taedong River and opposite Pyongyang Grand Theatre. 5 floors and 170 rooms.

Third-class hotels

Haebangsan Hotel Sungni St, Haebangsandong, Central District; tel: 37037; fax: +850-2-3813569; telex: 38050 HBS KP. South of the square, near Taedong Bridge, and the only third class hotel where foreigners can stay, mostly foreign students; 83 rooms. Rooms are clean but not luxurious. Bathrooms with hot water. Weird sentinel tower on one corner.

Hotels not yet accessible for tourists

Changgwangsan Hotel Chollima St, Tongsong-dong, Central District; tel: 48366. Second class. 3km west of the centre, at the Pothong River. Hotel with 420 rooms.

Moranbong Hotel Moranbong St

Ponghwasan Hotel Moranbong St

West Pyongyang Hotel Pipa St

WHERE TO EAT

All of the hotels have their own restaurants, and the top-class ones have quite a few each (some revolve!) but an interesting and ever-expanding selection of restaurants is sprinkled across Pyongyang. In general, expect to pay around ∈3 for a plate of kimchi, ∈8 for pre-BQQ beef and ∈10 for bean-curd soup with rice.

The **Yanggakdo** has a gamut of restaurants round the stairwell behind the foyer bar. Of the two Korean restaurants, **No 1** is small and enclosed, **No 2** is airier and has a

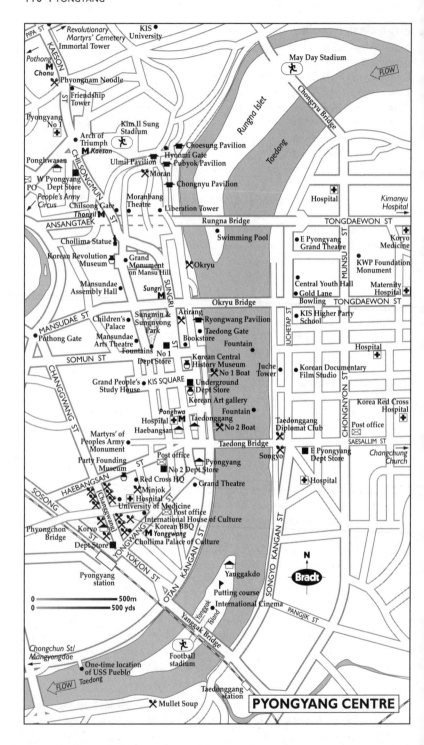

PIPA ST
Revolutionary Martyrs' Cemetery
KIS University
Immortal Tower
KAESON ST
Pothong
Chonu
Phyongnam Noodle
Friendship Tower
May Day Stadium
FLOW
Rungna Islet
Chongryu Bridge
Pyongyang No 1
Kim Il Sung Stadium
CHILSONGMUN ST
Arch of Triumph
Kaeson
Choesung Pavilion
Hyonmi Gate
Ulmil Pavilion
Pubyok Pavilion
Moran
Taedong
Ponghwasan
W Pyongyang Dept Store
PO
People's Army Circus
Chilsong Gate
Thongil
Chongnyu Pavilion
Moranbang Theatre
Liberation Tower
Hospital
Kimanyu Hospital
ANSANGTAEK
Rungna Bridge
TONGDAEWON ST
Cholima Statue
Swimming Pool
E Pyongyang Grand Theatre
Koryo Medicine
Korean Revolution Museum
Grand Monument on Mansu Hill
Okryu
MUNSU ST
KWP Foundation Monument
Mansudae Assembly Hall
Sungri
Central Youth Hall
Gold Lane Bowling
Maternity Hospital
Okryu Bridge
TONGDAEWON ST
MANSUDAE ST
Children's Palace
Sungmin & Sungnyong Park
Arirang
Ryongwang Pavilion
KIS Higher Party School
IUCHETAP ST
Pothong Gate
Mansudae Arts Theatre
Taedong Gate
Bookstore
Fountain
Hospital
SOMUN ST
Fountains
No 1 Dept Store
Korean Central History Museum
Juche Tower
Korean Documentary Film Studio
CHANGGWANG ST
Grand People's Study House
KIS SQUARE
No 1 Boat
Underground Dept Store
Korean Art gallery
CHONGNYON ST
Korea Red Cross Hospital
Ponghwa Hospital
Taedonggang
Fountain
Post office
SAESALLIM ST
Martyrs' of Peoples Army Monument
Haebangsan
No 2 Boat
Taedonggang Diplomat Club
Party Founding Museum
Post office
No 2 Dept Store
Pyongyang
Taedong Bridge
Songyo
E Pyongyang Dept Store
Changchung Church
SOSONG
HAEBANGSAN
Red Cross HQ
Grand Theatre
Hospital
CHANGGWANG ST
Minjok
Hospital
University of Medicine
Post office
Phyongchon Bridge
Koryo
International House of Culture
Korean BBQ
Yonggwang
Dept Store
YONGGWANG ST
Chollima Palace of Culture
KANGAN ST
N
Bradt
Pyongyang station
YOKION ST
Yanggakdo
Putting course
International Cinema
SONGYO KANGAN ST
PANGJIK ST
0   500m
0   500 yds
OTAN KANGAN ST
Yanggak Island
Yanggak Bridge
Chongchun St/ Mangyongdae
One-time location of USS Pueblo
Football stadium
Taedonggang station
FLOW Taedong
Mullet Soup
PYONGYANG CENTRE

river view. Both serve a compromise of basic Western and Korean foods. Enclosed **Japanese** and **Chinese** restaurants sit opposite them across the stairs to the basement, where is the **Macau Chinese restaurant**, a very popular spot with expats – although Koreans are not allowed in – with long opening hours and a menu to match (open 08:30–03:30, tel: 02 381 2134 x 10808; fax: 10807); around ∈ 12 each for a party of four. The Yanggakdo's warm revolving venue serves its last at 22:00.

Changgwang Street has two dozen restaurants and bars that accept foreigners and their money. They all advertise as being open from 12.00–15.00 and 18.00–21.30, but may not be in practice and some open only for large bookings, for works' units on reward whom you may see queuing outside with their vouchers.

Three restaurants are tucked into the block opposite the Koryo Hotel entrance. Cross Changgwang from the Koryo, heading for the side street on the right, and about 80 metres down on the left is a gated courtyard. On the immediate left is a white conservatory entrance to a multi-floored **Korean BBQ** (around ∈ 15 each) and a **Japanese restaurant**. On the far side of the yard is another **Korean** venue with karaoke upstairs. Both are open until 23.00.

The **Okryu restaurant** sits in full hip-saddle roofed swing on the Taedong's west bank. Large halls, high turnover of clientele, great in summer for cold noodles on the veranda overlooking the river, but a bit cavernous in winter.

Pyongyang No 1 Boat Restaurant Usually moors opposite the Juche Tower on the west bank. Excellent BBQs, around ∈ 30 for four. Can be hired out for events and cruises lazily along the river.

Pyongyang Boat Restaurant No 2 Smaller than the No 1, this usually moors about 200m south of the No 1, with pink net curtains and a welcoming smile. Serves black beer.

Mokran (Magnolia) is a Japanese-based Western restaurant in the Pothonghang Hotel, with excellent service and fine wine for ∈ 30 a bottle. In this hotel is a standard Korean restaurant that has recently had a make over.

Mingjok Siktang (also known as the **National**), next to the Red Cross HQ and Pyongyang University of Medicine over the road from the Koryo Hotel. Set dinners for about ∈ 15, with a fun floorshow most evenings and great ambience.

Taedonggang Diplomatic Club. Through its corridors are a few restaurants, including one '70s décor place with a dancefloor. Simple servings of soups and salads for up to ∈ 12 per person. Open for lunch and until 21.30, and the disco's open until 23.00 on Fridays and Saturdays. Opposite the Club is the **Songyo** Korean restaurant. Cross Okryu Bridge eastwards, follow Monsudong Street straight through a three-pronged fork, and on the right appears the drum-shaped **Taedongyogwan** Korean.

Pyongyang BBQ Duck restaurant is on the northwest corner of Thongil Street and Chungsong Bridge junction. Excellent food, good service, and popular with the locals. Open until 21.30. Around ∈ 30 for four. Diagonally opposite is the **Pyongyang Noodle House**, specialising in Pyongyang noodles.

Chongnyu restaurant sits on the Pothong riverbank before Sinso Bridge. Tel: 48257, four-storey building shaped like a ship. Serves usual Korean, including *sinsollo*, with rooms dedicated to particular dishes.

The **Pyongyang Botanical Gardens** has a Korean place next to its entrance, excellent in summer, open only during the day.

The nearby **ice rink** has a restaurant.

Pyongyang Friendship International Health Centre, next to the ice rink, has two restaurants, but the one on the terrace is only open in the summer. Both serve the higher end (and higher priced) of Korean fare.

The **Moranbang Hotel** has been revamped and has opened a Japanese-Korean terrace bar; lovely in the evenings.

Eyonphung BBQ restaurant Just off a side road from Photong Bridge. At € 20 per head including beer and soju – does a good barbecue.

Dog meat can be found at a restaurant on Tongil St. For € 30 you get the lot, nose to tail.

The **Pyongyang Botanical Gardens** has a Korean place next to its entrance; excellent in summer, open only during the day.

Chongchun restaurant is on Kwangbok Street, near the Tangsang Flyover, and along here too is the **Chongchun No 2** and the **Hyangmannu**.

Pyongyang (Computer) Programme Centre, in the shadow of the uncompleted Ryugyong Hotel, has a good, if expensive, Korean BBQ restaurant.

Phyongnam Noodle restaurant is on Kaesong Street, opposite the friendship tower.

Moran Korean restaurant is in the middle of Moranbang Park.

At the **Gold Lane** bowling alley are two restaurants serving draft beer.

New Diplomatic Club, in the Munsudong district, serves an eclectic mix of Chinese, Korean, Japanese and Western food. It also has a karaoke bar. It is in the same compound as the Diplomatic Shop.

Pyongyang Mullet Soup restaurant is on the Taedong's south bank between Chungsong and Yanggak bridges, but is fiddly to get to.

There's an English menu at the **Arirang**, 150m south of Okryu Bridge, with a BBQ, beer and salad for € 10 each.

NIGHTLIFE

For nightlife, there's not that much to do. The city was once famed for the wits and other delights of its 'kisaeng girls', akin to the geishas of Japan, but these days they're rather thin on the ground. Most of the hotels now have some form of karaoke, which open until your larynx is frazzled. There's an interesting Egyptian-themed nightclub in the Yangakkdo Hotel basement that's open till the small hours, next to the DPRK's first casino (staffed only by Chinese, open from 14.00 to 05.00). Many all-night beer tents open around the hotels during summer to give the impression of a burgeoning nightlife. Both the Koryo and Yangakkdo have white-boothed bars selling good, opaque, brown draft beer till midnight.

But the quietness of Pyongyang at night is another unique attribute; no capital anywhere is as silent or dark. One guest at the island hotel of Yanggakdo leaned out of his top-floor window and heard a baby crying, which he realised was coming from an apartment across the river. If it's a special time of year, or a state visit is on, the main sites are illuminated. If not, tiptoeing through the streets at night in the pitch black is one way to go round town without getting any kind of attention. Sometimes you only know someone's there as you hear voices suddenly going past you. Around Pyongyang railway station is wonderful at night; it's full of waiting travellers, smoking, chatting, playing cards and sleeping, maybe one playing a flute for haunting tunes to waft through the streets.

PRACTICALITIES
Shopping
Shopping is limited to the large department stores and hotel shops.

Publications
Korea (monthly) and the *Pyongyang Times* (weekly) are multi-lingual publications available from the hotel shops. Much of the available literature in the DPRK concerns the lives and works of the Kims, or foreign affairs' reviews like 'The US Imperialists started the war'. Otherwise there are glossy books on Korea's wildlife, and that's it. There is one foreign-language bookshop (09.00–18.00, except Sunday and Thursday afternoon) opposite the Pyongyang No 1 store on the same block as the Korean Culture Museum.

Post office
The main post office is in the centre, just southwest of Taedong Bridge. The International Post Office is in Haebangsan Street. The International Communications Center is in Pothonggang District, opposite the Pyongyang Indoor Stadium.

Changing money
You can change money in the big hotels and at the Trade Bank on Sungni Street, near Kim Il Sung Square. Foreign currencies should be changed in the DPRK to 'the money exchangeable for foreign currency'. Foreign exchange is available at the Trade Bank or its agents, hotels, and restaurants.

Hospitals and pharmacies
A doctor and a nurse are meant to be permanently based at the Yanggakdo Hotel. Note that the following telephone numbers are subject to change:

Red Cross General Hospital of Korea Tel: 28291 (621 1110) East-Pyongyang
Pyongyang Friendship Hospital Tel: 621 6145 (operator)
Pyongyang First Aid Hospital Tel: 22758
Pyongyang Foreigners' Hospital Tel: 22160
Kim Man Yu Hospital Tel: 28136 (621 3111) East Pyongyang
Pyongyang Maternity Hospital Tel: 621 1125 East Pyongyang
Mannyon Traditional General Pharmacy 1 Ongnyu-dong, Taedonggang
Mannyon Pharmacy 3 Ongnyudong, Taedonggang
Mannyon Health General Company 3 Ongnyudong, Taedonggang; tel: 23048, 31225, 22891

WHAT TO SEE
Guides and DPRK guidebooks give a lot of statistics: dates of construction, speed of construction, floor-space, and the number of tiles, bricks or measurements that have symbolism for the cult of the Kims. The anodyne statistics are also proof of progress. Communist states in the heady decades of success from the 1950s to the 1980s were fiercely competitive among themselves in terms of output and progress, and the proof of a more advanced,

more capable workforce was that they could knock up the biggest library in the world in the shortest time.

These statistics also make up for the dearth of other facts. It's quickly apparent that there are far fewer urban anecdotes than those you'd find in London, eg: 'This area used to be a red-light district, and that hotel used to be a brothel and Dickens was once caught there'. The issue is less that of a Year Zero whereupon the communist expunged all the history of the corrupt and wicked past, but Ground Zero, for by 1953 Pyongyang had been levelled by war. Nearly every building, including the 'ancient' ones, were built or reconstructed post-war, and the grander buildings are from the late 1960s and 1970s when the economy could afford more grandeur. In that sense, what you see is what you get. An apartment block is and has always been that, and the purpose for which a government edifice was put up is the purpose for which that building is used today. You might also disagree over what DPRK literature considers to be 'highlights', as the following from *Pyongyang Review* suggests:

> The Three Revolution Exhibition is a centre for recreation for
> working people, and for scientific research. It is made up of pavilions,
> recreation, management, entrance, car park and lawn area, which
> constitute an ensemble.

Kim Il Sung Square

This huge open plaza of 75,000m² of granite, set out in 1954, is seen as the heart of the city, through which the great military and torch parades and mass rallies pass and is as good a place as any to start a tour. The square is hemmed in by the **Grand People's Study House** to the west and affords a grand vista of the **Juche Tower** east over the river. The simple classical grandeur of the **Korean Central History Museum** (northeast side) and opposite, the **Korean Art Gallery** battle with the Korean-style Study House, while huge placards of the country's flags and weapons add vibrant colour to an austere place.

Dominating the whole square is the Grand People's Study House. 'Its architectural ornaments are of light and quiet colours, which contribute to its magnificent yet refreshing appearance. In architecture, it demonstrates the elegance and majesty of the traditional Korean-style building.' The 34 hip-saddle roofs, capped with 750,000 green tiles, rise one above another like unfolded wings of cranes. Built for Kim Il Sung's 70th birthday in 1982, it is the facility that allows the 'Study-While-Working' educational system for cadres and working people, and can accommodate 12,000 users a day. A huge white statue of the Great Leader sits in the marble-pillared entrance, flanked not by grand stairways but by two modern escalators. Enter the KIS reading room with its half computerised directory, half carded index, and you'll see the music library with the foreign music section – where Koreans can listen to foreign popular music such as Vera Lynn's greatest hits right up to the most modern – The Beatles. Maybe you'll see a language class in action (Repeat after me!) and big reading rooms full of dull, flickering lights to strain the eyes of the library's visitors poring over its 30,000,000 volumes, deliverable on a remote-controlled conveyor. Certainly the lifts are in tremendous demand on Saturdays. The upper balcony is also used to coordinate the march-pasts and evening torch parades, and you can look out on to the mature metal roofs of the surrounding buildings.

On the east half of the square is the **Korean Central History Museum** (Tuesday to Sunday), a long, detailed tour of the peninsula's history, a lot of which is invasions, resistance and repulsions, feuds and wars between provinces, kingdoms and surrounding countries. It's a complicated tale that's difficult to tell coherently, and the museum could assist visitors' concentration by adjusting the museum's lighting and ventilation. Look out for the world's first rocket batteries and the classic black ball and fuse of the world's first time-bomb.

The **Korean Art Gallery** is well worth a visit. From its excellent reproductions of early Korean tomb paintings, it follows with large (roll mat) screen paintings illustrating court and common life in Korea across time. The guides provide an excellent interpretation of the paintings, from the decadence of feudal Korea up to the real meanings of seemingly innocuous paintings under Japanese rule. The big, bright, socialist-realism paintings on the upper floors are fascinating, especially the 'Sailing Steel Works' that challenges Western notions of what constitutes beauty.

The rest of the city

Now, leave the square by going north along Sungri Street (that splits the square in two), and a block later on the crossroads with Somun Street you'll find the **Pyongyang Department Store No 1**.

> None of the lights were on in the shop when I went there, so only daylight glinting off the polished floor permeated the shop's centre. This meant I could get quite close to the tills (for practically all goods are behind counters) before the shop assistants would see me and wander off.
>
> Robin Tudge

Opposite to the No 1 is the **Foreign Languages Bookshop** (09.00–18.00 Monday–Saturday, closed Thursday afternoon). On the corner and riverwards along Somun Street is the **Korean Folklore Museum**. This is a much more manageable 3-floor exhibition of the daily lives of Koreans, and the English-speaking guide gives a good account of what work and fun entailed for Korean men, women and children in times gone by.

On the No 1's west side, and accessible via a huge staircase leading down from the Grand Study House, are the hard-to-miss **Mansudae fountains** (firing up to 80m high) providing cooling mists in summer and pools for locals to play in. The fountains befront the massive **Mansudae Arts Theatre**, with its spectrum-coloured tower, and in which dance and music performances can be seen by arrangement. In good contrast with the theatre's monolithic simplicity are the more humanly scaled **Sungmin** and **Sungnyong** temples, dating from 1325 and 1429 respectively. The latter was built as a shrine to Tangun and to the founder of Koguryo, Tongmyong. Continuing uphill and northwards to Mansu hill, a good view of the city to the west becomes visible. Soon, on the left appears the monolithic DPRK building of the **Mansudae Assembly Hall**, with a huge carved national emblem on its façade, surrounded by acres of empty car parks. Visiting Mansudae is possible by arrangement, ie: when it's not in use. Hallways hundreds of metres in length lined with statues of good workers (not aged lords and nobles as in the West) and wall-length paintings beam away from stairwells with chandeliers cascading through them. The main assembly hall is cavernous, with an awesome glazed ceiling. Observe the detail of the décor and count the number and location of microphones. Guides take you through the numerous private committee rooms and lounges that are usually smoke-filled.

From the Hall, the road tips down then up Mansu Hill towards the **Korean Revolutionary Museum** and what must be Pyongyang's most famous site, the **Grand Monument**. Here is the towering 20m bronze figure of Kim Il Sung, arm out pointing the way forward in front of a 70m wide mosaic of Korea's spiritual source, Mt Paektu. Flanking the Great Leader are the DPRK and KWP flags carved from stone and lined with 228 bronze figures (5m high) symbolising the anti-Japanese struggle, socialist revolution and construction.

> The Korean People erected the monument from their unanimous desire and aspiration to have the immortal revolutionary exploits of the great leader Comrade Kim Il Sung; remembered for all time and to carry forward and consummate the revolutionary cause of Juche which he initiated.

Slogans on the monuments' placards read as 'Long Live Kim Il Sung' and 'Let us drive out US imperialism and reunify the country'. A six-figure group on the left banner of the statue plot the overthrow of US imperialism, all imperialism, and the world revolution. The monument and the museum were built for Kim's 60th birthday, and the museum has over 4.5km of display halls of varying interest. Since his death in July 1994, it has become the focus for mourning. Local people come to the statue at all times of the day and night to lay flowers and observe a moment's silence. Foreigners also pay homage with flowers, available from nearby or down in the fountains for €5 a bunch. From the monument, far across the river can be seen the **Korean Workers' Party Monument**, at the end of a broad street aligned with the Grand Monument.

Northwards past the monument run little leafy paths down to Chilsongmun Street, that hugs the hilltop park of Chongnion on **Moran Hill**. First on Chilsongmun you pass the **Chollima** statue. Chollima is a fabled winged horse that could cover a thousand ri (400km) a day. The 46m-high statue was inaugurated in 1961 and 'symbolises the heroic mettle and indomitable spirit of our people who made ceaseless innovations for post war rehabilitation'. The rebuilding of Pyongyang after the Korean War was said to be carried out at Chollima speed.

> The statue is composed of a worker, a member of our heroic class, spurring the Chollima on to a leap forward with the red letter of the

Central Committee of the Workers' Party of Korea in his raised hand and a young peasant woman seated behind him with a sheaf of ripe rice in her arms.

Opposite Chollima is the classical portico of **Moranbong Theatre**, built in 1946 and where the first Supreme People's Assembly was held in 1948. It's nestled into Moran Hill, the slopes and trees of which provide shade and breeze as you descend to the Arch of Triumph. This road crosses over the road tunnel that bores under Chongnion and on to the Rungra Bridge. Kim Jong Suk nursery is on the left.

Eventually you reach the unmistakable **Arch of Triumph**. Made of white granite, the 60m arch is dedicated to 'the home return of the Great Leader Comrade Kim Il Sung who liberated Korea from Japanese colonialism' and has dozens of rooms in the interior. It was erected in 1982 in one year on the 70th birthday of Kim Il Sung (symbolised by the 70 azaleas, Korea's national flower,

PYONGYANG MARATHON

The Pyongyang Marathon was opened to international competition in 2001, with 200 spaces allowed for elite and amateur competitors from abroad. The flat and fast course starts and finishes at the 70,000-seat Kim Il Sung Stadium, weaving through Pyongyang with a stretch along the Taedong. Around 300,000 Pyongyangians cheered 300 runners at the 2002 run, including 15 elite internationals. "Several runners reported extremely tired arms as they decided to shake hands with the crowd over the last five kilometres,' said one of the organisers, Nick Horne. Foreign entrants paid US$1,000 for a four-day package, charter flight to and from Beijing included. The marathon is held in April, when temperatures are from 10° to 14°C.

South Africa's Zachariah Mpolokeng won the men's race in 2hr 15min 05sec, with DPR Korea's Kil Jae Son second and Jang Chong Il third. DPR Korea's Ham Pong Sil won the women's race in a course record of 2hr 26min 23sec. The current record-holder is Kenya's Nelson Ndereva Njeru with 2hr 11min 05sec. Marathon running is taken very seriously in Korea. Seoul has four annual marathons with 13,000 entries each, and the ROK's Lee Bong Ju won silver in the 1996 Olympics and gold in the 1998 and 2002 Asian Games. The DPRK's top ten male runners consistently run 2hr 10min–2hr 15min and there are ten DPRK women who can run under 2hr 30min, including Jong Song Ok, winner of the 1999 IAAF World Women's Marathon Championships.

FILA sponsored the 2002 marathon and numerous DPRK sports federations. Their sponsorship of the 2001 Pyongyang Skating Festival got their signage on DPR Korean television, the first foreign advertising ever seen in the country! For details contact Guy Horne on tel: (852) 22345338; fax: (852) 2529 9650; email: horne@netvigator.com.

that frame the arch). As written in the *Pyongyang Review*, 'Inscribed either side of the arch are the dates 1925–45 covering the period when Comrade Kim Il Sung set out on the 1,000 ri Journey for National Liberation to the time when he returned home in triumph after achieving his aim'.

The *Review* continues:

> The three-tiered roof embodies the structural features of the
> traditional architecture – the pillars, beams, brackets and eaves are
> formed in a way congenial to modern aesthetic taste.

Taller than the Parisian version we were told – interesting that the architectural styles are so similar! Opposite the arch is the large **Kim Il Sung Stadium**, where the Great Leader made a speech at the 'Pyongyang mass Meeting' after Japan's occupation finished in 1945. Originally called Moranbong Stadium, it was reconstructed with a capacity of 100,000 and renamed for KIS' 70th birthday. It is used for athletic events as well as Mass Games held on national holidays and commemorative occasions, where tens of thousands of performers perform choreographed socialist-realism displays, 'a form of mass physical culture which is combined with physical skills and ideological and artistic value'.

Next to the stadium is a large stone with Kim Il Sung's autograph carved on to it. In the immediate vicinity of the Arch is the West Pyongyang department store (just south of the arch), and the Pyongyang City People's Hospital No 1.

If you continue north on Kaeson Street, the 30m **Friendship Tower** arises on the right, commemorating the alliance of China and the DPRK. Opposite is the Chongsun restaurant and the Chongsun Revolutionary Museum and further along is the Phyongnam noodle restaurant. Kaeson Street crosses Pipa Street and there appears on the left the **April 25 People's Army House of Culture** (West on Pipa Street), a 'centre of mass cultural education for soldiers of the Korean People's Army and the Working People'. Within the 50m-high, 176m-long building is a cinema and two theatres (one with 6,000 seats). The westward road opposite, guarded by a giant trident called the **Immortal Tower**, dedicated to the onliving spirit of Kim Il Sung, heads to Taesong and Kim Il Sung's mausoleum.

Pressing on north on Podunamu Street, you pass the Ryonmot restaurant on the left towards the **Three-Revolution Exhibition**, about 6km from the city centre. It's a series of massive sheds in 100 hectares, and an almighty steel globe. The exhibition is made up of various halls such as New Technical Innovations, Light Industry and Agriculture, with exhibits from the ideological, technological and cultural revolutions. The objectives of these revolutions, a significant political milestone in DPRK policy, are 'to raise the ideological level of the people, equip the economy with modern techniques and to lift the people's technological and cultural level. They are considered essential for successful socialist construction'. The place comes across as a massive expo-centre for DPRK manufacturers, so you get to see loads of what's not in the shops, and if that doesn't appeal then see it as an exhibition of what's considered fascinating.

Pipa Street continues east straight to Mt Taesong. The street gets leafier and hillier along here as the land rolls up to Taesong's base, and where the city begins to peter out you pass **Kim Il Sung University**, a severe-looking complex of buildings for 12,000 serious students (including not a few foreign ones) to do serious study and by God they'll never have worked so hard in their lives nor ever will again. It's Pyongyang's top multi-curricular university of the thirty-odd universities in Pyongyang, that range from Pyongyang University of Foreign Studies to the University of Railways.

Staying at Moran Hill, the hill divides into two parks, Moranbong and Youth Park, but the hill's contouring paths lasso the parks together seamlessly. In spring this park drowns in pink blossom and it's a favourite area for strolling lovers. One path leads to the highly prominent **Liberation Tower**, built to commemorate the USSR's assistance in liberating Korea from the Japanese. It is on the hill's southern slope, overlooking the Rungna Bridge and Rungna Islet (itself a park) where the glint of steel from the fantastic **May Day Stadium's** grand arches soar. This stadium has a seating capacity of 150,000 and is the venue for the truly awesome Mass Games which reached a zenith with the Arirang Festival (see box below).

Should you stay on the mainland of Moran Hill, its paths connect a series of old pavilions, gates and sentinel towers that remain from old Pyongyang's fortress walls that protected the city and formed the divisions of its inner districts. Pyongyang's walls were first built between 552 and 586 as the city was then the Koguryo capital and at the height of its prosperity had over 210,000 houses. The walled city went south from Moran Hill, filling the sac of land

THE MASS GAMES AND ARIRANG

Nearly every year, 100,000 artistes, young students and children perform in the four-act show, with ten scenes of ethnic dances, gymnastics and giddying acrobatics and folk songs. It's a compact story of the DPRK in dance, with everything celebrated from the might of the armed forces to how cute children are, the victory of the country in completing the 'arduous march' to the success of the cooperative farms; you have to go just to see 2,000 people-sized eggs running about. Thousands of performers are on stage in each scene, in a stunning feat of choreography, not only for the precision of the dances during the scenes, but how they all leave the stage in a flash in total darkness. Behind the floor show is a huge screen of images made from pixels of coloured card held by 20,000 students. Watching them warm up with a massive test-card before the show proper begins is entertainment in itself. Usually scheduled from the end of April to the end of June, it can run until mid-August, so go if you can. For the 2002 Arirang, US tourists were given special dispensation to visit. That year, tickets cost US$50, US$100, US$150 and US$300, with upgrades of seating and service, but the foreigners are congregated where they get a central view.

RIVER WALKS

The willowy Pothong River park is a balmy place to stroll. Both banks of the River Taedong, from Rungna Bridge down beyond the Yanggak, have raised dykes topped by paths shaded by trees, making for good strolls of the city with broad panoramas of the capital and a chance to see the locals relaxing. On the west bank opposite Juche Tower, pedal-boats operate in summer, and the river can freeze thick enough for skating in winter.

that rests between the Taedong and Pothong rivers, natural defences for the city. All of the wall's gates and posts have been rebuilt at one time or another, with many rebuilt in the 1710s following a great fire. But before we look at the old pavilions, under Moran Hill are tunnels and caves, where the government functioned during the Korean War.

On Moran Hill's Chilsongmun side is **Chilsong Gate**, known as the 'gate of happiness' or 'gate of love' since the 6th century. On the hill's riverside is **Chongryu Pavilion**, another gate to the walled city. **Pubyok Pavilion** (so named from the 12th century) on the Chongryu cliffs was an annex of the **Yongmyong Temple** built in 393. Pubyok name means 'floating walls' as if it floats on the river. **Ulmil Pavilion** was originally 6th century, a northern command post, rebuilt in 1714 and named after General Ulmil who defended the place, and is famed for its picturesque location during spring. Just 100m downhill is **Hyonmu Gate**, the northern gate of the walled city during Kogruyu times, named after the black tortoise-serpent god Hyonmu that was fabled as this city district's spiritual defender. On Moran Hill's highest peak is the **Choesung Pavilion**, originally 6th century and rebuilt in 1716. The height of the hill made it the natural choice as the city's central command point. **Jongum Gate** was the southern gate of the Koguryo's northern fort and was rebuilt in 1714. All were part of Pyongyang's Inner Fort, the walls of which traced down the riverbank a kilometre southwards past the Okryu Bridge to **Ryongwang Pavilion** and **Taedong Gate.** Ryongywang dates from the Koguryo period and the Taedong Gate was originally 6th century, as is the eastern gate of the inner fort. One plaque on the gate reads 'Uphoru', meaning a 'pavilion facing a clear stream', and one below it reads 'Taedong Gate'. Next to it is the 13.5- ton Pyongyang Bell, cast in 1726 and used until the 1890s to tell the time and also to warn of danger.

Continuing south a few hundred metres and you're back slap between Juche Tower and KIS Square, or from Okryu Bridge you can follow Mansudae Street west to the **Pothong Gate**. This was the west gate of the walled city, first built mid-6th century under the Koguryo, and rebuilt several times since, most recently after the Korean War. It now marks the Pothong Bridge crossing into Pothonggang District, a heart-shaped area moated by two arteries of the Pothong River. From here the Pothonggang Pleasure Park curves northwest and is a beautiful venue for walking amid willow trees, confirming Pyongyang's moniker as 'city of willows'. Pyongyangians are seen relaxing and fishing all along the river. Compared to other Asian cities, Pyongyang is exceptionally quiet at most times of day, but the thin and lazy Pothong is charmingly gentrified and quiet. The park's paths can be followed as they curve northwest, past Mansu Bridge and the adjacent dome of the People's Army Circus, towards the **Victorious Fatherland Liberation War Museum** on Yonggung Street. This is brilliant, with halls of compellingly arranged documents and artefacts from the Korean War, its build-up and aftermath. It's impossible to take it all in in a day, but along the way are fabulously intricate models and dioramas, that help to inspire a feeling of shame that such a devastating war can have been so largely forgotten in the West. Up a rounded stairway is a spectacular 360° revolving panorama of a battle. In the basement are the remains of numerous southern and American vehicles, boats and aircraft, juxtaposed with the intact Korean People's Army machines responsible for blowing them up and bringing them down (well you would only have the enemy's wrecks to display, wouldn't you?). There are the remains of American reconnaissance craft intercepted since the Korean War, and the gruellingly written confession of one US helicopter pilot whose handwriting suggests what broke him to spill all beyond his name, rank, serial number.

Behind the museum, across the Jongsong Bridge into Pothonggang district, is the **Monument to the Victorious Fatherland Liberation War 1950–1953**, erected in 1993 'on the occasion of the 40th anniversary of war victory'. The setting consists of a 150,000m² white stone-flagged park with ten group sculptures in dark bronze depicting various battles on sea, land and air. It is dedicated to the 'Korean People's Army and Korean people who defeated the US imperialists and its allies in the Fatherland Liberation War'. On a sunny day, the contrast of the dazzling white floor and the nearly black sculptures is eerily impressive. The **'Victory' Sculpture** is the monument's focal point, its bronze sculpture represents a soldier shouting 'hurry', at the top of his voice, in the direction of the nearby Ryugyong Hotel. From every viewpoint can be seen the great unfinished **Ryugyong Hotel**, a vast pyramid stabbing the sky that was simply a hotel too far. It stands as an empty, unclad shell, and has done for years, with no date set for completion. Its 105 grey-brown storeys topped by five revolving (what else?) restaurants have space for 3,000 rooms and the building's planned facilities would have warranted it as a district in its own right. The guides roll their eyes when asked about this magnificent folly. Another site on the Pothong River's western artery is the **Monument to the Pothong River Improvement Project** and further west is **Pongsu Church**.

Heading south from Pothong Gate along Chollima Street, it seems that the road broadens out and the buildings are given more personal space to flaunt themselves, lined up along the Pothong and taking in the sun. You pass the huge traditional Korean-style **People's Palace of Culture**, a labyrinth of rooms and halls for the 'ideological and cultural education of the working people', and in front of which grand public dances are held on national holidays. Next to it is the **Pyongyang Indoor Stadium**. Spacious roads break west to cross the Pothong by the Susong Bridge (just over which is the silvery tower of the International Communications Centre) and Sinso Bridge. Just before Sinso is a knot of buildings including the Changwang Health Complex, Ragwon department store, Chongryu restaurant and the **Ice Rink**, the 12 supports on its conical shape resembling skates.

Continue south on Chollima Street until it intersects with Sosong Street and follow the rail tracks to **Pyongyang railway station**, where you may have first arrived or perhaps will leave the country. The clock overlooking the square is said to be the time-standard for all the DPRK. The entrance door on the left is for foreigners, entering through the right door will lead to your swift exit back through it. The copse of trees in station square is full of waiting travellers at all hours of the day, who choose not to peruse the wares of the Pyongyang Station Department Store on the opposite corner nor follow Yongwang Street towards the river, taking in the simple classical design of the **Chollima House of Culture**, the bad day for modernist architecture that created the **International House of Culture** and the sweeping fancy of the neo-Korean **Pyongyang Grand Theatre.**

Now, in front of the classical portico of the **State Theatrical Company**, you can go west along Haebangsan Street past two post offices to the **Party Founding Museum.** This schoolish edifice was a Japanese company headquarters before 1945, whereupon it became the HQ for the Party's Central Committee immediately following 1945, and has the hallowed rooms and residence where Kim Il Sung mapped and slept upon the Party's future. It also contains the pond in which Kim Jong Il's younger brother drowned when the Dear Leader was a child. You're walking in the grounds where the state germinated, just over the road from the 'Forbidden City' where the state lives today. A complex of apartments and governmental buildings for the DPRK elite exists in the area between Changgwang, Chollima, and Jebangsan streets, with roads blocked off and guarded between strips of metal fencing, though you'll certainly see numerous saloon cars cruising in and out. Return to Sungri Street dog-legging past the **Monument to Martyrs of the People's Army** and you're going back towards Kim Il Sung square, or cross the Taedong Bridge to the city's eastern half.

East Pyongyang

This side of town is quieter and there's less to see. The Taedonggang and Tongdaewon districts of East Pyongyang are home to the city's diplomatic quarter, a dozen universities and a few hospitals, including the top-flight 1,500-bed **Pyongyang Maternity Hospital**. Some have claimed this was built to dispel the myth that pregnant women were banished from the city but it would seem to be a somewhat dramatic response to a persistent rumour. Just off Saeserim Street running from Taedong Bridge is the **Changchun Catholic Church**, reportedly built in 1989 to dispel the myth that religion was banned from the country.

Perhaps you can load up at the Taedonggang Diplomatic Club or the Songyu restaurant opposite, both on Taedong Bridge's east end. Then head along Juchetap Street for the **Juche Tower** dominating the eastern riverbank.

This 150m stone-clad tower, with a 20m, 45-ton metal flame flickering atop it, was built, as its name suggests, to celebrate the Juche philosophy of self-reliance as expounded by Kim Il Sung and developed by Kim Jong Il. The two words Ju and Che appear in large form on the east and west sides. The sides' tiers add up to 70, Kim Il Sung's age in 1982 and for that birthday the tower was built, while each stone is for a day in his life.

At the east base is an open shrine to dedications to the Juche idea, containing over 500 tabulets from around the world given in deference to the man and his idea. The entrance to the tower is down the steps on the southeast corner. Pay €5 entry then head through a long tunnel, with guide, before climbing into the lift that in its minute climb passes the floors of no known purpose up to the plinth of the flame from whence a very impressive view of the city is available. This guide dodges photos with a boxer's skill, and has a very good memory for faces. Coke was available from one of the karaoke rooms along the tunnel.

The statue fronting the tower on to the river has three people, intellectual, worker and farmer, holding their tools aloft into the KWP insignia, and looking out on to the 150m-high fountains blasting out of the Taedong. Behind the tower across Juchetap Street is the Korea Documentary Film studio where all things Juche are produced. Further north along this road is a tall, plain building with a deep bronze tint that's noticeable only for the large KWP sign on its roof. This otherwise innocuous high-rise is the **Kim Il Sung Higher Party School**, where Korea's brightest and best get trained in ruling the country.

Then further north along Juchetap come the peculiarly sculpted **Central Youth Hall**, with its anvil and armadillo roofs, and the slide machine of the **East Pyongyang Grand Theatre**. Around 3,500 people can pack in to see music or revolutionary opera here. Midway between these two buildings is a symmetrical street, and you realise it's in perfect alignment with the Mansu Grand Monument west across the river and the **Monument to Party Foundation** to your east just across Munsu Street. This staggering piece of work was erected in 1995 to celebrate the 50th anniversary of the Korean Workers' Party: a hammer, sickle and calligraphy brush grasped in the hands of a worker, farmer and intellectual. The sculpture's 50 granite-faced metres mark one metre for each of the Party's 50 years. The belt uniting the three tools has bronze reliefs lining its interior, emblazoned with the slogan, 'Long live the Workers Party of Korea, the Organiser and Guide of the Victory of the Korean People!' The inscription on the pedestal refers to the development of the Party from the roots of anti-imperialism.

Further out of town
Korean Film Studio
Far out into Hyongjesan district, about 10km due northwest of Kim Il Sung Square, is the other great factory of the DPRK's view on the world, the Korean Film Studio. With nothing to note on the way to this massive Korean Hollywood (except the Railways University) it's a must-see, churning out such thrillers as *Daughter of the Revolution*. You'll likely watch old melodramas

KIMILSUNGIA AND KIMJONGILIA: FANATIC FLOWERS

Deriving from the *Dendobrium* genus of the orchid family, Kimilsungia is a tropical perennial with deep pink flowers, cultivated in Indonesia and named after Kim Il Sung in 1965 when he visited the country: 'The Indonesian president said that his respected excellency (Kim Il Sung) had rendered great services to mankind and deserved a high honour. The Indonesian president was so firmly resolved that Kim Il Sung could no longer decline his offer.'

Kim Jong Il received his own species of Kimjongilia, a blood-red bloom of tuberous begonia, in 1988 from a Japanese botanist, Kamo Mototeru, 'in the hope of achieving amity and friendship between Japan and Korea'. Both plants have inspired songs, won international competitions, and are cultivated countrywide for local shows and an annual festival for Kimjongilia flowers held in Pyongyang in February.

being filmed and tour through reconstructed feudal villages which give a good insight into ancient Korean life, so it's partly a moving museum (although the crops grown in the village are for real). Note the German town, pre-revolution Chinatown and the totally decadent Seoul city, awash with US and Japanese-run brothels, go-go bars, casinos and all so decadent that they don't eat dogs but pamper them. Despite having to pay to take photos (of the actors at least), the studios are well worth visiting to experience the dream world within the dream city.

The number 5 tram ventures there from West Pyongyang railway station.

Mt Taesong

Beyond the sprawl, about 10km northeast of the city centre, are Mount Taesong and its hills. The road with **Kim Il Sung University** and **Kumsusan Memorial Palace** (see page 129) continues to undulate eastwards, crossing the Hapjang River, which seems to be a border for town and country.

Physically, Mt Taesong is one peak, Jujak (192m) surrounded by a series of vegetation-covered summits capped with small pavilions, while many small lakes pock the valley that curves around Jujak and its surrounding peaks. A series of paths weaves the lakes and hills together and make for a good afternoon's walking in balmy air, finding amid the scant ruined walls of **Fort Taesong** viewpoints over distant Pyongyang. The peaks were linked by a fort wall from the 3rd century, and the fort was bolstered for Pyongyang's defences after the Koguryo moved their capital to the city in AD427. Fort Taesong's walls reached 9.2km in length, and of its 20 gates, the most prominent 'survivor' is the **Nam Gate**, rebuilt in 1978.

Looking from the bus terminus at Taesong's southwest foot, on the left is **Pyongyang Central Zoo**. It may have 600 species of all breathing things, many of which were gifts to Kim Il Sung, but it's a zoo in the very, very traditional sense. Attractions include Korean tigers in a seriously miserable cage, elephants penned in by spiked plates on the floor, and a collection of cats and dogs. Only the unconvincingly escape-proof baboon pen merits much more attention.

Opposite the zoo are the **Botanical Gardens**, of note for any of the 5,000 species there. The chance to see Kimilsungia and Kimiljongilia out of season is possibly the best reason to visit, and to investigate what's being bred in the gardens' 'experimental' section. The gardens also have some ancient tombs, possibly of Koryo origin. The gardens are next to the **Taesongan Fun Fair**, with a charming Buddhist temple within its grounds (open on request) and beyond that, past a handful of restaurants lies the main path for the pavilions of Jangsu and Sumon peaks around Jujak.

These are all light distractions compared to Jujak's crown, the **Revolutionary Martyrs' Cemetery**. Unless driven to the top, you pass through the large Korean-style gate and ascend a breathless flight of 300 granite steps up to a road (where the van otherwise stops), then the cemetery begins on a shallower slope up to Jujak Peak. Between a large medal and a huge crimson granite flag are interred over 200 leading figures from Korea's resistance to Japanese colonial rule and the Korean War. A bust of Kim Il Sung's wife is before the flag. Many were scarcely adults when they fell fighting the Japanese and in the War. Now their bronze busts look out on to Pyongyang as somber music is piped around them, in what is an exceedingly austere but very moving setting. It is expected that you pay respects at the medal and the flag.

Exiting left of the flag, there appears a road heading back to the bus terminus and another path heading for the peaks.

Buses 1, 2, 3, 28, 29, 30 terminate at Mt Taesong. Only the 3 is useful in running into central town along Hyoksin, Pipa and Mundok streets. Back at the terminus, the 1 trolley bus trundles southeast for a mile, past **Pyongyang Astronomical Observatory** and another 500m to the Koguryo's **Anhak Palace**. It must have been a major sight to behold, for within its four walls (each measuring 622m and 6–12m high), the remains of 52 buildings, most linked by lengthy cloisters, have been found amongst gardens and waterways.

Over Taesong's west side is the **Kwangbok Temple**, tucked up a small valley and with a handful of monks still seen to practise their religion. The site, if not the buildings, is one of Pyongyang's most ancient, for a temple has been here since AD392. However, the original burnt down in 1700 and its replacement was razed during the Korean War, hence the gleaming one you see today, built in 1990 following the 1989 World Festival of Youth and Students.

Mangyongdae

Following the river road down to Mangyongdae you may see the USS *Pueblo* moored around Yanggak Bridge. This Cold War trophy is now a floating museum.

In January 1968 the 850-ton spy-boat USS *Pueblo*, with Captain Pete Bucher and 82 crewmembers, left Japan supposedly on an oceanographic research mission but really to conduct electronic surveillance off the DPRK coast. The North Koreans had recently expressed their heightened irritation over spy-ships loitering in its waters; indeed in January 1967 North Korean

GENERAL SHERMAN

By the 1860s, the Ri court was deeply alarmed that despite the prohibition and persecution of Christianity and its followers, Koreans were still converting by the thousand. The Tonghak rebellion of 1864 further shook the court and it boded that any more foreign proselytisers would get very short shrift.

So it was ill-timed that in August 1866, the armed steam-schooner the *General Sherman* should steam up the Taedong River, ostensibly to broach trade with Korea, but on board was the young Protestant missionary, Robert Jermaine Thomas. The *Sherman* had been a trader used by both sides of America's Civil War, following the end of which the *Sherman* was pressed into service in East Asia. Captain Page piloted the ship into Korea but it was evidently Thomas that called the shots. The *Sherman* was first greeted by an emissary for Governor Park Kyoo Soo of Pyung-an, who told Page, Thomas and the other Westerners aboard (including the ship's owner) that trade with Korea was illegal, but that provisions would be provided for the ship's departure from Korea.

Nonetheless, on Thomas' insistence, upon the emissary's departure the *Sherman* continued upriver towards Pyongyang, where heavy rain and high tides allowed the ship to sail an unusually deep river and get to Turu Islet, near Mangyongdae, from whence Thomas proselytised and his companions tried to trade with locals. Deputy Commander Lee Hyon-ik of the Pyongyang garrison was sent to the ship to convey the king's displeasure at the *Sherman*'s further intrusion. The Koreans now heavily suspected that this was less about trade than about Christian evangelism, and a testy confrontation was imminent when, upon the call-out of the Pyongyang garrison, Lee found himself taken

battery fire from their shores had sunk the American patrol-boat *PCE-56* near the DMZ, but their threats of an even more vigorous response weren't heeded. Surely, though North Korean planes and boats buzzed the *Pueblo*, its captain and crew considered they were safe (the US insist that it was never closer than 15 miles from the DPRK, ie: in international waters), until one North Korean vessel approached to board it. Bucher ordered the *Pueblo* to weave away at speed, but the *Pueblo* received gunfire from the north. In the ensuing chase and boarding, one crewmember was killed and several were wounded. Realising that the *Pueblo* was outpaced and outgunned, Bucher surrendered the ship. A haul of secret documents and equipment, neither destroyed nor dumped in time, fell into North Korean hands, later gleefully shared with the Soviets. More importantly, they had 82 Americans captive to torture and with which to torture President Johnson's administration for eleven months. The weight of American commitment in Vietnam (1968 being a year of heavy casualties for the US there) precluded more aggressive attempts to get the crew returned. The crew's captivity was harsh and only improved upon the signing of confessions. The crew were ultimately handed back, with hostage as the ship turned. However, the wet weather had abated, the tide was turning, then fog sealed the futility of the ship's escape and it ran aground. Accounts differ as to whether the Pyongyang garrison or the *Sherman* fired first. Keeping Deputy Commander Lee as a hostage to forestall any attack while the *Sherman* turned may have provoked the garrison to attack, but the *Sherman* may have opened fire to seal its getaway before running aground, or to repel boarders afterwards. Either way, the garrison attacked with fire-rockets and cannon, and the *Sherman* returned cannon fire on anything that moved, civilian and military alike. After four days' battle, on September 2, Korean turtle-boats were tied together, set afire and pushed towards the *Sherman*. All the Westerners and the ship's Asian crew that had escaped gunfire or the fumes of the burning ship were caught, executed and mutilated. Thomas apparently followed his Bible riverward from the burning ship's deck, and was captured. Whether he died the brave martyr or was slain begging for his life is not clear. The *USS Wachusett* was sent the following year to investigate the incident, but little was learnt except that the *Sherman* had indeed been destroyed. In spring 1868, the *USS Shenandoah* reached the Taedong River's mouth where Captain Febiger received an official acknowledgment that all the *General Sherman*'s crew were dead. The *Sherman*'s destruction was cited as but one 'depredation against Americans' that justified a punitive attack on numerous sites and forts by American forces in 1871: the incident and its repercussions also justified to the Ri that politeness was ultimately wasted on these foreign devils and their duplicitous ways, and stelae were put up nationwide that read 'Posterity should remember that unwillingness to fight the intrusion of the Westerners means reconciliation, and that insisting on negotiations for peace mean selling the country'.

the remains of the dead crewmember, through Panmumnjom on 23 December 1968, but the equipment remained. The North Koreans kept the *Pueblo* in Wonsan until the late 1990s, then moored it in Pyongyang near to where the *General Sherman* was burned in 1866. It was moved in mid-2002, but may yet return to Pyongyang if not to Wonsan.

Mangyongdae district is the westernmost area of Pyongyang city, filling the banks of the River Pothong's western artery. Two boulevards, **Kwangbok Street** and **Chongchun Street**, divide and rule this area in their roles as open galleries for the art of concrete architecture. Kwangbok Street, finished in 1989, is described as a city in its own right, with 25,000 flats racked and stacked along this 6km-long, 100m-wide strip. Beginning at the Pothong's Palgol Bridge, Kwangbok has the hexagonal spaceships of the **Circus** on its west side. Here you'll see a fun mix of high-wire acrobatics and grotesque parodies of American troops and South Koreans. Kwangbok ends in the embracing arms of the **Mangyongdae Students and Children's Palace** and its bronze-coloured 'Chariot of Happiness' amid sculptures from numerous tales told to children by the Great and Dear Leaders. Many of the various 690 rooms are for group classes where children learn the violin, accordion, dance, public speaking, Taekwondo, boxing, etc, and a tour should prelude an electrifying, technically razor-sharp 90-minute show of music and dance by the children trained at this DPRK version of 'Fame'. Halfway along Kwangbok, Chongchun or 'Gymnasium' Street undercuts it. A series of nine sports' halls, each dedicated to one sport, line this road down to the Angol Flyover on the Taedong. Each hall's design apparently represents some facet of their nominated sport, but unless you're going to watch one, the buildings are bizarrely impressive enough. To increase the social interest in physical sports the government set the second Sunday of October every year as Sports Day.

You may traverse Kwangbok and Chongchun going to or from the **Mangyongdae Revolutionary Site,** where the Great Leader was born and spent his first few years. Otherwise, you may hug the road on the Taedong's west bank down to Mangyongdae, spying the huge thermal power plant to the east belching fumes skywards.

Just before Mangyongdae, you'll notice that the river has split around the rather large Turu Islet and its satellite islets. Here it's thought that the American missionary-trader USS *General Sherman* was beached and destroyed in 1866. Official histories credit the burning of the ship to Kim Il Sung's great-grandfather Kim Ung U, but the story's details swirl in debate (see box on pages 126–7).

Mangyongdae Shrine and its environs
Follow the Taedong's west bank southwards and the landscape becomes rapidly green and rural. Some 12km south of the city centre, just before the River Sunhwa empties into the Taedong, is a site of nearly religious significance, the former village of Mangyongdae. Here Kim Il Sung was born and spent his childhood, and the handful of tiny thatched huts where his parents and grandparents tilled the land are now enshrined. They form the centre of some well-trimmed parkland to which throngs of Koreans are taken on Party, factory and school tours to pay homage. The huts sit beside the small lotus pond, and are surrounded by small sites of significance, including the graves of Kim Il Sung's forebears. The full, official history of Kim's forebears is within the **Mangyongdae Revolutionary Museum,** 100m from the huts. On the lotus pond's opposite bank is a line of trees, each donated by visiting leader from the communist bloc, a reminder of the world of comrades that has so recently disappeared. Mangyong hill has a small pavilion atop it, and has two sites where Kim Il Sung studied and another where, according to legend, he wrestled with a larger foe and won.

Fighting through the throng of **Mangyongdae Fun Fair**'s reported 100,000 daily visitors, you'll find the Grenade Throwing ground and Machine Gun stalls as well as fifty other amusements visible from the fair's gondola and monorail rides. You might also get to see the DPRK's own little Eton, **Mangyongdae Revolutionary School,** just over the hill from the shrines. Here are trained the 'children of revolutionary martyrs to be political and military cadres. Kim Il Sung Higher Party school and Pyongyang Communist

University (just east of the Koryo Hotel) train Party workers or give reorientation to them' (*Pyongyang Review*).

Ryongak Hill
The refreshingly untouched Ryongak Hill sits about 4km north of Mangyongdae. On the edge of town, it's largely unvisited and appeals for being what it is, a hill set in greenery with a few forgotten sites around it. The Koguryo-dynasty Pobun Monastery and the Ryonggok Academy, dating from 1656, are to be found there. At 292m, Tae peak is the highest on Ryongak and gives splendid views of the city.

Tomb of King Tangun
The 5,000-year-old bones of the mythical King Tangun were identified in the early 1990s, an event so ground-shaking that 'Comrade Kim Il Sung was so please [sic] he asked dear Comrade Kim Jong Il if it was true'. At the base of Mt Taebak in Munhung-ri, Pyongyang, Tangun's tomb was reconstructed and opened in October 1994 (reflected in the number of stones used to rebuild the tomb), a nine-tiered granite pyramid without a point at the end of two colossal flights of steps. Inside, in polished wooden coffins are kept the remains of Tangun and his wife, guarded by a stone tiger, the 'biggest in the world' at 3.5m height. The steps to the tomb are flanked by statues of Tangun's sons and ministers, while another monument celebrating the reconstruction stands between the two flights. Followers of the Taejong religion, a Korea-centric religion built around the deity of Tangun, can now worship at the site, which also receives two pilgrimages on October 2 and March 15 every year, so the tomb has been awarded profound spiritual and political resonance.

Kumsusan Memorial Palace
Kim Il Sung's final resting house is the Kumsusan Memorial Palace. Set in 100 hectares of trees, this was formerly where Kim Il Sung lived, worked and entertained and its interiors are lavish, so it is not a monolith built around a mausoleum but was refurbished to make it one. The cuboid mausoleum isn't dissimilar in design to Lenin's, Mao's or Ho Chi Minh's, but isn't open to the general public just to turn up. The road leading there (and to Kim Il Sung university) begins opposite the classical façade of the April 25 People's Army Palace, where stands a towering stele like an almighty trident lanced into the ground, straddling the road. This stele's red letters wish long life to Kim Il Sung, reminding the populace that Kim Il Sung's spirit shall forever be with them, and is the master-copy of the many smaller stelae you will see dominating town squares all over the country. Anybody can go to the Kumsusan Memorial Palace, providing they give notice, on a Friday or a Sunday, but note that visitors to the palace should be smartly dressed, which for men means long trousers, a shirt and tie. Koreans like it if you ask to visit.

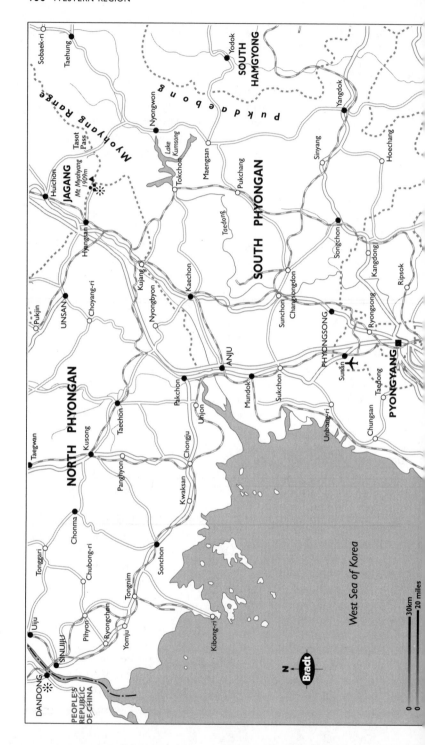

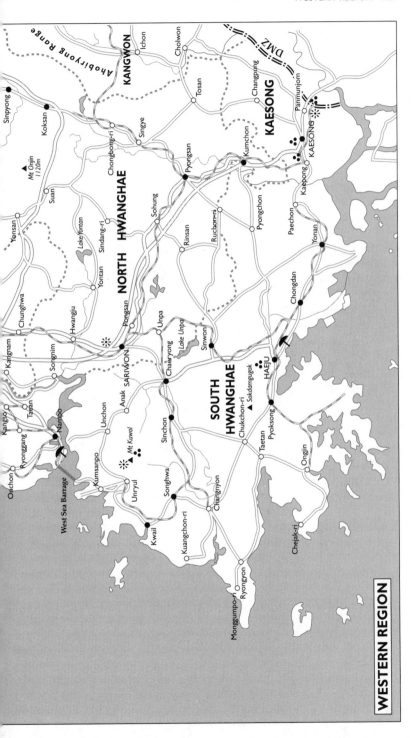

WESTERN REGION

Pyongyang

Above Mass Games being held in Pyongyang's Kim Il Sung Stadium (NB)

Left A member of the 1966 DPRK World Cup football team (NB)

Below Young athletes hope for victory as they head by train for China (RT)

Above King Kongmin's tomb, near Kaesong (RT)

Right Thongil Street, Kaesong (RT)

Below This monument to reunification towers over the road south from Pyongyang to the DMZ (RT)

South: Pyongyang to Kaesong and Panmunjom

Pyongyang to Kaesong, three hours by train and 90 minutes by road. Pyongyang to Sariwon 50km, Pyongyang to Kaesong 161km

Going to Kaesong from Pyongyang by road involves cruising down Thongil Street, a monolithic housing development completed in 1993. The road rises up and under the extraordinary '**Three Principles Monument**', a 30m granite statue of two women from both Koreas leaning together over the highway. Its symbolism is accentuated by its location on the road towards the ROK. The Army Film Studios are quite near this monument. Through the checkpoints, and 9km from Pyongyang, is the country's only turnpike, indicating Wonsan 191km and Kaesong 152km. As you cruise to Kaesong you observe the farms and the long slogan boards planted in the fields, then you can admire how well tended the verges are on the road itself. Most of this highway, like the rest, is as straight as a runway, but the turns get sharper as the landscape gets hillier going south. And yes, the roads are always this quiet, although they didn't used to be: 'In this country, in which sumptuary laws prevent the humbler classes from travelling on horseback, and where wagons and steam roads are unknown, the roads are lively with numerous foot passengers,' wrote Griffis, listing pupils, pilgrims, pompous functionaries on horseback, travelling players, picnickers, postal slaves on the pony express, pack-horsed merchants, beggars, refugees of war and weather, and 'men dead of hunger in times of famine'. But the well-trodden roads did not support ye olde motel industry: 'The country is very deficient in houses for public accommodation. Inns are to be found only along the great highways, and but rarely along the smaller or sequestered roads. This want arises, perhaps, not so much from the poverty of the people, as from the fact that their numerous proverbial hospitality does away with the necessity of numerous inns.' If a household hadn't the food to replenish a traveller, the travellers would be invited in anyway to cook their own.

SARIWON

38.3° north, 125.4° east; capital of North Hwanghae Province

Forty minutes' drive from Pyongyang is the North Hwanghae Province seat of Sariwon. The city skyline is broken up by heavy and light industry factories

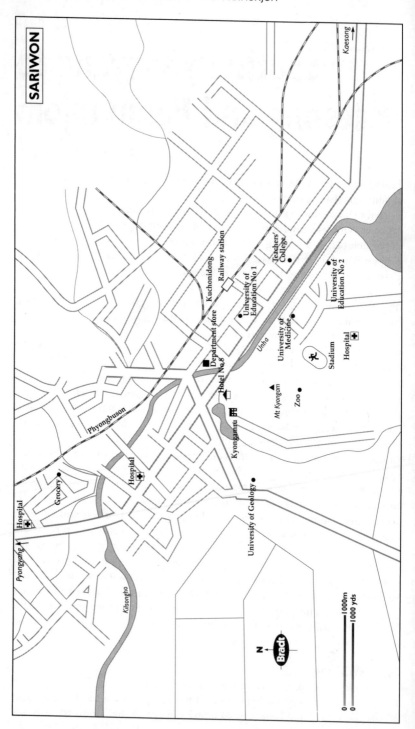

SARIWON

Kaesong →

Kuchonidong

Railway station

Teachers' College

University of Education No 1

University of Education No 2

Department store

University of Medicine

Hotel No 8

Unha

Stadium

Hospital

Mt Kyongam

Zoo

Phyongbuson

Kyongamnu

Grocery

Hospital

Hospital

University of Geology

Pyongyang →

Kilsongho

N

Bradt

1000m
1000 yds

0
0

strewn between the Kyongam and Sangmae hills, and although you may be attracted to the **Sariwon Orchard,** noted for its 'Sariwon Grape', or be seduced by the allure of the **Sariwon Potassic Fertiliser Complex,** there's little of interest in an otherwise attractive town. It's easier to breathe in the **Jongbang Mountains** 8km north of the city, which were decreed as a park (Jongbangsan Pleasure Ground) by Kim Il Sung. On the mountain slopes is the **Fort of Jongbangsan,** which actually laps up to the Jongbang tunnel of the Pyongyang-Kaesong highway. It was a good enough site for the fort to be rebuilt in the mid-1600s and within its 12km walls can be found the remains of its main armoury, garrisons, and bits of 48 long-destroyed temples. The buildings of the Buddhist temple Songbul still stand, although they've been rebuilt many times since 898.

Drive 30km due east from Sariwon via Chaeryong and you'll come to Sinchon, with the **Sinchon Massacre Museum** which, in customary micro detail, tells of an appalling atrocity committed by the US forces during the Korean War, wherein thousands of civilians were cut down by advancing US troops.

Where to stay
March 8 Hotel (29 rooms) Located at the foot of Mt. Kyongam. Hotel with 2 second-class rooms and 27 third-class rooms.

Otherwise, press on 30km further from Sariwon towards Kaesong until you reach the **Sohung Tea House,** where you can 'recover from fatigue and enjoy the nature' and have some tea. As well as the usual ginseng, embroideries and paintings, it might have a load of ostrich eggs in stock (∈5) for there is an ostrich cooperative farm somewhere nearby. You could also pick up a CD-ROM about dogs.

The road has finally quit trying to avoid the hillsides and by now just bores straight through them. The tunnel entrances have precariously-supported concrete obstacles, waiting to fall in the path of any invading tank or tourist bus. Evidence of a far older invasion is some 28km before Kaesong, just before Ryunggung Tunnel. On the left at the bottom of a hill are a series of **dinosaur footprints,** 30 great plate-marks from 180 million years ago, found during the road's construction.

Eventually, you pass through the mist of the last seeping tunnel and a long flank of apartment blocks appears on the left, your vehicle curves right round under the highway and on to Thongil Street, the other end of the one you left Pyongyang on. The street darts down and up a hill to a bronze statue of Kim Il Sung, who hails your arrival into Kaesong.

KAESONG
37.55° north, 126.3° east; city and area under central authority
This former capital of Koryo is really a pleasant and interesting place to pass a couple of days. Most of the sites are within walking distance of each other and the city has the broad boulevards of Pyongyang but none of the traffic (!), giving

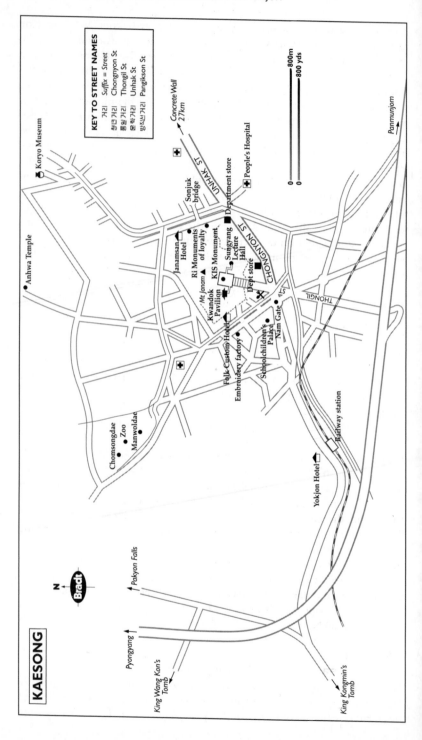

KAESONG

KEY TO STREET NAMES
거리 Suffix = Street
청년 거리 Chongnyon St
통일 거리 Thongil St
운학 거리 Unhak St
방직선거리 Pangikson St

800m
800 yds

Koryo Museum

Concrete Wall
27km

People's Hospital

UNHAK ST

Department store

Sonjuk
bridge

Janamsan
Hotel

Ri Monuments
of loyalty

CHONGNYON ST

Sungyang
Lecture
Hall

KIS Monument

Mt Janam ▲

Dept store

Kwandok
Pavilion

Anhwa Temple

THONGIL

Folk Custom Hotel

Embroidery factory

Schoolchildren's
Palace

Nam Gate

Railway station

Chomsongdae

Zoo

Manwoldae

Yokjon Hotel

Pyongyang

Pakyon Falls

N
Bradt

King Wang Kon's
Tomb

King Kongmin's
Tomb

Panmunjom

the city a relaxed air that you wouldn't expect so close to the DMZ (only 8km away!) Except for those lining the thoroughfares off Thongil Street, the buildings are low-storey and leave the surrounding hills to provide the shelter.

Kaesong means 'castle gate opening' and the city had long been a significant fortress city before King Wang Kon made it the capital of Koryo in 932, deeming it best located as a centre for the Koryo kingdom. In the next four hundred years, Kaesong grew and prospered not only as the kingdom's political centre but one of great commerce and learning. Buddhism was made the official religion and Kaesong its heart, as the aristocracy poured money into monasteries, temples and schools of learning. Although no longer the capital, the city remained a significant commercial centre and military staging post throughout the Ri dynasty, and became a centre for the cultivation and trading of the great medicinal cash-crop, ginseng (*Koryo insam*), still a highly prized crop produced locally today. Until World War II, visitors noted a bustling business town, a great centre of the grain trade, with various mercantile guilds and roaring businesses in sesame oil, paper products, tobacco pouches, umbrellas and sheetings for walls and windows, and imports from Britain and Japan. Kaesong was fortunate to be set in a 'no bomb' zone that exempted it from the attention of US carpet-bombing, but it didn't escape the effects of the Korean ground war. The first armistice talks were held here in June 1951 before being moved to Panmunjom. In 1955, Kaesong was declared to be under direct central authority, and now constitutes one city and three counties.

Today, the city's main commodity is ginseng, with good trade in rice, barley, and wheat until recently. The city's also known for its embroideries and porcelain, textiles, and heavy industry, but there's more dust and rust here than in Pyongyang. Little remains of the city walls that once circled 15km around, its scores of temples and monasteries are largely vanished, and its population, at 335,000 is a sharp fall from its height of 800,000 under the Ri. Floods in recent years have damaged the city's surrounding farmland, and look out for any food-aid sacks with the stars and stripes on them. However, an industrial complex is planned for foreign investors, particularly those from the ROK, and the city's tourist potential is to be built upon as part of the forthcoming Kaesong Industrial Zone.

Where to stay
Kaesong Folk Hotel Traditional one-storey houses built aside a stream during the Ri Dynasty, and furnished as such. Absolutely charming place, with little courtyards set in the city's old quarter, great fun. 50 second-class rooms.
Janamsan Hotel Next to Mt Janam up the road from Sonjuk Bridge. 43 second-class rooms.

Where to eat
Thongil Restaurant at the foot of Mt Janam serves local cuisine like *pansnaggi*, *insam takgom*, Kaesong *posam kimchi*, Kaesong *yakbap*. The two hotels have their own restaurants.

What to see

Overlooking Kaesong is the pine-tree covered Mt Songak, with the smaller Mt Janam 'kneeling before it like a cute child to its father'. But it's around the latter hill that Kaesong centres, and Mt Janam is all the more dominant with its crown of bronze, in the form of Kim Il Sung, gesturing to the south. At night the statue is the lucky recipient of the city's only regular power supply, with the huge searchlights illuminating the statue and setting its shadow against low-cloud. By day, the 17 hectares of leafy slopes around it include a revolutionary museum, monument and 'on-the-spot guidance' from the Great Leader. It's good for views of the city's old quarter. To the statue's left is the **Kwandok Pavilion**, built in 1780, where archery was practised in feudal times:

> The chief out-door manly sport in Corea is, by excellence, that of archery. It is encouraged by the government for the national safety in war, and nobles stimulate their retainers to excellence by rewards. At regular times contests are held, at which archers of reputation compete, the expense and prizes being paid for out of the public purse.
>
> William Eliot Griffis, *The Hermit Nation*, 1882

Cut into the eastern slope of Mt Janam is the charming **Sungyang Lecture Hall**. Confucianism was taught in this private hall, where lived the Confucian official Jong Mong Ju in the dying days of Koryo (he was assassinated on the Sonjuk Bridge). On a north–south axis, the school buildings were in the front and those annexes for sacrificial rites in the rear of the site, while to the east and west lie the dormitories.

All around Mt Janam's base are narrow-as-a-man alleys of single-storeyed, clay-brick houses, with gently sweeping roofs and an old-world appearance that both charms and appals. Though not all the roof tiles can be accounted for, it's fortunate that these densely packed houses are no longer thatched.

There's an unmissable neo-Korean edifice, the **Kaesong Schoolchildren's Palace**, for 3,000 children to engage in after-school activities.

From Koryo times, Kaesong had been a great castle city, with a royal palace stashed within an inner and outer castle. The southern gate to the inner castle, **Nam Gate**, has been reconstructed and dominates the crossroads just off from Thongil Street. Originally built in 1391, it stood as the southern gate of Kaesong's inner castle until it was destroyed during the Korean War. The gate houses the **Yonbok Temple bell**, made in 1346 for Yonbok Temple and moved to the gate in 1563 when the temple burnt down. Weighing 14 tons, it's covered with figures of tortoises, crabs, dragon, phoenix, deer, and images of the Buddha, and the two dragons on top of the bell indicate 'intrepid spirit'. The bell can be heard 4km away.

Bishop (see page 222) wrote that the road was lined with monuments to good governors, magistrates, faithful widows and pious sons. Very few such sites remain, but walking east along Chongnyon Street, possibly the same road

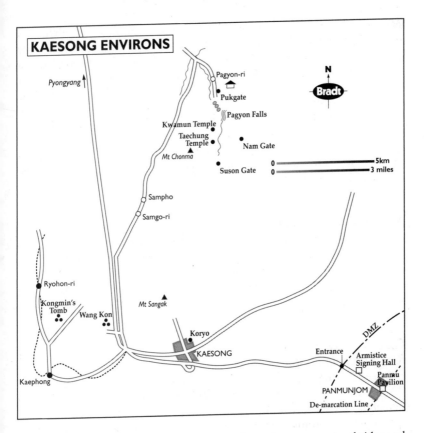

that caused Bishop to call Kaesong a 'one-road town', you come to a bridge and a road going left. A hundred metres up here on the right is **Sonjuk Bridge**, a tiny stone crossing built in 1215 that now has a small fence round it and another crossing next to it. Ri Song Gye assassinated Jong Mong Ju, a civil servant and loyalist to the Koryo dynasty, on this bridge in 1392. Where Jong's blood fell, it stained the bridge (visible today?!) or from the blood grew bamboo. To commemorate the incident, a descendant of Jong fenced off the bridge in 1780.

Jong's loyalty is also celebrated at the **Songmin Monument** just beyond the bridge, erected in 1641 along with two monuments, one to the memory of the government official Gyong Jowho who was killed with Jong. Loyalty to the Ri dynasty inspired the monuments set across the road from the bridge, with two large stelae set on the backs of tortoises. The left dates from 1740 and King Yong Jo and the right from 1872 by King Ko Jong.

Songyungwan

This large education complex of 20 buildings was founded in 992 as the Kukjagam, the highest educational institute for the civil service as Kaesong was directed towards being the intellectual heart of Koryo as well as its political capital. The children of Koryo and later Ri aristocracy attended the school to learn the Confucian ways of administration and sacrifice. Renamed Songyungwan from 1308, it was expanded but burnt down during the Japanese invasion of 1592 and was rebuilt ten years later. The main buildings are in a typically Confucian north-south axis, with a pleasure ground for archery and swinging over the west side. Since 1987, the site has been home to the **Koryo Museum**, a good little museum with a thousand pieces of pottery, iron work, prints and relics from the Koryo dynasty, with readable presentations of life in those time, and some thousand-year-old pagodas rescued from Hyonhwa, Hungguk and Pulil temples, all overlooked by 500-year-old Ginko trees and a 900-year-old Zelkova. East of the museum are two mounds of a tomb that are worth investigating.

On the southern foot of Mt Songak, 2km north of Nam Gate, sits the site of the Koryo royal palace of **Manwoldae**, dating from the 900s, with a part of the Kaesong Outer Castle and the Chomsongdae astronomical observatory, in most use between 1024 and the late 1300s. The Koryo Museum has much more on the observatory.

A fleeting excursion could be made to Anhwa Temple, 4km from Nam Gate and built in 930 on the mid-slope of Mt Songak. Here studied Wang Sin, a cousin of King Wang Kon. Obaek Hall's thousand Buddhas protected it from the ravages of war, and the seven-storey pagoda survived too.

Out of town
King Kongmin's Tomb

Fourteen kilometres southwest of central Kaesong is the charming tomb of the 31st King of Koryo from 1352. King Kongmin was a skilled painter and draughtsman, and when his wife died in 1365 he designed two tombs side by side (construction completed in 1372), the right one housing his wife and the left he entered upon his death in 1374. The statues are of military and civil officials. The 'older' military figure is on the outside, better able to defend the king from attack through his veteran experiences, and the older civil officials are nearer the tomb than the youthful assistants, as maturity guarantees better advice to the king. The tiger outside the tomb is representative of the Koryo ancestry and the sheep of his wife's Mongol descent.

Wang Kon's Tomb and the Pakyon Falls

Just over 3km due east of Nam Gate in Haeson-ri, on the road to Pakyon Falls is the **Tomb of King Wan Kon** (877–943), the founder of Koryo. He was born into a wealthy farming family and his father held great influence as a local aristocrat and landowner. Wan Gon served as a civil servant from the age of 20 and achieved high rank. His coup d'etat in June 918 overthrew the Thaebong state and founded the Koryo, inheriting Koguryo's remnants and bringing Silla and Paekche under the rule of Kaesong. His died in 943 and they built his tomb there, with lawns carpeting up to it. Statues of officials and animals, stone lamps for burning incense, an offertory table, and images of 12 guardian gods all guard the tomb.

Pakyon Falls

Moving north from the tombs, the road gets grottier and tighter as you head up through the Jongmyongsa Pass and down into a valley of *insam*. You're en route to Pakyon Falls, a delightful waterfall 24km from Kaesong, tucked into a sharp valley fort on Mt Taehung.

As you turn right through the village of Pagyon-ri, there appears on the left a monument to the falls. Then there appears Puk Gate, a large edifice that fronts the Taehungsan Fort surrounding the falls. The fort itself was established before Koryo but was substantially beefed up to defend the new capital of Kaesong, and its walls lace around the hills for 10km. Puk is flanked by a hotel and restaurant.

Passing through the gate and past some large ponds, you come to the falls, dropping 37m down from Pakyon pond. To the right is the **Pomsa Pavilion**, dating from Koryo times, that gives a good view and a sit-down. A kilometre further up the valley from the pond is the beautiful **Kwanum Temple**, built when the fort was expanded. With its seven-storey pagoda, it's a fabulously tranquil location that could inspire the most Godless to concede that, living in such settings and high architecture, the Buddhists were possibly on to something. Nearby is Kwanum Cave that was blessed with two marble Buddhas in 970 by the temple's high priest.

Another 2km upwards is the private school where Wang Kon's son studied in 921. The old temple of Taehung that was here burnt down. Later the school building was converted into the temple it is today. This is set dead in the centre of a reserve for the white-bellied black woodpecker, which could be spied from the paths around Taehung Temple that lead to the fort's remaining gates.

PANMUNJOM AND THE DMZ

Many moons ago there was a road linking Kaesong to Seoul. The road crossed the River Sachon, a tributary of the River Rimjin. People built a bridge with logs and boards and named it Panmun, but rains would wash the bridge away and prevent anyone from crossing, so an inn was built for delayed travellers called Panmunjom (board-framed shop) that lent its name to the village built here. The village itself was wiped from the map during the Korean War, but the name survived and it's now known as the venue for the Korean Armistice Talks. It's here that the 'US imperialists bent the knees down before the Korean people' when the US 'gave up' in 1953, and is the epicentre of the De-Militarised Zone (DMZ). The actual division line of Korea is the Military Demarcation Line (MDL) that snakes across Korea from the mouth of the River Rimjin in the west to the east coast Walbisn-ri, and the DMZ is a 4km-thick buffer straddling the MDL. The DMZ is anything but de-militarised, and is one of the most heavily guarded, heavily mined frontiers in the world. This isn't surprising as a combined total of 1.5 million Korean and 40,000 American soldiers would clash along this frontier, and the DMZ bristles with artillery and troops ready to let rip at the drop of grenade. As you are driven in and out of the area, try and spot as many disguised sentry points, pill-boxes, tank-traps, machine-gun and artillery posts as you can. Having said that, the atmosphere is overall surprisingly relaxed, especially compared with the Friendship Exhibition in Myohyangsan, and while here more than anywhere permission for photos is needed, the officer guiding you will yay or nay with a friendly bat of his hand.

DMZ wildlife and the Peace Park

So little actual human activity for good or ill goes on in the DMZ (for obvious risks of being shot or blown up) that wildlife, particularly endangered species, have been seen to thrive in this fenced-in strip of land. It is unsurprisingly difficult for any ologists to get in and check what hops amid the mines, but Manchurian crane, ringtail pheasant, spot-billed duck, black-tailed gull, white-naped and red-crowned cranes, and the black-faced spoonbill have been sighted, as have bears, wildcats, leopards, deer and Siberian tiger in the hillier parts, as well as freshwater turtles, terrapins and butterflies. The DMZ has become such a haven for species that are endangered elsewhere that plans are afoot to turn this buffer zone to keep the peace into a 'peace park', to protect a substantial slice of the peninsula's biodiversity. Nelson Mandela has put his name to the scheme that supporters are asking the United Nations to endorse. The park would symbolically convert the DMZ from a symbol of division into one of peace and unity. However, in an ironic twist, the haven is being threatened by those same forces of reconciliation; rail and road links across the DMZ will require the area's de-mining, and may destroy these fragile habitats. For updates about this plan, visit www.dmzforum.org or email its president, Seung-ho Lee, at shl6@nyu.edu.

You may lunch in a resthouse on the way in to the DMZ. Gritty rice.

What to see

The entrance to the DMZ is 8km south of Kaesong, and the first building at the entrance is the **General Lecture Room**. Its small shop sells a masterpiece book of propaganda about the Americans and their lackey puppets. It's here also that, over an impressive map of the area, you meet your Korean People's Army officer, who leads you around the DMZ sites.

The officer (and any others needing a lift) board your vehicle at the entrance gate, through which is a little lane kitted out with an amazing array of anti-tank traps, from block-obstacles, drop-down barriers, ditches and moats, leading towards the **Armistice Talks Hall,** a pretty little hut with a small stele outside. This is 1km into the DMZ and is where the Korean War armistice talks were held. It took a year of fighting from 1950 for both sides' armies to grind to a halt pretty much back where they'd started, and talks began in June 1951 in Kaesong itself. Two more years passed in which hundreds of thousands of lives were squandered while talks continued in this hut, in what is now an eerily quiet part of the world.

Next to the Armistice Talks Hall is a large, light-coloured building with a dove on the roof, the hall where the armistice was **signed** on July 27 1953, and the chairs, tables and flags are all preserved there. Here is a museum with the usual impressive display of enlarged photos, documented 'proof' of US aggression and maps of the war, but it's mostly in Chinese.

THE ARMISTICE

On June 23 1951, nearly a year after the Korean War had started, Soviet delegate Yakov Malik suggested that both sides should try peace negotiations. The DPRK's forces had nearly succeeded in uniting the country, as had the United Nations Command (UNC) coming back the other way. A week later, UNC General Ridgeway got word that the communists might be favourable to armistice talks, which were arranged, unarranged and rearranged for Kaesong. The decision to move the talks from Kaesong to Panmunjom in September 1951 was the easiest decision reached by the communists (consisting of Korean People's Army and the Chinese People's Volunteers) and the UNC, and it totally dominated discussions for two weeks. The agenda finally decided upon was to agree what a ceasefire meant, how it was to be implemented, where (which involved drawing a demarcation line while fighting continued) and what to do with prisoners of war. Two years of long, tedious and tortuous negotiations followed, while talking peace took second place to another day's fighting that could tip the balance in a side's favour. Both delegations, the communists led by Korean General Nam II, and the UNC by Lieutenant-General William K Harrison, engaged in time-wasting tactics and talks descended into vitriolic slanging matches, with the most colourful language coming from the communists. As soon as a point of conduct or principle of a ceasefire was agreed, one side accused the other of violating it and raised hell if they didn't storm out, resuming negotiations by letter days or weeks later.

The repatriation of prisoners of war (POWs) took the most debate. The UNC declared they held up to 132,500 POWs, and the communists held around 11,400 UNC and 7,150 ROK troops (a disputed figure), with fierce debate over how a POW would be defined. The lists lengthened as fighting went on and shortened as dribs and drabs of POWs were repatriated through Panmunjom. The communists demanded their POWs be repatriated whether they wanted to or not, which the UNC insisted was a matter of free choice. Thousands of POWs on both sides were slain after capture and others held in camps so foul that prisoners grew sick and died while their captors looked on. Nam II and Harrison signed an armistice on July 27 1953. Accusations of violations of the armistice have flown from all sides every other week since.

The Panmun Pavilions and the Joint Security Area.

About 1km southward from the Armistice Halls, you cross the 72-hour Bridge over the Sachon River into the **Joint Security Area** (JSA). The JSA radiates 400m around a row of blue and white huts in which armistice talks continue to this day. From the DPRK side, you approach the huts from behind the elevated Panmungak Hall, an austere, Soviet-style building flanked by the carved signature of Kim Il Sung. Opposite Panmungak on the ROK side was once only a small, raised pavilion but now there is also a remarkable building fusing hi-tech modern materials and traditional Korean building style. Between these two architectural emblems of Korea is a tidy row of huts straddling a thin concrete path indicating the military demarcation line between north and south, and the huts are seemingly all that staple the two states together. The hut you will enter is the **Military Armistice Commission Conference Hall,** still used by the Military Armistice Commission and the Neutral Nations Supervisory Commission. In the middle of the hall is a table, across which are strung microphone leads, indicating the demarcation line in the hall, and it's at this table that representatives from the UNC, Korean People's Army and Chinese Volunteer Army sit and thrash out how each side is upholding the armistice, not always in the most cordial fashion. It's also been used for negotiations with the Red Cross and Olympic committee. However, tourists can orbit the table and thereby technically cross into the ROK, but do not touch the microphone leads and do not try to cross the concrete demarcation line outside (one Soviet defector made it in 1983). In the hall there's also a list of participatory countries in the Korean War against the DPRK side that the guides refer to apologetically as you may well come from one of them.

The JSA itself used to be pocked with equidistant United Nations

PANMUNJOM AXE INCIDENT

On the lane to the Bridge of No Return, southwest of the huts, occurred a bizarre incident on August 18 1976 that became known to the US side as the 'Panmunjom Axe Murders'. A group of ROK and US soldiers arrived near the bridge to prune a large poplar tree obscuring the view of two proximate UNC checkpoints. Captain Arthur Bonifas with First Lieutenant Mark Barrett and a Korean officer oversaw the task as a group of Korean People's Army (KPA) soldiers arrived. The KPA officer demanded the pruning be stopped; when it didn't, the KPA soldiers attacked the group with axes, knives and clubs, killing Bonifas and Barrett and injuring ten more. The KPA claimed that the tree pruning was a cover for provocative attacks on KPA checkpoints. Over the next few days, tensions ran high as the KPA shot at patrolling US aircraft while both sides readied for further bloodshed. The US response was Operation Paul Bunyon early on the 21st. US and ROK infantry and artillery trained their guns on KPA positions as US air-force bombers readied from across Asia and the US scowled the skies. A US 'task force' completed the pruning. The Americans now call the JSA 'Camp Bonifas', and the JSA was summarily divided, with The Bridge of No Return going into the southern half. The KPA built themselves a new bridge in three days, calling it '72-hour bridge'.

Command and Korean People's Army checkpoints, for, until 1976, both sides had free run of the JSA and jointly maintained its security. This changed in September that year following the bizarre Panmunjom Axe Incident (see box), and the JSA was divided into North and South.

At various points along the road to the JSA, you can see the two flags of Korea flying atop vast masts opposite each other. The DPRK flag mast is in the **Panmunjom-ri coop farm**, a series of brightly painted apartment blocks that comprises the northern half of a divided village, the southern side of which is Taesong-dong where the ROK flag flies. The ROK call the northern coop 'propaganda village', claiming it has no purpose but to broadcast high volume abuse at Taesong-dong. ROK literature contrasts the villages with ROK photographs of Taesong-dong showing a beaming, happy population that are regularly helped in the fields by smiling soldiers, before darkness falls and the 11pm curfew begins.

Elsewhere along the DMZ you can see an 8m-high concrete wall, the **Wall of Division**, in the southern half, built from 1976 to 1979 by US forces along nearly all the DMZ. Going due east for 27km from Nam Gate you will eventually get to a good viewing point, to see this coldly impressive Korean wall.

Visiting from the ROK

On the DPRK side you'll be spied upon by UN troops with binoculars and may be dazzled by the flash-photography of a tour group from the other side, mainly Americans, ROK citizens and Japanese who might otherwise never have a chance of stepping into the DPRK. Panmunjom is only a 90-minute drive from Seoul, and day-long bus tours running from Seoul can include commentaries on the area's history and visits to the tunnels that the DPRK dug under the demarcation line into the south to sneak fully armoured attacks on Seoul. A series of monuments to the 15 countries' forces dot the route into the DMZ, and should you stray past a sky-blue obelisk saying DMZ you know where you are. Tours do not run every week day and not on holidays, so check with operators.

Tour operators

Korea Travel Bureau 1465-11 Seocho-Dong, Seocho-Gu, Seoul, Korea 137-073; tel: +82 2 585 7072 4; fax: 82 2 585 1187; email: tour@ktbinc.co.kr; web: www.ktbonline.com. One-day tours are around US$70. You must bring your passport on the day, your hair must not be unkempt and your safety in the DMZ cannot be guaranteed:

Panmunjom Travel Center Lotte Hotel 2nd floor (Main Bldg), Chung-Gu, Sogong-dong, Seoul City; tel: +82 (0) 2 771 5593 5; fax: +82 (0)2 771 5596; web: www.panmunjomtour.com

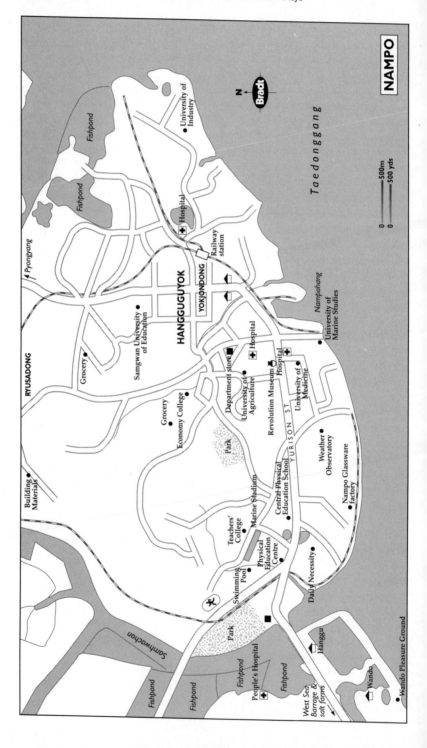

NAMPO

West and Southwest: Nampo, Mt Kuwol and Haeju

From Mangyongdae, follow the 'Youth Hero Motorway' along the Taedong 55km westwards to reach Nampo city. Sticking to the river, you pass the **Chollima Steel Complex** and the **Taean Heavy Machine Complex**, both sites having great significance in the progress of the DPRK's post-war industrialisation strategies.

Another road goes from Pyongyang past the tombs of **Kangso** and **Tokhung-ri** (outside Taepyong) and then **Kangso** town where the 18-hole **Pyongyang golf course** awaits to give the golfing experience that no golfer could ever miss. Legend has it that the Dear Leader played a round here and scored 18 holes-in-one (quite a record and quite a drinks' bill), but the legend is rumoured to be of Western origin. Hmmm.

NAMPO
38.4° north, 125.2° east, 55km west of Pyongyang, South Pyongan Province, Taedong River estuary, West Korea bay
The workers among Nampo's population of nearly three-quarters of a million unload cargo bound for Pyongyang, build ships, smelt copper, manufacture electrodes and glass products or eke a living on the seas, which is fortunate for them as there's little else to do.

Where to stay
Hanggu Hotel Waudo recreation ground, 109 C-class rooms.

What to see
Nampo's few features include the 1970s' buildings in **Nampo Sports Village** and the **Waudo Pleasure Grounds** of Wau Islet and Wau Peak. Going west, salt farms (not mines) extend to the horizon until 6km west of Nampo, is the **Nampo West Sea Barrage**. All vessels going to Pyongyang come through this barrage that controls the tides and has been central to the large schemes of land reclamation and irrigation for agriculture in this region. It is a terrific feat of engineering, opened in 1986 after five years' construction to cross the 8km-wide Taedong River estuary. The monument at the barrage's northern entrance celebrates the sacrifice of the KPA and others who built it, and the Pi Islet

Pavilion shows a stirring video of the barrage's construction. With not much else on, the Nampo beach awaits and is a major resort for foreign residents.

Unryul

The southern end of the barrage connects with Unryul County, on the northwest coast of South Hwanghae Province.

Unryul's dominant industry is iron ore extraction and processing, for which the Unryul conveyor-belt, almost as long as the sea barrage, was built and is worth a look for the sheer scale of this great black tongue of rock. In Unryul town, diversion may be made to the **Unryul Revolution Museum**, dedicated to Kim Il Sung's father, Mr Kim Hyong Jik. From there speed onwards to the town of Kwail in the so-named county, where fruit farms cover most of the cultivated land, especially around **Songgok-ri.** The farms and mines crop up amid the shallow, afforested slopes and trickling streams sliding away from the **Kuwol Mountains** that command the district.

MT KUWOL

38.3° north, 125.2° east, South Hwanghae Province
Mt Kuwol is a gentle, handsome range of peaks, hills, waterfalls and spas, with a healthy sprinkling of temples and hermitages, roped within a nature reserve covering 110km². The highest peak is the 954m Sahwang peak, neighboured by **Samsong Pleasure Ground**. The next peaks are O at 859m, Insa at 688m and Inhwang and Juga peaks. The area seems to have fallen off recent tourist itineraries, despite being one of the five celebrated mountains of Korea along with Paektu, Kumgang, Myohyang and Jiri, and having a more recent association with Kim Hyong Jik's revolutionary activities. The faded beauty of the 9th-century **Woljong Temple** hides in the southern Jol Valley, east of Asa peak, despite being rebuilt during the 15th century. The restored **Samsong Temple** was originally dedicated to Korea's spiritual founder, Tangun, and during Koryo times Tangun's grandfather and father were added to the rolls of reverence. While campaigning against Japanese colonialism, Patriot Taejonggyo Ra Chol committed suicide here. Japanese forces later razed the site.

There may be time after a day ambling around these hills to visit the **Mausoleum of King Kogukwon** in Anak County. Built in the Oguk-ri, Anak County in the mid-4th century of early Koguryo, its seven sections are part of an unusually large and complicated design, and its murals of the pomp and ceremony of court-life, along with the less salubrious goings on, are fine historical treasures.

The mountain of **Sokdamgugok** (nine valleys of pools and rocks) sits on the River Sokdam, 12km north of Haeju. In its Unbyong (the finest among nine valleys) lurks the 15th-century Sohyon Academy, where the famous scholar Li Ryul Gok taught, and the names of Sokdamgugok's features denote an aged reverence and penchant for meditation and all things quiet, from the Munsan (the best place for reading), Kwan rock (horsehair hat), Chwibyong (a flower-patterned blind), Chohyop (fishing place) to the Kumtan (stream murmuring like Komungo).

HAEJU

38.05° north, 125.45° east, 140km south of Pyongyang, capital of South Hwanghae Province, located on Haeju Bay, Korea's West Sea. Population 236,000.

This is the only west-coast port city in the DPRK that doesn't freeze in winter, and has regular trading links with Nampo by land and sea. The province is of major agricultural significance to the country, and the city's industries are heavily involved in processing the farms' produce, most notably for the fruit and wood of the Haeju pear. But the region's farm output has been acutely reduced in the cruel vice of the energy crises and the appalling droughts that began in the mid-1990s, with knock-on effects for the locals and the country. Haeju has become the second west-coast city for receiving food, fuel and fertiliser aid to the country, after Nampo. Haeju joins Nampo, Kaesong and Pyongyang as cities increasingly bereft of stable rainfall. So a visit to Ok Chong Cooperative Farm, 25km from Haeju, may not be on.

Hopes for the area's industrial rejuvenation lie with the South Korean conglomerate Hyundai's proposed investment in the city's port facilities and the building of rail links to Haeju, along with a large-scale, ten-year redevelopment of the city and its industries, focusing mainly on textile, shoe and toy manufacture. Haeju is also a noted manufacturer of semi-conductors.

Haeju's been a regional seat since 983, when it was made one of 12 civilian-run regional capitals under the Koryo King Seongjong.

Being only 3km from the 38th parallel, Haeju has the bizarre distinction of being the first city taken by the ROK forces in July 1950 in a short-lived counter-attack. Refugee columns passed through Haeju in both directions throughout the war, and it's claimed that thousands were killed in strafing and bombing by UN forces. For sure the region around was bitterly fought over by both sides.

In town, there's little remaining of the Puyong Temple, destroyed in the Korean War, and the Cheonwang (Heavenly King) Monument from Koryo times, and an arbour called 'the Sami Arbour' in the Ri Dynasty.

At the foot of Mt Suyang is the **Five-Storeyed Pagoda**, built from granite during the early Koryo, and close to it is the gaping arch of the **stone ice house**, once faced with loam and peat, first built around 1000 and rebuilt in 1735, and the **Koryo Sami Pavilion**. Another temple, long disappeared, is oft mentioned in local literature and may have been the Haeju Temple, one where a stone in the forehead of the Great Buddha would turn red every time Japan threatened to invade.

Mt Suyang is an impressive mound (946m) lying some 7km northwest of Haeju city, and is dotted with statues and slogans commemorating the 'Great Leader'. Changdae Peak is a southern point right on the city's edge, where sits the Koryo **Fort on Mt Suyang**. Within its 8km of walls (in parts up to 7m high) 14 command posts and gates of the barracks are identifiable. In 1894, the Tonghak army attacked the Haeju Fort but was repulsed. From the hill's southeast side flow the waters of Suyangsan Falls, the 128m fall split halfway by a large pool.

Two small rocky islets of **Hyongje** (Brother islets) lie 20 minutes' boat-ride southwest of the Haeju mainland in the bay noted for its shrimps. For a few hours each day the tides recede to reveal long stretches of beach around them,

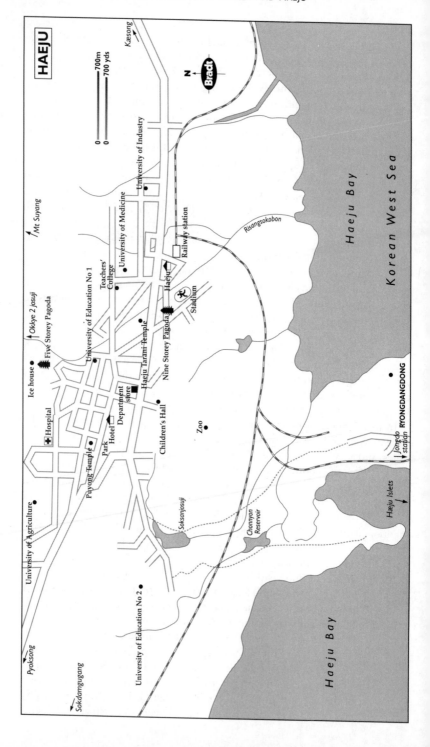

so a few solitary hours of sunbathing or crustacean catching can be done before the tide returns.

Where to stay
Haeju Hotel 42 third-class rooms, on the edge of Haeju Square.

It's 54km north from Haeju to the resthouse of Chaeryong town, and another 20 to Sariwon, from where you can go back south to Kaesong or loop up back to Pyongyang. A road running directly eastwards to Kaesong exists, via the spa-towns of Yonan and Paechon, but the accessibility of this route is tenuous.

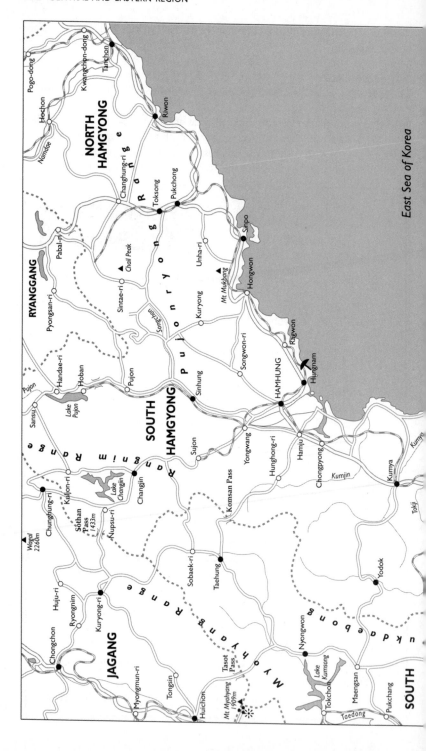

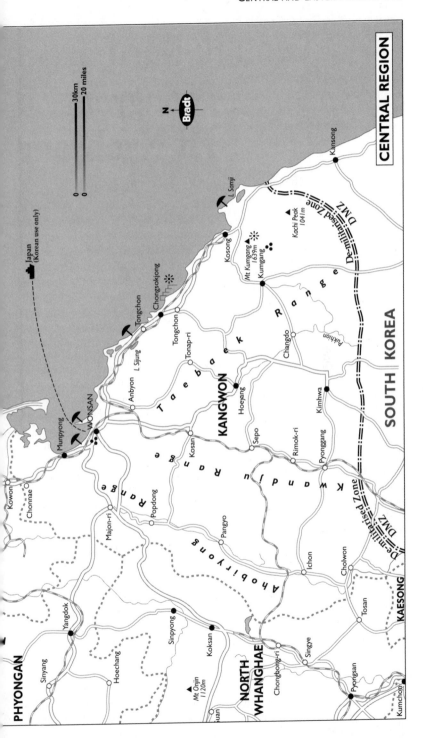

CENTRAL REGION

Central: North from Pyongyang to Mt Myohyang

40.05° north, 126.2° east, 150km north of Pyongyan. Chagang, North and South Pyongan provinces meet around it. Weather: January –11.6°C, August 23.7°C, average 8.3°C. 1,300mm rain, mainly in July and August.

Kim Il Sung put it quite succinctly: 'You can see scenic beauty everywhere in our country, but Mt Myohyangsan is particularly well known from ancient times for its wonderful and exquisite geographical features and idyllic scenery.'

Mt Myohyang is a fabulous pocket of peaks and forested valleys in the centre of the country. Its temperate climate makes it a worthwhile visit in all seasons, although in July the windless slopes make it a humidity trap. Mt Myohyang (meaning 'mountain of a single fragrance') is one of five of Korea's holy mountains, with a famed 1,000-year-old temple at its heart that drew pilgrims for centuries. The DPRK state has reconfirmed the holiness of the area by siting the extraordinary International Friendship Exhibitions here.

It takes four hours by the very early morning train from Pyongyang, with the dawn lighting the route along the way. By road, it's a 160km drive from Pyongyang via Anju, or 150km via Pyongsong and Sunchon. Away from Anju is **Paekchang Pavilion** and the nearby **Namhung Youth Chemical complex** on the River Chungchon, which the road follows for a long way. Either way, both roads converge at Kaechon and go through Kujang. Where the River Myohyang meets the River Chongchon, there is a sharp turn-off (to avoid a sharp finish to the road) towards Hyangsan town that is the gate to Sangwon Valley though it has little else to say for itself. Eight kilometres past Hyangsan barrage is the pyramidal Hyangsan Hotel and the valley-proper begins.

Myohyang mountain is like a wet hand resting on a table, with four valleys running up between the fingers and thumb to the knuckles, or peaks. The River Myohyang runs along the fingertips towards the River Chongchun, and from the road tracing the river begin all the valley walks, some taking a morning, some all day.

WILDLIFE

Wild goat, musk deer, hare, badger, racoon, wild boar, and flying squirrels occupy these parts, and leopards and bears occasionally forage in the deciduous forests from the valleys beyond. The thick tree canopy up to 1,000m is structured by 200 species of trees, including Korean maple, many Asiatic oaks, pakdal, Aceraceae, Korean spindle tree, ash, agaric, Asian hazelnut, Chinese sumac, Japanese red pine and Asian white birch. Bark-climbing fern and a multitude of moss, lichen and bryophytes thrive in the humid micro-climate, as do 460 species of herb, with medicinal poppy and aconitum. Azalea, apricot and wild cherry blossom bombard the valley with colour in spring, and magnolia, clove tree and guinguecostatus take over in summer. Blue bird, grosbeak, Korean crested-lark, oriole, Korean scops owl, goldfinch, grey wagtail, woodpecker and cuckoo take in the scene from the skies and char, silver fish, rainbow trout, eel and Moroccan oxycephalus view from the streams.

WHERE TO STAY
Hyangsan Hotel 5km from Hyangsan Town on the Myohyang River, 15-storey pyramid, all manner of amusements, brilliant foyer with waterfall, and the hotel's capped by a revolving restaurant that doesn't quite succeed with the night views. 228 A-class rooms, serviceable décor.
Chongbyong Hotel 22 C-class rooms, 15 minutes from the station by car. Small and cosy looking.
Chongchon Hotel Neo-Korean grandeur. 33 rooms from first to third class. Five minutes by car from the railway station.

WHAT TO SEE
Just across the River Myohyang, 1km from the Hyangsan, are two huge traditional Korean-style buildings burrowing into the mountainsides, housing the **International Friendship Exhibition** dedicated to the world's gifts for the Great Leaders. On the left of a classical edifice is Kim Il Sung's building, and the right one is for Kim Jong Il. From the moment you see the guards with their silver-plated machine guns, be on your best behaviour, and cast your gaze upon the concrete beams and rafters decorated with Kimilsungia and azaleas. You may (with gloved hands) be allowed to open the four-ton, bronze-coloured doors of the Kim Il Sung exhibition, doors that open so easily it 'makes you feel mysterious'.

Inside, it's hats off, cameras into a kiosk and plastic socks covering your shoes as you pad around the exhibition's 100 rooms. Be on your best behaviour. It contains 71,000 gifts of homage to the Great Leader, starting with a large room with his statue and a map showing the country and 'rank' of the gifts. Look out for Billy Graham's offerings. Then, off corridors that disappear into the distance, and between groups of Korean tourists who swiftly disappear from view, you tour long, windowless rooms of gifts, categorised by continent and arranged chronologically. Time-lights buzz on and off from room to room, as you marvel at Mao and Stalin's railway carriages (Mao pays homage to Kim Il Sung!), a stuffed crocodile drinks' tray holder, fossil-topped tables, Kalashnikov-shaped vodka bottles, gold tanks. It's a pantheon of the great and the dead from lost worlds of politics and style. This enormous collection is like a vast collage of gifts charting the chronology and reach of DPRK foreign relations, as gifts from some countries begin and finish. It's observable how by the early 1990s the gifts become more discreet in the Kim Il Sung Hall, but by the late 1990s improved relations with the ROK saw Kim Jong Il blessed with some excellent consumer durables among 40,000 other gifts.

Crossing the river, it's left some 4km to the Hyangsan, or a few hundred metres right into the Sangwon Valley to find the historically holy **Pohyon Temple**. The Pohyon Temple was founded in 1042 by the monk Kwanghwak, and was named after the saint that guards the morals of Buddha. Half of its original 24 buildings were levelled during the Korean War. Prior to then, the temple housed 60 monks, a fifth of whom were students. Substantially fewer monks await as you enter into Pohyong through the 14th-century Jogye Gate. Beyond this sits a monument to Kwagnhwak and another monk Thamil, founder of the Ansim Temple, and embedded among 1200 characters relating their lives are bits of bomb shrapnel.

You then have your sins cleansed as you pass through the Haethal Gate that marks the crossing from the mortal into the Buddhist world. The Boddhisattvas of Pohyon (the moral guardian) and Munsu (the guardian of wisdom) inhabit this gate. Four guardians of the Buddha check you for heathen status as you cross through the final, largest gate, Chonwang, dating from 1042. Beyond is the courtyard of Manse Pavilion with its nine-storey pagoda, 6m of granite and with its lotus-covered pedestal indicating its Koryo heritage. In Manse were kept the one-ton bell and drums struck for prayer every morning. Behind Manse is the Koryo-dated octagonal 13-storey pagoda, nearly 9m tall, and there sits Taeung Hall, Pohyon's main temple room. This was the grandest building from 1042 to be destroyed during the War. It was rebuilt with its stunning paintings and carved detailing.

Decades ago, at around 03.00, the valley would shake with the reverberations of the temple gong being struck in the darkness. This was the first call to prayer of the day, and would be overlapped by the throaty chimes of the bell that hung in Manse Pavilion. The monks striking these instruments sang Buddhist hymns in low, monotonous incantations. The one beating the gong would move to striking the large bell, then the drum and then a large wooden fish before leaving the temple to join a score of monks in another hall who had congregated in the passing half-hour. Lights burned before the altar, and monks, some dressed in black and others in white, sat cross-legged in a semi-circle, intoning hymns in high-pitched voices. They then stood and raised their hands in prayer to the Buddha, bowing and kneeling so their foreheads touched the floor, repeating this as they filed to another altar before resuming their seating and their prayer. The whole sequence would be repeated several times a day.

Next appears **Manse Hall**, a residential building originally built under the Ri and rebuilt in 1875, either for the messengers or the head of Pohyon Temple. The **Kwanum Hall** is an original Pohyon edifice and in this heated setting was most Buddhist doctrine taught. The 1794 **Suchung Temple** commemorates the Army of Righteous Volunteers who fought in the Imjin war against Hideyoshi, with the great priests Samyongdang, Choyong, and Sosan, the leader of tens of thousands of monk soldiers that liberated Pyongyang. Every spring and autumn, memorial services are held here to their memory.

On the far side of the temple complex is the newly built, traditionally styled archive for the 80,000 blocks of the Tripitaka, a massive containment of Buddhist scripture and literature from the Koryo and Ri dynasties and considered a world treasure.

The first books of Buddhist scriptures, 6,000 volumes, were made in the tenth century, followed by another 4,770 volumes. All the prints and printing blocks were destroyed in 1231 during the Liao occupation. Exiling itself to Kanghwa Island from 1236 to 1251, the Koryo Court spent its time productively, remaking the entire text in 80,000 blocks of magnolia, pakdal and birchwood. Each blocks measures 50 x 23 x 4cm with 22 lines of 14 letters per line, with a lacquer protection. Scholars come from far and wide to review the blocks and the scriptures. Nearby is the Bell House and Korea's largest bell at seven tonnes.

WALKING

There are three main hikes that can be done in one day or less up the Sangwon Valley, Manpok Valley and up to Piro peak. The Sangwon Valley route totals 14km and starts a little way west of the Puhyon, at the monstrous mushroom shapes of stupas in the monks' graveyard.

Sangwon Valley

Near the westernmost stupa is the large rock of Sangwon Gateway, which you pass under towards the collided rocks of Kumgang Gate. Past here is the Kumgang Pavilion overlooking Kumgang Falls, and 1km on are the misty Taeha Falls. It's only half as far again to the spectacular Ryongyong Falls, cascading 84m from the Ryong (dragon) pool, preceding the Sanju Falls and Pavilion. Inho rock sits up to the left of Ryongyong Falls, and the pavilion up there has great views. Carry on up to the stepped Chonsin Falls (86m), that overlook the charming, Koryo-era Sangwon Hermitage (rebuilt in 1580). The Su Pavilion here has the legendary milk of Buddha that cures all ills. Walking 2km onwards, rising 500m, you come to Nungin Hermitage, the highest in Myohyang at 1,000m, rebuilt in 1780. Then it's only another 1km to Popwang Peak at 1,389m. From Popwang Peak it's possible to trace the knuckled ridge about 10km to Piro Peak, a three-hour jaunt but watch the winds.

Coming straight down from Popwang, from the back of Sangwon Hermitage is the Chuksong Temple, built in 1875. A 2km diversion tumbles down to the Puryong Cloister and its massive sweeping eaves dating from 1700. Kumgang Pavilion is just another 1,000m away.

Manpok Valley

Roughly 4km from the Hyangsan Hotel along the River Myohyang is Manpok Valley, with a 6km roundtrip drenched in waterfalls. First, 500m along the way

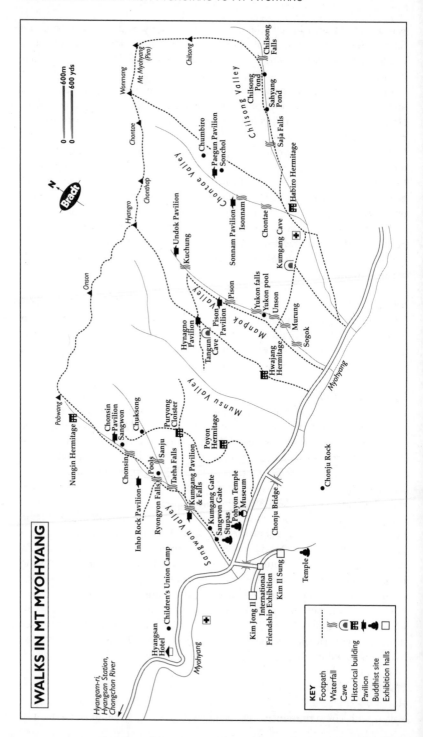

WALKS IN MT MYOHYANG

KEY

Footpath
Waterfall
Cave
Historical building
Pavilion
Buddhist site
Exhibition halls

is the Sogok (prelude) Falls that prelude the valley's 'symphony of falls'. It's then 250m to Murung Falls, where eight brothers used to rest here after collecting firewood. On to Unson Falls, then the Pal pools where fairies used to frolic. Onwards to a bridge spanning the 66m Yukon Falls that break from a sheer slope amid the trees into eight pools. A steel handrail goes up to the highly protrusive Changes Rock, and it's 300m to the twin Pison Falls that drop some 46m. Then past Pison Rock and Pison Pavilion, it's 1km to Nine-Tier Falls and Undok Pavilion. Seven hundred metres down west of here is Hynagno Pavilion and the nearby Tangun Grotto, where legend says was born the founder of Korea, Tangun. Down from there appears the 30m-wide Mujigae (rainbow) rock, a rainbow that the fairies rode down to earth. It's 2km downhill to the Koryo Temple of Hwajang Hermitage, and then you're back on the road.

A third hike goes up to Myohyang's highest peak, the 1909m Piro Peak. Starting 5.5km from the Hyangsan, it's 9km up the Chontae and Chilsong valleys and along to Piro, with stunning views from the knuckled ridge leading to it.

First, past Pirobong lodging for travellers, it's 2km up to Habiro Hermitage, originally 16th century (rebuilt in 1882), where the Chontae Valley and Chilsong Valley streams meet. From here are two routes, one going directly to Piro Peak up Chilsong Valley, the other up Chontae Valley to Wonmang peak and along. Up Chontae, it's 400m to Chontae Falls and 200m more to Isonnam Falls, then the three-pillared Sonnam Pavilion. Paegun Pavilion sits at 1,200m, 2km from Habiro, and nearby is the heavenly (drinkable) spa of the 'sachol' spring. Behind Chunbiro Hermitage is Paegun Rock, affording a bird's eye view. Alpine flora found here include Thuja, Sabina *Sargentii Nakai* and cloves. Wonmang rock is 2km up, at 1,825m, third to Piro and Chilsong peaks. Up Chilsong Valley, it's 2km to Saja Falls and another 2km to Chilsong Falls, and then 6km to Piro Peak, from which point the whole world is yours and on the finest days can be seen the West Sea of Korea.

Ryongmun and Paengryong Caves

Ryongmun Cave is an amazing grotto of cavernous halls with their vaults soaring 40m, populated by stalactites and stalagmites and separated by long pools. Discovered in the 8th century, it's been used as a hiding place for refugees evading the numerous wars that have swept the peninsula (hence the many marked fireplaces), and to stash Buddhist images and other treasures from greedy local chieftains. A lone Buddhist monk spent 18 months down here among the bear skeletons. In the rainy season, the waters rise to make pools big enough for boats to traverse over long distances. It's 2km all the way through, and is situated 30km east of Hyangsan town, 1.5km from Unhung-ri. Seventeen kilometres further east, 5km beyond Taephung-ri, is Paengryong Cave, smaller but no less full of giddyingly weird limestone protrusions and damp chambers populated by damp dwelling spirits.

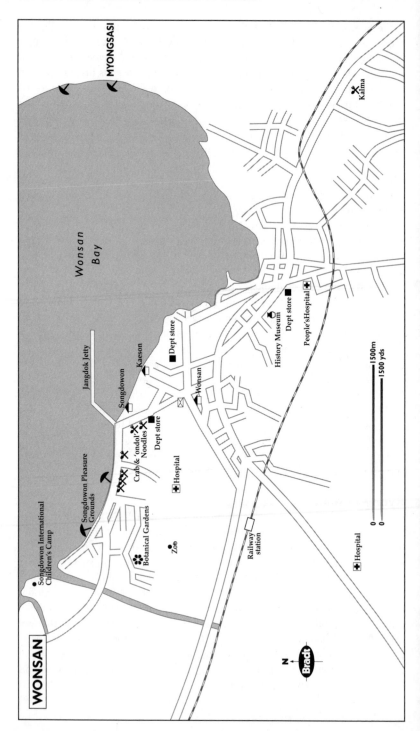

WONSAN

MYONGSASI

Kalma

Wonsan Bay

History Museum

Dept store

People's Hospital

Jangdok Jetty

Kaeson

Dept store

Songdowon

Wonsan

Songdowon Pleasure Grounds

Crab & 'ondol' Noodles

Dept store

Hospital

Songdowon International Children's Camp

Botanical Gardens

Zoo

Railway station

Hospital

N

Bradt

1500m

1500 yds

0

0

East Coast Central: Pyongyang to Wonsan

39.1° north, 127.28° east, 200km east of Pyongyang, capital of Kangwon Province, Gulf of East Korea.

The two-hour drive to Wonsan via Koksan takes in few sites. **King Tongmyong**, founder of the Koryo Kingdom, has his reconstructed tomb 25km from Pyongyang, and 15km further on you pass the **Hugu-ri**, with early Palaeolithic remains and a nice cave.

The road winds and coils up tighter and tighter round conical hillsides, until it breaks out on to a large, lush plateau hemmed in by slopes.

About 110km from Pyongyang, **Sinphyong Resthouse** appears on the shore of a small reservoir in steep-sided hills that in autumn become canopied by blazing red maple trees. Sinphyong's current expansion and healthy stock of good liquor and champagne (including a tank of real snake-wine) suggests it is frequented by well-moneyed people and does good business.

From then on it's dripping tunnels and grand bursts of paddies until finally the Sea of Japan comes into sight and you sweep into **Wonsan**.

WONSAN

With a population of 331,000, Wonsan is at the centre of this well-populated strip of coast and is the connecting hub from Pyongyang northwards to Hamhung city; it also acts as the gateway to the Kumgang Mountains in the south. The surrounding land is the most fertile in the province, and under the soil, gold is mined.

As the Kangwon provincial capital, Wonsan is a major port for trading goods with Russia and Japan, and ferryboats to Japan loiter along the quays. Served by ten universities and colleges, the city's industries include fishing, rice processing, oil refining, and the manufacture of ships, locomotives, textiles, chemicals and brewing (particularly rice wine). Since the 19th century, the city's been well known for its leather and fur goods. Wonsan's connections to the forested, mountainous north meant it was the first point for many hunters, whose appetites for game were provoked by the large bear and tiger skins treated and traded through the city. Now visitors come for Wonsan's access to Kumgang and the beaches all along this coast.

History

The city has existed here since the early Koguryo period and was named Wonsan under the Koryo, and was for centuries a trading settlement with incoming junks anchoring in its natural harbour.

By the 1880s, Wonsan was one of three ports being run by the Japanese (who called it Gensan) and had around 15,000 inhabitants, with two small settlements, one for the 700 Japanese inhabiting the city (with their own police force), and the other for other foreigners, mainly French, Russian and British. There was also a small Chinese population, filling minor official and entrepreneurial roles and selling imported goods, and staffing their own small police force as a counter to the Japanese. As the Chinese and Japanese both ran the country, Captain Cavendish couldn't tell 'which race the inhabitants hate most'.

It was under Japanese colonialism that Wonsan underwent unprecedented urban growth, as its role in exporting commodities to Japan grew and the city's major industries were founded for producing and shipping cheap manufactures to Japan, and a railroad hub for Japanese goods and men into Korea. These same port and shipping facilities made Wonsan ideal as a Japanese Navy operations base during World War II. Five years after that conflict's end, US marines landed here to a reception of South Korean soldiers as the UN forces pushed back the Korean People's Army in late 1950, but the city was retaken by the north in the coming winter. Ground fighting and bombing had levelled the city by the middle of 1953, and all that you see has been built since then. Wonsan was where the USS *Pueblo* was taken in 1968 and where it was moored for decades as a museum, before being moved to Pyongyang.

Where to stay

Songdowon Hotel On the seashore opposite Haean Square, 164 second-class rooms.
Tongmyong Hotel Second class. Prism-shaped, perfectly serviceable with billiards and a bookshop. Located where the Songdowon beach and base of the artificial Jangdok Islet meet.
Songdowon Tourist Hotel Songdowon Pleasure Grounds. 83 third-class rooms.

Where to eat

The seafront roads running on both sides of the Tongmyong Hotel are lined with restaurants. Recommended are two places right opposite the Tongmyong, a large eaved building named **Korean Noodle House** with stairs going up. But at the car park level is a doorway going into a much smaller, cosier place with two rooms, one with baking *ondol* heating. Here a slap-up steamed crab feast for four is about ∈ 25. Arrange in advance.

What to see

Wonsan's concrete cityscape is bolted to a backdrop of steep hills that screen in the natural harbour and give the city its name of 'Folding Screen'. The high-rises that fire out of the hillsides resemble the Chongsokjon rock formations further south down the coast. Wonsan's port proper is bracketed by the **Songdowon** pleasure grounds to the north and the southern Kalma peninsula resort of **Myongsasimni** and its 4km of beaches.

The **Songdowon** begin just beyond the man-made Changbok Islet, with the seafront road flanked by sandy, segregated beaches on one side and a gamut of restaurants on the other. You stroll along towards a forested area, watching locals hurl themselves from rusting water towers or lolling on the beach.

Songdowon is dominated by a deep windbreak of pine trees, some 700 years old, in which are hidden a zoo and **botanical gardens** (with stores of Kimilsungia and Kimiljongilia) that makes for a good half-hour's ambling around. Locals picnic and dance in the clearings amid the pine trees. An aged canal abruptly cuts the windbreak and the beach, across which is **Songdowon International Children's Union Camp**. It's a nice three-star hotel built in 1993 with lots of activities and events for up to 1,200 children, but don't visit unless children are there or you're touring a Holiday Inn without guests.

Along the quay are supposedly boats that can do small trips of the coast down to Tongchok, but this hasn't been verified.

The **Old Castle of Tokungen** holds the tomb of the founder of the Chosen dynasty, but it's not known where. Other reported sites include an airfield and an 'experimental station for marine products', so go see those three-eyed fish.

Well worth a look is the **co-operative farm** 7.7km south of the city centre. Cross the last bridge on the edge of town, turn right, then turn left at the next big stele 6km later. This idyll of rustic harmony and model of co-operative farming (see box opposite) has been frequented by Kim Il Sung and Kim Jong Il, which suggests why it's on the tour map, and it's interesting to see to what ends the finest stone is put.

Try to cadge a drag of a local's newspaper cigarette. You may get to 'drop in' on a farmer's household to meet some very well mannered children, although their songs may be interrupted by broadcasts from the radio high up the wall. This may be your only chance to visit a house of this kind in the country, and these are good quality, well-made houses, shown by their tiled roofs. You won't see any houses with thatched roofs. Older houses used to have wooden chimneys wrapped in thatch, but the air from the stove would have lost all sparks as it was piped under the floor in the *ondol* heating. Many of the poorest rural dwellings didn't have raised floors for *ondol*, and were built on the earth, so were notoriously dirty. Cattle and pigs were brought in to protect them from tigers, and the floors were veritable bug farms, such that travellers would barricade themselves in with fresh straw, hoping this would prove impenetrable to bugs during the night.

Unless made of concrete blocks, today's single-storey houses are built as they were from clay-brick coated with cement, with gardens fenced in by split-bamboo. As you enter (and take off your shoes!) there's an obvious lack of furniture, beyond the shelves and cupboards against the wall. Very little clutters the smooth, lacquer-papered floor, except a low table and floor cushions brought out for eating meals. As you sit and notice the heated floor,

CO-OPERATIVE

Co-operatives are units of up to 300 households that jointly own and run the land. Each co-op is controlled at the *kun* (prefecture) level, that sets output targets to be met by the co-op. Produce is traded and sold for external goods like tractors and fertiliser. In the co-op the farmers own their own houses but work in units on the land, in specialised work teams, like the rice-work team, or the cow-work team. Similarly assigned teams can compete for speed and output, with results posted up in the village square so all can see who's leading and by how much. At the end of the crop-cycle or year, those more than fulfilling their targets are rewarded in cash and kind, those failing lose payments.

Each day, members of co-ops gather at around 08.30 after a signal bell to receive instructions for the day's tasks. Lunch is at noon, held at home or in the communal hall, with dancing and music groups. During the ten-minute breaks per hour are 'news reading meetings'. At each day's end the work is evaluated and points are put in farmers' Labour Notebooks according to the work done. This ultimately affects their level of pay. They then go to the communal bath-house, cinema, political meeting or home, unless they're needed for other 'voluntary' tasks of irrigation building or factory work; otherwise they tend to their own plots. Farmers have small private plots for bees, pigs, chickens, and rabbits, which can be sold. This element of private ownership differentiated the DPRK's collectivisation programme from China's that happened almost concurrently in the 1950s, for China had much greater emphasis on communal living and state ownership. Where surplus has allowed, in recent years there has been an increasing number of farmers' markets appearing across the country, as a private supplement to state rations. However, with regard to the famines, these markets are scarce.

don't forget not to point your soles at anyone. These houses often have no more than three rooms, including the bedroom and kitchen, so the third room is multi-purpose, for entertaining, studying, eating, and listening to the announcements from the radio. Two gleaming pictures of the Great Leaders will hang high somewhere. The rooms are not divided by doors but maybe by screens. In the kitchen you'll see large earthenware pots for *kimchi* and holding dry comestibles. Having been duly entertained by the wife and her children, it should be time to bid farewell and get back on the way to Kumgang.

South Coast to the Border: Wonsan to Mt Kumgang

The road from Wonsan to Kumgang sails alongside the railway across a green sea of paddies before tacking right on to the shoreline, racing the electric fence all the way to the DMZ. En route there are many modern stelae on the roadsides, which the guides can translate, and cranes keeping an eye over the fields and lakes.

Around 37km from Wonsan is **Tongjong Lake**, formerly a seawater bay, and the beach of Chona Port. Ten kilometres further south is **Lake Sijung**, which the road and railway keep separate from the sea. On the lake's shore is a small, very hot guesthouse specialising in mud treatment and massage. The mud at the bottom of the lake is formed by a rich, thick layer of rotting God-knows-what, but very likely contains the carcasses of carp, sardine, mullet, lobster, clam, abalone, eel and snakefish that otherwise harass the row-boats floating from the guesthouse. This mud is heated up and packed on to your bits so that its nutrients may seep in and sooth your inner ills. It also pongs and can be too well heated, but a soak in the stuff helps cure numerous skin complaints, bronchitis and heart trouble.

The guesthouse is about a kilometre north of a private beach, entered through a reception pavilion that provides towels and showers for a nominal fee and sells the good booze (it's an area popular with Russians). The little islets dotted along it can almost be walked to across the beach's long shallows, in which the holidaying Koreans scour for shellfish and will share with you. Agree to any drinks the Russians might offer you.

Further on, the town of Tongchon has little to excite the visitor, but is adjacent to the beautifully geometric **Chongsokjong** rocks that protrude from the sea like great teeth. Another 42km along is Kosong, the last major town before the glories of Mt Kumgang.

WILDLIFE

Four hundred species of butterfly flit through the steep, forested slopes of Kumgang. Of the dozens of animal species in these mountains are musk deer, roe deer, antelope, bear, wild boar, and flying squirrel. The area ranges from deciduous to lower alpine forests, in which are stashed some 1,200 plant species, from bamboo to fir, oak, chestnut, hawthorn and varieties of maple and pine, thuja, Sabina chinensis, mountain cranberry and blueberry. The mossy ground is shielded with azalea, yellow clematis, primulas, and lilies; Japanese red pine and herbaceous fern protrude from the cracked cliffs. Local species to be spotted include Kumgang stephanandra and Kumgang bellflower. Indeed, botanists to these parts are warned by the local tourist information agency: 'There are some plants that will attract you. If you fail to see them, you will regret for your lifetime.' Flying in and around are kingfisher, yellow fisher, pied wagtail, pheasant, black-naped oriole, migratory grosbeak, Korean scops owl, cuckoo, wild geese, heron, and gulls apuses. The streams hold carp, trout, salmon, and ten species of batrachians, including the bell-toad.

MT KUMGANG

38.45° north, 128.1° east, 108km south of Wonsan, Kangwon Province, near to the DMZ and East Korea Sea.

Mt Kumgang is situated in the northern part of the Thaebaek mountain range on Korea's central-eastern coast, and covers an area of some 40km east–west and 60km north–south. Mt Kumgang means 'diamond mountains', so-called as the granite peaks and hillsides glitter in the sunlight, but they have had different names in each season, being the Pongnae Mountains ('spirits enjoy visiting') in summer, Phungak ('variety of views') in autumn and Kaegol Mountains ('snow sided') in winter. The highest is Piro Peak at 1,639m and another dozen touch over 1,500m, with a hundred or so over 1,000m and peaks as sharp as 'the tips of paint brushes' – although there may be fewer than the commonly cited 12,000 peaks.

Kumgang's been considered sacred for millennia. 'Buddhism,' wrote Isabella Bishop in *Korea and her Neighbours*, 'which possesses itself of the fairest spots of nature, fixed itself in this romantic seclusion as early as the 6th century'. Access was through Tan Pa Ryong (since renamed) that means 'cropped hair pass', a Rubicon for anyone seeking a life of Buddhist solace. In feudal Korea, bachelors had heavy braids of hair, married men's hair was coiled into a topknot, but monks, unencumbered by considerations of marital status, shaved all their hair off. The town of Choanjri once housed a great concentration of 16 temples and halls dating from the 6th century. Even by the late 19th century, when Buddhism had long fallen from official (and therefore financial) favour and most Koreans were succumbing to Christianity, 45 monasteries, nunneries and shrines were counted in the area. Thirty-two remained pre-World War II, but today less than a handful remain in any use.

However, tourists have long been filling out the space left by thinning pilgrims. Cavendish observed in 1887 that:

> The Koreans are great lovers of nature and admirers of scenery, and
> are also great pedestrians; they – that is, the men, who always seem to
> have plenty of time to kill – often make pilgrimages to places whence
> a fine view may be obtained ... annually they [Diamond mountains]
> are visited by hundreds of Koreans.

The Japanese turned the area into a park, and today Kumgang's spiritual splendour has allowed it to be the only place in the DPRK that ROK Koreans can visit relatively freely. Kumgang is divided into three areas, Inner, Outer and Sea of Kumgang, with 22 sub-divisions within it and so many different routes of peaks, pools, lakes, waterfalls and temples to follow that a serious walker would need a week to cover the place. Inner Kumgang has recently been opened to the foreign public.

The following contains a selection of good walks in the area but is by no means a definitive account of all the routes and sites in Kumgang.

Outer Kumgang

The Kumgangsan Hotel is a juncture for many hikes. It's 300m from the **Kumgangsan Spa**, the silica-imbued water of which simmers nicely between 37° and 44°C and is good for hypertension and heart troubles. Nothing gets the blood going like a bit of revolutionary fervour, mind, and you could find yourself being lured into the **Kumgangsan Revolutionary Museum**. Alternatively, get your boots on and head for the hills.

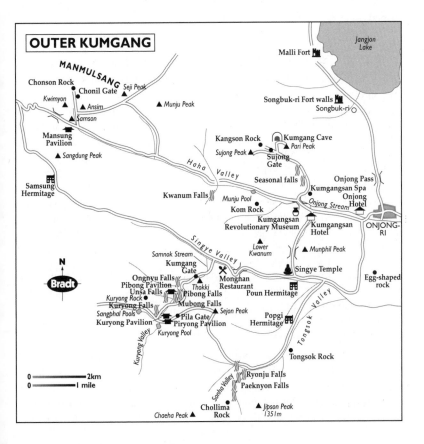

Sujong Peak

Sujong Peak, a good place to watch the sunrise casting its net of mist over the mountains, is 3km northwest from Kumgangsan Hotel. From the hotel, cross the Onjong stream towards the Kumgangsan hot springs, behind which is a track that an hour's jaunt up the Sujong Valley to Sujong and Pari peaks. First is a small drinking spring, and then follow 30m and 100m 'seasonal' waterfalls. Beyond a stone gate is the roundish flat rock of Kangson where the fairies used to come. Look out for three rocks, shaped like a turtle, a flying pigeon and a man in bed.

The trail forks towards a suspension bridge that leads to an 'observatory' beneath the ridge on which sits Sunjong Peak, like a cluster of artichokes. From here can be seen the sea. The right fork goes to the hollows and water of Kumgang Cave, then the ridge goes right to the smooth dome of Pari Peak, like an upturned bowl. The Onjong stream flows from west to east through Onjong-ri, flowing past the Kumgangsan and Onjong hotels on the way. A road follows the stream, sometimes referred to as Hanha stream. Following the road due east away from Onjongr-ri, the Sujong Peak area is on the right, Singye Valley is away on the left, and Hanha and Manmulsang valleys lie ahead. Hanha (cold fog) Valley is the broadest valley in Mt Kumgang and splits into many sub-valleys between peaks. Sanggwanum Peak (1,227m) aligns with the other oddly shaped peaks of Nunggot Rock, Kom Rock and Tol Gate.

On the left appears Kom Rock, a bear with its paw raised against the cliff. This bear once mistook the gemstones in the stream below for acorns, but got stuck on the way down to get them. It's near the Onjong's Munju Pond and Munju bridge, a couple of hundred metres from the 43m-high Kwanum Falls also on the left or south of the stream.

Continue west for about 10km from the hotel until you arrive at Mansang Pavilion, the start of an odd walk of curious boulders. First is Samson Rock, like three spirits, then Kwimyon Rock, the figure of a goblin or a massive petrified tree. Look out for the 'man on seven rocks', and those resembling eagles, bears and tortoises. It's a steep, sharp path up Jolbu (axe chop) rock to Ansim (saddle) rock.

Fork right 100m to the spring of 'Forget stick' (*mangjang*), whose rejuvenating waters are said to make the old forget their sticks. Then it's a climb to Kumgang's highest gate, Chonil (sky) Gate, to see over Chonson Rock, which doubled as an observatory. From here you can see the weird, smashed white glass face of Manmulsang. Look out for the Samsong Hermitage and the looming peak of Sandung. An off-shoot from the track goes north-east and then divides, the right fork looping back to the main road, the left continuing for a good few kilometres to Chonpok Valley, with its series of falls, odd-rocks and caves.

Sejon Peak

A different road heads due south of Onjong-ri and then bends westwards. Take this road through Sulginomi Pass where the egg-shaped rock appears on the left. About 1.5km beyond the bend in the road, a short-cut from Kumgangsan Hotel appears, joining the road just where sits one of Kumgang's oldest temples, Singye, that dates from 519. The temple and its three-storey pagoda mark the entrance to Singye valley. From this pagoda are brief excursions up to Munphil and Lower Kwanum peaks, flanking the path going north to the Kumgangsan. From the main road, two paths loop southwards and converge on Sejon Peak. The first route starts a few hundred metres east of Singye Temple, going up the shallow Tongsak valley on a very pretty jaunt of mild exertion. Tongsak hold the shaking Tongsak rock that weighs tonnes and shivers with the lightest prod. It leads into Sonha valley with its Ryonju and Paeknyon waterfalls and where sits the Kobuk (turtle) rock, a turtle that stretched its neck to drink water but was so captivated by the falls, it turned to stone. From Ryonju, look southwards to the 1,351m Jipson Peak, Kumgang's sharpest point, high on the northern range with the cloud-shrouded Chaeha peak to its right, and the Chollima rock (like Pyongyang's statue) between them. The path from Ryonju carries on westwards along a ridge to Sejon Peak.

East of Jipson Peak is the 4km Ryongsin Valley, a track tacking round waterfalls and pools, with the 7m-deep Jonju pool and 8m deep Ryongyon Pool. In south Ryongsin valley is Palyon valley with a stone-arch rainbow bridge, and the 8th-century Palyon temple beside it.

The **second route** to Sejon Peak starts some 2km further west along Singye Valley from Singye Temple. Going west, Pogwang Hermitage appears on the right, and you cross a bridge where insam and deer antlers are dissolved, and come to Mongnan restaurant. The road, now a track, forks to the south, from whence Ongnyu and Kuryong valleys extend like a twig from a branch from a tree, each littered with waterfalls and pools going up to Sejon peak, about four km from the restaurant.

The Samnok stream trickles from Ongnyu (clear water) Valley, so you follow it up and south, past the left Thokki (tortoise) Rock on the left. Sliding through the eye of Kumgang Gate seals your presence in the valley. Look for the flower-like Chonha rock. Ongnyu Falls channel through flat-sided trenches to the 6m-deep Ongnyu pond, over a bridge and 200 more metres past Ryonju rock and falls, then the spectacular Pibong falls (Phoenix falls, from the swirling mists) tumble 140m down a thousand broken dinner-plates and past Mubung Falls.

From the Pibong Pavilion, Unsa (silver string) Falls are next as you continue upwards towards Kuryong (nine dragons) Pavilion, stacked onto the hillside of Kuryong valley. Here's a fine view of the 74m-high Kuryong Falls, one of Korea's largest. Nine dragons reportedly lived in the 13m pool at the bottom, defending Kumgang from interlopers. About 100m up from the Kuryong Pavilion is Piryong Pavilion with grand vistas of all around.

From Kuryong Pool, cross Yondam Bridge and traverse 700m of rocky cliff and ladders to arrive at Kuryong rock, from where are visible the eight large green pools (the Sangphal Pools), noted as bathing spots for good spirits. Sneak through Pisa Gate and nothing but a ridge-hike remains until you get the grand overview from Sejon Peak, now reached from both sides.

Further possibilities

Other areas to enquire about in Outer Kumgang are the Songrim District, which has Songrim Cave and Songrim Hermitage, but be careful! 'If you are enthralled by the views, you are liable to get behind from your companions.' Unsudae District is the site of the 9th-century Yujom Temple; Kumgang's largest temple, it was destroyed by US bombers and only the foundations remain. Chonbuldong District is in the Chonbul stream basin in east Manmulsang District, with the 1,000 Buddha-shaped rocks of Mt Chonbul, and Sonam, Chonpok and Conbul valleys.

Inner Kumgang

The long road towards Inner Kumgang from Kumgang town (Kumgang province seat) is of goodish quality, hugging the hillside as it wiggles higher and higher up a very spacious valley marked by new pavilions to stop and admire the view from. A long, lush plateau stretches out, flanked by wall-vertical cliffs with mines burrowed into their bases. The road quality deteriorates as it descends from the plateau past the hamlet of Naegang-ri, 10km from Kumgang, into a copse of trees and the final checkpoint. Herein its dirtracks crudely cut from the sheer cliffs and battling to prevent the foliage from taking this exposed earth for its own. The final climb and descent is slow going and through thick greenery, but spectacular peaks flit into view, locked in frozen battle with the tentacles of tree-roots and ivy. Eventually you pass the Inner Kumgang resthouse, and the road forks. Right goes past the Okgyong pond, for 2km to Myonggyong Rock, like a great split mirror 90m high. In legend it read the minds and showed the sins of those who saw it. Two caves emerge further on, and then the path splits as the stream splits. The right fork goes to Ryongwon Hermitage, south of Jijang Peak, and continues for 4km to Paekma Peak. The left fork goes around Jijang Peak's north side and takes in a series of waterfalls en route to the Mun, Jungmyong and Tabu pagodas. However, this is quite a trek.

Back at the main road from Naegang-ri, the road snakes along, hugging the stream, past the three-storied, 7th-century pagoda of Jangan temple, one of the four major temples of Mt Kumgang. Continuing north past Ul Pond is the Sambul bridge, 3½km from Naegang-ri, is the diversion of Sambul Rock, covered with three large and 60 small Buddhist images, dating from the last century of the Koryo. Legend has it that the images were carved by two bitterly rivaling monks named Raio and Kinko, who challenged each other to carve the greatest Buddha. The loser would have to commit suicide, and the locals didn't consider Kinko's 60 small Buddhas as fine as Raio's three big ones, so Kinko threw himself into the river nearby. It's at this bridge that a track loops east-south-east to the paths around Sibwang and Jijang Peaks.

Staying on the main track going north, you pass a monument erected in 1632 to the great Buddhist priest Sosan, a local who valiantly led monk-soldiers against Hideyoshi's invaders in the late 16th century. Then, round a bend and over a bridge is Phyohun temple, first built in the 670s under the Koguryo and was for centuries one of the largest temples in the area, with 50 monks. Its original buildings were destroyed in the 16th century by Hideyoshi's invaders, and the reconstructions were flattened during the Korean War, but the rebuilt temple is still technically active.

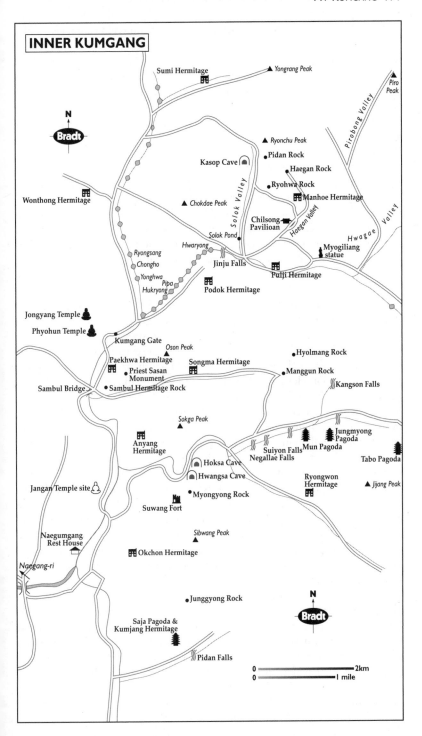

INNER KUMGANG

Sumi Hermitage
Yongrang Peak
Piro Peak
Pirobong Valley
Ryonchu Peak
Pidan Rock
Kasop Cave
Haegan Rock
Ryohwa Rock
Manhoe Hermitage
Chokdae Peak
Solok Valley
Haegan Valley
Chilsong Pavilioan
Hwagae Valley
Wonthong Hermitage
Solok Pond
Myogiliang statue
Ryongsang
Hwaryong
Chongho
Jinju Falls
Yonghwa
Pipa
Podok Hermitage
Pulji Hermitage
Hukryong
Jongyang Temple
Phyohun Temple
Kumgang Gate
Oson Peak
Hyolmang Rock
Paekhwa Hermitage
Songma Hermitage
Priest Sasan Monument
Manggun Rock
Sambul Bridge
Sambul Hermitage Rock
Kangson Falls
Sokga Peak
Jungmyong Pagoda
Anyang Hermitage
Suiyon Falls
Mun Pagoda
Negallae Falls
Tabo Pagoda
Hoksa Cave
Hwangsa Cave
Ryongwon Hermitage
Jangan Temple site
Jijang Peak
Myongyong Rock
Suwang Fort
Naegumgang Rest House
Sibwang Peak
Naegang-ri
Okchon Hermitage
Junggyong Rock
Saja Pagoda & Kumjang Hermitage
Pidan Falls

0 ——————— 2km
0 ——————— 1 mile

A hundred metres from here is the 'valley of ten thousand waterfalls', and – to make sure everyone knew where they were – a 16th-century calligrapher wrote 'Kumgang Mt and Manphok Valley' just below the large Kumgang rock. The Chinese graffiti is actually the names of visiting dignitaries carved in Chinese script by the monks in thanks for their patronage, and here the valley splits.

Strolling up the right valley, bathe your feet in the dark blue Hukryong Pool and listen out for the mandolin sounds of Pipa Pond, if not for the hiss of the flaming dragon in Hwaryong Pool.

Beyond a flimsy-looking suspension bridge, the lowly turret of Podok Hermitage appears up on the right, seeming to hang off a cliff or perch precariously atop a brass pole. Podok was built in 627 under the Koguryo and solitary monks would inhabit the site for their monastic lives of devotion to Buddha, looking down on to the ravine through a hole in the floor. Be careful that you are not so overwhelmed by the beauty of the monks' solace that you kill yourself, as one foreign visitor is fabled to have done. At least see the Jinju Falls first, just beyond Podok.

Alternatively, back at the graffiti, take the left valley up past a series of ponds. Continuing north you come to Sumi Pagoda and Sumi Hermitage, nestled at the base of Yongrang Peak. Before that, however, the path cuts right (east) to circle the Chokdae Peak. A complex network of converging valleys make the paths loop and doublebacks to surround a wealth of rocks, peaks, pavilions and hermitage, known as **Paegundae District**. The path almost loops back to the Podok Hermitage. Paegun Valley has good views of Inner Kumgang, but its main attraction is the sliced buttresses of Paegun Rock. It's said that the clouds here scatter in the morning and return in the evening to play with the cranes. Pobki peak along here is heavily inscribed, before Junghyangsong (rampart of smoke from a million incense). Here also is Kumgang's finest spring of water. Solok Valley has the good views from Ryonhwa Rock, Ryonchu Peak with its cactus-shaped crown and the sensuously smooth Pidan Rock.

The final gulley in this knot of valleys is the fabulous **Hwagae Valley**, with its climbing, winding paths that pass the extraordinary Myogil Statue, a huge 15m Buddha carved onto a rock. It's thought that the victorious monk Raio completed it as a sculpture of honour in late Koryo. The 7th-century Manhoe monastery is nearby and it's 4km up through Pirobong to Kumgang's highest point, the 1,639m Piro Peak, where you're some 8km from your start point of Phyohun Temple.

Sea of Kumgang

Just inland from the spectacular rock formations that dot this part of the coast is Samil Lagoon, or 'three-day' lagoon, where a king stopped for a rest and stayed three days, captivated by its beauty. The Tanphung (maple) restaurant and Chungsong Pavilion are on its shores.

East Coast to Tanchon

Robin Paxton

MUNPYONG

39.16° north, 127° east; Kangwon Province 12km northwest of Wonsan
Munpyong is famed for its lead smelter, a 1930s-built
relic of the Japanese occupation. Slag heaps dominate
the horizon: behind its imposing gateway, the
ageing factory employs around 1,800 people
and produces lead bullion for use in the local
battery industry and for export to China.

From Wonsan, the town is reached along an
attractive tree-lined road that runs for several
kilometres without turning a corner. There is also
some agriculture in the region, with farmers labouring under rows of
fluttering red banners on the outskirts of town.

HAMHUNG

39.5° north, 127.35° east, 110km north of Wonsan, South Hamgyong Province
Hamhung is North Korea's second city. The birthplace of the founder of Korea's
Ri dynasty and the site of a famous battle during the Korean War, Hamhung has
since developed into a spacious industrial city of around 750,000 inhabitants. The
city is renowned as a heavy engineering centre and is also famed for the
enormous Hungnam ammonium fertiliser plant, the largest in the DPRK.

Hamhung's whitewashed apartment buildings and tree-lined streets are best
viewed from Mount Tonghung. The historic hill is home to several ancient
temples and stands at the southern edge of town. The city is located close to the
northern end of Hamhung Bay and is served by the nearby port of Hungnam,
one of the country's largest export centres. A little further down the coast lies
the Majon beach resort, reputedly eastern Korea's answer to Club Med.

Relative to other cities in the region, Hamhung is bustling with activity.
Though there are few cars, cyclists tear along the pavements and pedestrians
stroll past the grandiose theatre building. The occasional street vendor does a
brisk trade by the roadside and there is some construction work in evidence in
the medium to low-rise residential areas.

Hamhung also boasts a proud academic tradition. The city's branch of the
Academy of Sciences is particularly strong in the field of chemical research,
developing a PVA, limestone and anthracite compound known as vinalon,
produced en masse for the textile industry at the February 8 Vinalon Complex.

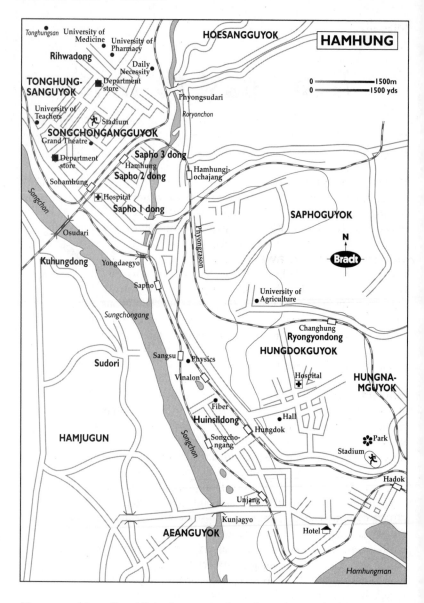

However, this well-publicised expertise has given rise to suspicions among western intelligence sources that the city is also a potential centre for chemical weapons production.

The Majon resort at Hamhung is actually pretty good, with villas, which can be taken whole or by the room – the rooms have their own bathrooms. Meals can be good, with local seafood. The aid agencies/NGOs work out of the resort, so there will probably be some foreign company if you stay there. The beaches are very good.

History
A settlement at Hamhung dates from at least the 12th century AD. A walled city around Mount Tonghung is believed to have been built in 1108. The ancient city is believed to be the birthplace of the founder of the Ri dynasty, which ruled Korea from the late 14th century until Japanese occupation in 1910.

The Hamhung/Hungnam area was also the site of a major battle during the Korean War. Twice in 1950, the city was evacuated, with the Songchon River Bridge destroyed several times over. US and South Korean troops took the city in October 1950 before being driven out by advancing Chinese-backed North Korean troops in December of the same year.

Hamhung's subsequent development into a major industrial centre has occurred largely since the independence of the DPRK. Much of the architecture is post-war. Kim Il Sung was a frequent visitor to the city.

Getting there and away
Hamhung is accessible by train from Pyongyang. The east coast line from Wonsan to the Russian/Chinese border passes through the city.

By road, Hamhung is three hours' drive north of Wonsan. Vehicles are checked on entry to the city. The road surface deteriorates into a two-lane dust track a few kilometres north of Wonsan, winding across mountain terrain. The landscape to the immediate north of Hamhung is flatter, where the road traverses the Hamhung Plain.

When to go
The most favourable seasons are spring and autumn, when the climate is cool and dry. Summer can be hot and rainy.

Where to stay and eat
Sin Hung San Hotel Tonghungsan district, Hamhung. The hotel is located on Hamhung's main thoroughfare, close to Mount Tonghung. There is a large car park at the front. 76 rooms, a first-floor restaurant serving basic Korean food and a smoke-filled billiard hall and bar on the ground floor. In true communist style, the corridors are wide and ostentatious with thin, well-worn carpets. The hotel is next door to a large restaurant built in traditional Korean style.

Majon Resort Majondong, Hungnam district. Located by the beach, around 25km from Hamhung itself, the resort is a self-styled tourist village offering sea views and bathing facilities.

What to see
Mount Tonghung
This 300m hill at the southern end of Hamhung offers good views of the city. It is home to several temples, including the Kuchon Temple and the Sonhwa Hall. The buildings and city walls are believed to date from the early 12th century, though most of what is standing today has been rebuilt more than once.

Hamhung Theatre

The large grey theatre, fronted by an expansive square, was opened in April 1984. The building is said to contain around 800 rooms and its main hall hosts various cultural performances.

Songchon River Bridge

Effectively the entrance to Hamhung from the south, the wide low-level bridge spans the Songchon River estuary. The droughts of recent years have taken their toll on the once-mighty river, now little more than a trickle as it drains towards Korea's East Sea.

TANCHON

40.28° north, 128.55° east, 150km northeast of Hamhung, capital of South Hamgyong Province

When the river in Tanchon runs grey, say local residents, it's a sure sign that the lead and zinc mines further upstream are in full swing. This bodes ill for any remaining marine life, though is a boost to the industrial needs of the northeastern port city. Environmentalists balk at the metallic content of the Pukdae River as it drains into Korea's East Sea but Tanchon has taken a prominent position in the national economy following the construction of a zinc smelter and magnesia plant on the coast.

Tanchon is one of several major ports along the eastern Korean coastline. The city lies in the delta of the Pukdae River, below the imposing foothills of the Paektu mountain range. The city's uniform white apartment blocks give way to more ramshackle, rural housing closer to the coast, where oxen haul carts along the road from the nearby fields. Tanchon is also a regional agricultural centre though, like other parts of the country, has suffered from the droughts of recent years.

A long, straight road runs from the city centre across sandbanks and the river delta to the zinc smelter and magnesia works. The approach to the plants is marked by a string of prominent letters, proclaiming: 'Long Live the Dear Leader Kim Jong Il, Sun of the 21st Century!' At shift's beginning and end, the road is packed with workers in brown overalls cycling to and from the factories.

The city is also a useful stop-off point for travellers to the far northeast of the DPRK. World Food Programme convoys plying the Pyongyang-Chongjin aid route often spend the night in Tanchon, grateful for the respite from the treacherous, winding roads.

History

Though an important eastern port of the DRPK, Tanchon is traditionally behind Wonsan, Hungnam, Chongjin and Rajin in the pecking order. Its prominence has grown since the flat stretch of land between the town and the coast was selected by Kim Il Sung himself as the site of a new zinc smelter in the early 1980s.

Smelting began in 1985, using ore from the Komdok mining complex some 80km inland. A brand new magnesia plant followed in 1997, fed by magnesite ore from Ryongyang. There has been talk of a plan to expand the port's facilities to accommodate an increasing level of exports. The zinc plant's owners are proposing an overhaul that would cost as much as US$100 million. These plans are at an early stage, however.

Getting there and away
Tanchon is on the main rail route linking Wonsan with the Chinese/Russian border. A branch line runs the 80km inland to Komdok.

By road, the city is a five-hour drive from Hamhung and around eight hours from Wonsan. The road between Hamhung and Tanchon is a winding two-lane dust track, extremely scenic in parts as it flirts with the East Korea Sea before disappearing back into the mountains. The route is certainly not conducive to high-speed travel.

When to go
The most favourable seasons are spring and autumn, when the climate is cool and dry. Summer can be hot and rainy.

Where to stay and eat
Accommodation is available in a hilltop hostel, situated around 2km from Tanchon itself among well-tended gardens. The hostel's VIP suite offers a double room with desk, fridge, deck chairs and some startling colour schemes. The en-suite bathroom has running water only periodically and there is no hot water. Also attached to the suite is a spacious meeting room decorated with several photographic portraits of Kim Il Sung.

Meals are served in a cafeteria housed in an adjacent building. The range of food is substantial and the dining-room boasts a fresco of the Tanchon shoreline across one entire wall.

What to see
Kim Il Sung and Kim Jong Il murals
Like every town in the DPRK, Tanchon displays extracts from Kim Il Sung's and Kim Jong Il's writings on large, stone walls. In Tanchon, the monuments can be found in a courtyard set slightly back from the main avenue through the town's modern housing.

Tanchon Zinc Smelter
A huge, red gate and heroic picture of Kim Il Sung and his subjects welcome visitors to the plant. Though opened only in 1985, the smelter is already in need of a facelift. Positive steps are being taken to engage international investors. The factory employs around 2,300 people.

Riwan
The attractive town of Riwon nestles at the end of a river valley, only 40km south of Tanchon. The town is a fishing centre and is home to a high concentration of naval officers. The town hugs the coastline of Riwon Bay,

where the road from the south dips to sea level before climbing inland into the mountains again. The east coast railroad skirts the western edge of town.

KOMDOK

41.05° north, 128.55° east, South Hamgyong Province, 80km northwest of Tanchon
Most Koreans associate the town of Komdok with one thing above all other: mining. The town, nestled around 600m above sea level at the end of a valley in the Paektu Mountains, is revered throughout the DPRK as the country's leading source of several metallurgical ores, primarily lead, zinc and silver.

Komdok translates roughly as 'Spider Plateau', a reference to the arachnid form apparent in maps of the area, which show seven major mine shafts scuttling outwards from the main body of the town. The eighth leg is now being developed.

Komdok also forms part of the 'Precious Mountain' area that encompasses the adjacent Ryongyang mining centre, the DPRK's primary source of magnesite ore. The name stems from an age-old eulogy attributed to President Kim Il Sung about the mineral wealth held within the mountain.

The Great Leader's words are everywhere. Enormous letters superimposed upon the hillside remind workers to 'move forward together under the red banner of socialism'. Colourful murals and stone-carved extracts of his writings dominate the town's central square, while piped instructions and reports on the day's production achievements are barked through speakers hung strategically around the town.

There are 7,000 lead and zinc miners living in Komdok, plus their families and many of the workers at the Ryongyang magnesite mine. The town's main institutions are built around the square, though the workers' houses cascade haphazardly across the hillside. A single-track tarmac road climbs up the valley side to an isolated ore processing plant at 1,200m above sea level, offering a breathtaking panorama of the valley and town below.

Komdok is also close to the source of the Pukdae River, though its waters often run milky-grey rather than blue. At times, up to 10% of the lead concentrate produced on site is believed to escape into the river. As the town seeks to improve its industrial base by engaging foreign investment, environmental considerations must be high on the agenda. Agriculture is limited, though potatoes are grown in small plots of land on the hillsides above the town.

Komdok suffered heavily in the floods of the mid-1990s, which caused widespread damage to the town, interrupted mining and severed transport links with the Korean coastline. However, in attempting an ambitious modernisation of its facilities, the town is entering a new era. Residents of Komdok exude pride in the mining achievements for which their town is renowned throughout the DPRK.

History

The site was first mined in the 14th century, though silver was discovered in the area as early as the 10th century AD. There are two major mining complexes at Komdok: the first mine reached along the road from Tanchon, the Ryongyang mine, produces magnesite ore, while the second is the larger lead and zinc complex, which produces silver as a by-product. Komdok has operated as a fully-fledged mining complex since 1946, though has suffered periodic stoppages along the way.

The complex has grown in stages. The lead and zinc complex has seven operational mines and three processing plants, the latest of which was built in the early 1980s. One hundred million tonnes of ore have been mined since 1946 and another 300 million tonnes are estimated still to be underground.

The great leader and eternal president, Kim Il Sung, visited Komdok twice during his lifetime, in April 1961 and May 1984. During the second of these visits, he supervised the opening of the third ore processing plant high on the mountainside. Outside the main entrance, a red line on a billboard depiction of the plant traces his every step that day. His words, including the immortal line that the factory resembled a 'sea of machinery', are reproduced in large letters inside.

The most celebrated visit, however, was that of Kim Jong Il in July 1975. The younger Kim is reputed to have ventured inside the main mine shaft and expressed horror that workers were spending up to fourteen consecutive days underground in order to surpass production targets by as much as 150%. He immediately decreed, or so the story goes, that every miner must return to the surface at the end of every eight-hour shift.

Kim Jong Il made his second visit in June 2002. In the 27 years since his previous appearance, Komdok has endured some difficult times. For much of the late 1990s, chronic flooding caused widespread damage at the mine and knocked out vital road and rail routes linking Komdok with the coast. Rusting railway cars still protrude from the river further downstream in grim tribute to the succession of natural disasters.

However, things have recently taken a turn for the better. A new body with ministerial status, the Korea Zinc Industrial Group, has been established to revitalise the mine as part of its wider industrial remit. The eventual target is a US$200 million investment that would double mining output from just over seven million tonnes annually to around 14 million tonnes.

Though cautious, there has been some interest from foreign investors. The mines and associated infrastructure were built entirely by the North Koreans, though the last few years have seen some equipment imported from Europe.

Getting there and away

A dusty mountain road and railway traverse the spectacular 80km stretch between Komdok and Tanchon, both following the route of the Pukdae River. The road journey takes around three hours, less time than it would take to travel by train. Road travel is by private transport; there is no regular bus service. The rail route is used primarily, though not exclusively, for goods transportation.

The road surface is poor in places, making for a bumpy ride, but the scenery more than compensates for any mild discomfort. From Tanchon, the road ascends quickly, passing through rocky valleys. Around halfway, the route passes through a mountainside settlement producing phosphorus for use in the manufacture of fertiliser. The railroad spans the Great North River by way of two large iron bridges and runs along the valley floor to Komdok, while the road passes along the side of the valley, cutting through a succession of tunnels on the approach to Komdok.

The road is also notable for several cartoon stone sculptures. The most impressive, around 10km from Komdok, is that of a small bear carved underneath a rocky outcrop with arms aloft, in a manner that suggests he is lifting the enormous boulder with his tiny arms.

When to go
April–June and September–October are the best months to visit. Winter temperatures fall well below freezing; due to the altitude, night-time is cold all year round. Rain is common in the summer months.

Where to stay and eat
Accommodation is available in the hostel that forms part of the Komdok Mining Complex's headquarters, overlooking the central square.

A single room has en-suite bathroom and living area with TV and couch. Hot running water is available on request for one hour per morning. Hotel staff will fill the bath for the duration of your stay.

There's a sauna in the basement.

Meals are available on request in the en-suite dining area. The building has a canteen.

What to see
Central Square
The central square is the focus of the Komdok community. A huge fresco at one end depicts the visits of the two Kims to the town. Two pictures are mounted on a grey, craggy background: the smaller picture shows Kim Il Sung, in dark hat and trench coat, flocked by the enthusiastic womenfolk of the town, while the larger picture shows a young Kim Jong Il, in a dazzling white coat, holding court with the miners deep underground. A jagged mountain backdrop adds to the dramatic scene.

Along another side of the square, Kim Il Sung's writings are carved in red upon another large stone structure. Opposite stands the main company offices and hostel. A bridge leads off from the square towards the stone obelisk, again inscribed with the words of Kim Il Sung, that marks the centre of every North Korean town. From the obelisk, it is a small climb to the entrance of the main mine shaft.

The square is best viewed just before eight o'clock in the morning. Practically the entire adult male population makes the trek to the mine entrance to begin their shift. Their journey is illuminated by Komdok's wives and mothers, ranks of whom sway gently in time with their songs of Korean reunification and the fulfilment of daily production targets. The female choir

Above Beach on the east coast, between Wonsan and Mount Kumgang (RT)

Right Children at the Taesong Fun Fair, Pyongyang (NB)

Below Eaves detail of traditional Korean building, Mount Myohyang (RT)

Left Calligraphy covers the rockface and valley around Podok Hermitage, Inner Kumgang (RT)

Above Mount Chilbo (NB)

Below Phyohun Temple, Inner Kumgang (RT)

and dancers are resplendent in national costume, each waving bouquets of bright pink Kimilsungia.

Komdok Museum of Mining

The museum is housed in the lower stories of a medium-rise building near the central square. The building is easily recognisable by the two large Korean characters, reading 'Juche', out front.

In addition to the pictures of Kim Jong Il's reputed Mt Paektu birthplace, ubiquitous throughout the DPRK, the museum has painstakingly preserved memorabilia relating to the younger Kim's 1975 visit. His wicker helmet is displayed along with a host of black-and-white photographs. The centrepiece of the Kim Jong Il display, however, is the mining car in which he travelled into the mountainside. Everything, from the dark green exterior to the red-and-cream upholstery, has been preserved for posterity.

The museum also houses an interesting scaled-down model of the Komdok mining complex, viewed as a cross-section of the mountain. It is possible to trace the underground route of the miners. And with the flick of a switch, the curator can set a motorised train in motion, turning the model into a giant train set.

Underground Mining Museum

The train journey into the main mining shaft takes around 35 minutes, barring any derailment (a not infrequent occurrence, though more inconvenient than perilous given the slow rattle at which the train travels). On disembarkation, it is a surprise to find a small shrine dedicated to the first visit of Kim Jong Il.

The room in which he sat, talked and wrote during his several hours underground is preserved as it was in 1975. The room is basic, with whitewashed walls and ceiling, and is lit by a single electric light bulb with no shade. Kim's small wooden desk and chair remain untouched, though miners can make use of the bench seating that runs either side of the office.

Directly outside the office, with a splurge of colour not seen anywhere else underground, billboards display an array of socialist artwork and reproductions of workers' bulletin boards of the time. One such placard relates the tale of the miner that worked a 14-day unbroken spell to exceed production targets by 150%; this poster reputedly prompted Kim's decree that all miners must return above ground at shift's end.

Number 3 Ore Processing Plant

Built in the early 1980s at the behest of Kim Il Sung, the plant is the newest building within the mining complex. The journey is notable for the views along the road from Komdok town, which rises 600m in a series of wide twists and turns. Along the roadside, there are a number of small, attractive cartoon carvings: a cow heading a football, a bear drinking from a bottle and a rabbit downhill skiing.

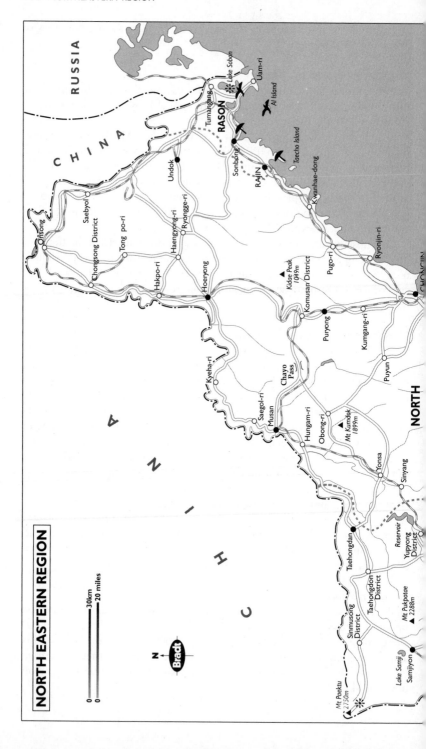

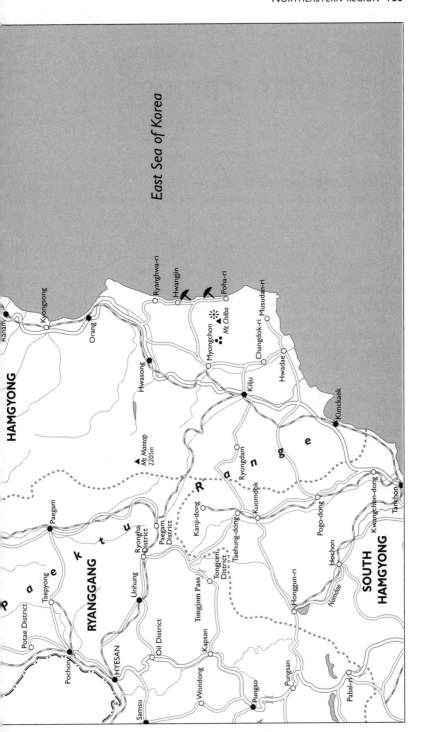

East Sea of Korea

HAMGYONG

Kanam
Kyongsong
Orang
Ryanghwa-ri
Hwanjin
Poha-ri
Myongchon
Mt Chilbo
Changdok-ri Musudan-ri
Hwasong
Hwadae
Kimckaek
Kiju

▲ Mt Mantap
2205m

Ryongdam

R   a   n   g   e

Kanji-dong
Kuomdok
Kwang-chon-dong
Tanchon

Paegam
Paegha
District
Paegam
District
Taehung-dong
Pogo-dong

P a e k t u

Unhung
Ryongha
District
Tongjom
District
Tongjom
District
Hongun-ri
Hochon

Taepyong
Namdae

RYANGGANG

Tongjom Pass
Namdae

SOUTH
HAMGYONG

Potae District

Pochon
HYESAN
Oil District
Kapsan

Wondong
Pungso
Pungsan
Pabal-ri

Samsu

Northernmost Corner

RAJIN-SONBONG

42.4° north, 130.4° east; North Hamgyong Province, bordering China and Russia

Wedged up in the DPRK's northeasternmost corner is the Rajin-Sonbong free trade zone. This 750km² area was dedicated in 1991 as a foreign investment zone and prospective hub of investment, industry and exporting by road, rail and sea to Russia, China and wherever the Pacific can take it. Two-thirds of the region's 150,000 people inhabit Rajin and Sonbong, many working in Rajin's port, Sonbong's oil processing refineries and the iron, magnesium and ceramics industries on the cities' outskirts. As such, it's been promoted less for tourists than for businessmen, but even then the zone's development is taking time, and the Rajin and Sonbong zone, collectively known as **Rason**, encloses an area of forested hills and wetlands, lakes and the Tuman River delta with an abundance of wildlife. The 150km-long coast running down to Mt Chilbo chops from long, sandy beaches in lazy bays to dramatic cliffs and rock outlets engineered by Vulcan. The winter along this part of Korea's East Sea is cold and windy and temperatures can fall to –10°C, while August peaks the summer's warmth at 25°C.

Wildlife

The variety of the landscape, with its forested hills falling into the sea and the Tuman River Delta wetlands, makes it home to a similarly wide variety of waterfowl and migratory birds; the area is considered by experts as a key staging post in this part of Asia for long-range birds. At the northern end of Rason is a series of shallow lagoons, including Korea's largest, the metre-deep, 41km-round Lagoon Sonbong. These are home to tens of thousands of ducks, while crane types known around here are red-crowned, white-naped, Siberian and hooded. Baikal teal and Baer's pochard breed here, too. In Rason Bay is the **Al Some (Egg Island) Bird Sanctuary**, which is the main home for 100,000 seabirds, including Temmincks' cormorants, common and spectacled guillemots, ancient murrelets and white-winged scoter. Other birds spotted in these parts include widgeons, tufted ducks, gargany, common teal, mallard, pintail, shovellers, mandarin duck, grey and white heron, snipe, dusty redshanks, sandpipers, quail, pheasant, harrier, osprey, kite, sparrowhawks, tit-larks, wagtails, skylarks, and eagle-owl, red-throated and arctic divers, black and red-necked grebes, and many types ofegret and goose. A comprehensive guide to the birdlife of the Rason zone, by Dr Philip Edwards, Nicholas Pertwee and Peter Garland, is printed in the summer 2003 Journal of the Korean Ornithological Society.

Also in Sonbong Bay is the **Uam Seal Sanctuary**, reachable by boat. Up in the Rason hills dwell bear, wild boar, racoon, fox and musk rat, ground squirrels and hare. Two thirds of Rason's surrounding land is forested hills and mountains, on which grow Korean pine, larch, oak, maple, fir, spruce and birch, although local needs for firewood have had a notable effect on the forests.

Getting there

Rajin to Hamhung is 488km by rail and more or less the same by car, following the east coast. Air Koryo runs a charter plane to Orang airport. In summer, a charter train runs from China's Tuman city to Rajin (currently for Chinese tourists only). There is the Quanhe/Wonjong Bridge across the Tuman River in Wonjong in the zone's northwestern corner. It's three hours by car from Yanji to Quanhe, and 90 minutes' drive from Wonjong to Rajin.

International tourists do not need a visa to visit the Rajin-Sonbong Zone but will need a visa to get into the DPRK which must be crossed. An invitation letter is required from the Rason City Tourism Administration (minimum three days processing), together with a passport valid for one year after entry to the Rajin-Sonbong Zone, faxed copies of relevant passport pages, a curriculum vitae with contact details, and itinerary.

Where to stay

Rason's tourism facilities are being beefed up by the DPRK and Yanbian region's tourist authorities, helping guide welcome investment into restaurants, hotels and taxi services:

Rajin Hotel First-class hotel in large, white, modern building on eastern shore of Rajin Bay. 98 rooms. Karaoke, sauna, massage, revolving restaurant.
Pipha Hotel Second class. Foot of Mt Ryongsu, four guesthouses, 36 rooms. Karaoke. Low level, quite pretty.
Namsan Hotel Third class. Heart of Rajin district, 30 rooms.
Pipha Tourist Hotel Third class. Seashore near the Pipha hotel. 200 guests.
Sonbong Hotel Third class. Heart of Sonbong county. 52 rooms. Grey barracks.
Uamsan Hotel Fourth class. Near the Sonbong Hotel. 24 rooms.

Where to eat

(Rajin) International Club
Phalgyong Restaurant
Pipha Restaurant On Pipha islet.

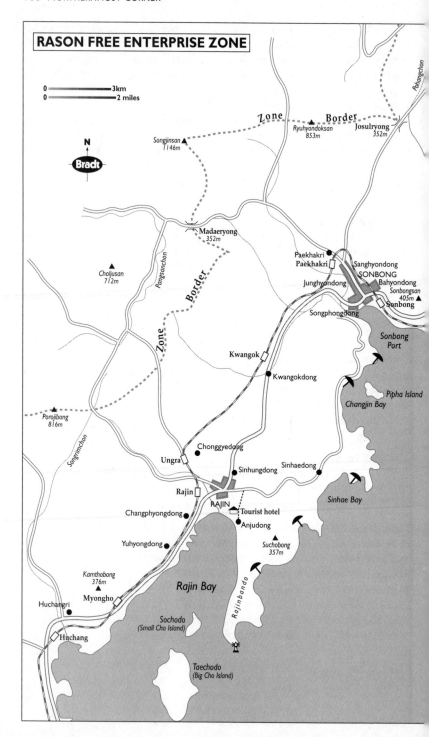

RASON FREE ENTERPRISE ZONE

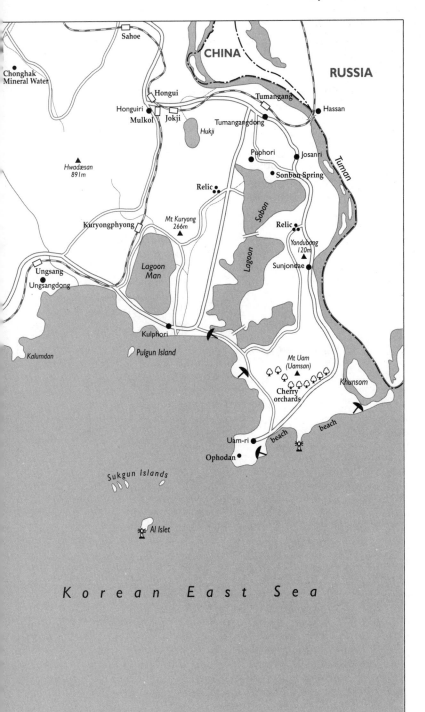

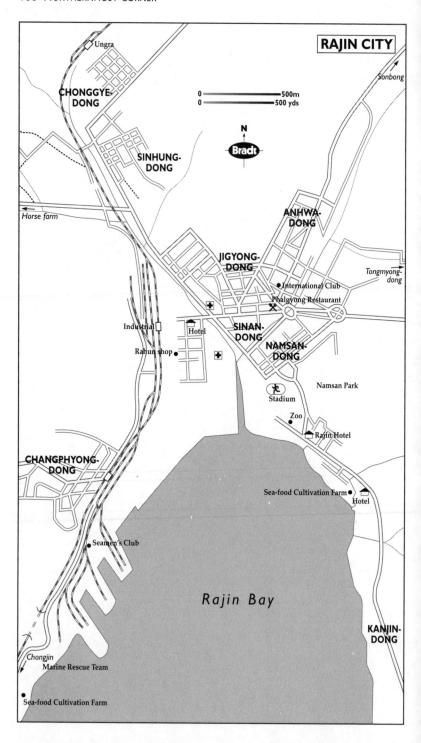

What to see

You may have taken a flying guess that most of Rason's prescribed tourist sites are of the 'Kim Il Sung Was Here' ilk, and both Rajin and Sonbong have their revolutionary museums dedicated to the Great Leaders and their family, plus a battery of revolutionary sites and spots. These rest uneasily alongside the

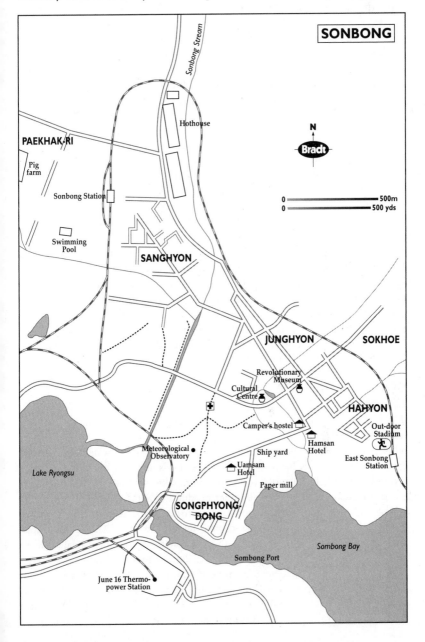

newer amusements of karaoke and the Haeyang Casino frequented by Chinese and Russian businessmen, but Rajin city's 1500-seat cultural theatre is frequented by martial arts and traditional dance troupes. Contact the tourist board for details.

However, Rason's coast is a series of bays and islands, with beaches and capes that are clean and clear locations to relax along, with all forms of water sports, and the whole Rason area is fenced in by a series of hills. So days between business can be spent bathing or hiking with a picnic stocked from the Rajin city market and a book from the foreign language store to keep you idle in the day, waiting for seafood dinners in the evening. Rajin's beaches include the headland to Taecho Island, Chujin, Sinhae-ri and Pipha Islet, and Sonbong has Unsang and, right on the final tip of the DPRK's north coast, Uam-ri. From Uam-ri it's easy to access the cherry orchards surrounding the base of Mt Uam, the northernmost hill in Rason's natural frontier. Mt Uam is flanked by the Korean East Sea and the wetland lagoons of the Tuman River, in which the ancient Kulpho ruins are found. A westward road runs from Uam along the Tuman to other historic fortresses in Tumangang, and all along you can see across to Russia and China, until you arrive in the sweet briar fields around Wonjong, Rason's land departure point for China. A taxi is needed for these journeys, however the Sonbong bus services get you close.

Keep going west and you're ultimately in the Tuman River Area, and Hoeryong border city opposite its Chinese counterpart, Jilin. Hoeryong is known for its white apricots and as the centre of this province's metallurgical and coal industries. Hoeryong is the base for many monuments to Kim Jong Suk, revolutionary anti-Japanese fighter (look him up on www.english.dprkorea.com/special/kim/photo_list.php?ca_no=706&no=2).

For more information try **Rason Tourism Administration Bureau**; tel: +850 8 21008; fax: +850 8 21009.

SOUTH OF RASON
Chongjin
41.45° north, 129.45° east; capital of North Hamgyong Province, Korean East Sea coast, 81km south of Rajin.
This port city specialises in ferrous metal industries. Although the average rainfall is low, the city has a good few weeks of mist drawing in from the forests around it. Similarly shrouded is **Kyongsong**, 35km southwest of Chongjin on the coast, living mainly from ceramics production and fishing. It's one of the oldest counties, and mostly consists of forested hills. **Kyongsong Onpho**, 12km northwest of Kyongsong's capital, features an excellent health resort, with the Onpho Resthouse where the spa waters are naturally heated up to 57°C. **Kyongsong Spa** lies in Haonpho-ri, 2km from the county seat, with spa and sand baths, and there are spas in nearby Songjong and Posan. Koryo-built **Fort of Kyongsong Seat** is 1km northeast of Kyongsong, and was rebuilt and enlarged between 1616 and 1672 under the Ri. The **Kyongsong Nam Gate** has been rebuilt many times. But more relevant for our purposes, Chongjin is

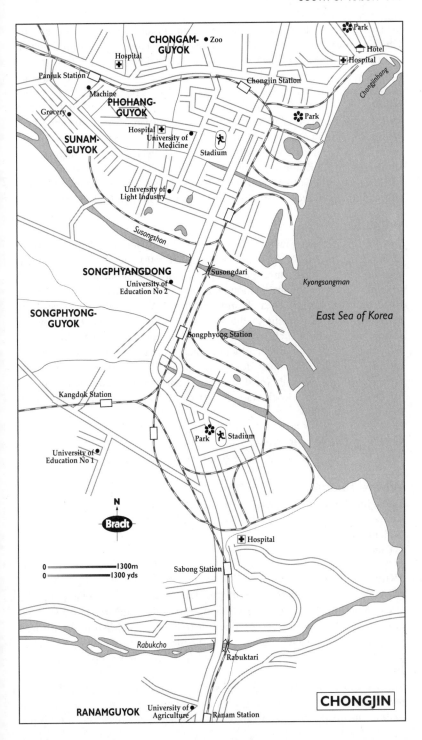

CHONGJIN

the nearest city to the real jewels in the crown of North Hamgyong's coast, the **Chilbo Mountains**. The name Chilbo means 'seven buried treasures', which must include the magma that made the area. It's a volcanic area formed one million years ago from lava blasting out of the nearby Paektu and Hamgyong Ranges, and such activity has been recorded as late as the 3rd and 4th centuries AD. The igneous rock that structures the area has been carved by wind and rain into the most fantastic peaks and valleys, with suspended rocks hanging over vertiginous hillsides, and these scars in the earth's crust seep spa-water but are healed with the greenery that the rich soil and diverse climate support. In a similar way to Mt Kumgang, Chilbo is divided into three districts, Inner, Outer and Sea, covering 250km² and lorded over by the 1,103m Sangmae Peak – although the peak securing the most attention is Chonbul Peak at 659m.

Wildlife
Sea, fresh water, deep ravines, dense forests and barren, lofty pinnacles offer ideal habitats across the spectrum of fauna. Of 250 known species of animal, wild boar, black long-haired pigs, leopards, wildcats, mountain squirrels and ground squirrel vie for space among the pine, azalea and maple trees alongside roe deer, bears, badgers, weasels and hedgehogs. A hundred bird species have been identified as resident to the area, with scores more migrating by the season, including nuthatch, tree-creeper, coal tit, great tit, marsh tit, long-tailed tit, golden crest, rose finch, blue magpie, hazel grouse, wrens, pheasants, magpies, carrion crows, turtle doves, jays, eagles, sparrowhawks, kestrels, blue tails, hawk owls. wagtails (pied and grey), starlings and red-tailed thrushes. Stickleback, dace and loach start the list of a score of fish species found in Chilbo's fresh waters.

Getting there and away
From Rajin, it's a 90-minute drive or a four-hour boat ride to Chongjin.

Where to stay
Chongjin Hotel In Chongjin city, 18 rooms.
Komalsan Hotel At the base of Mt Komal in Chongjin.
Naechilbo Hotel
Haechilbo Hotel

What to see
Chilbo itself is a triangular mass of rocky hills and outcrops that fan out to the sea. Chilbo Peak is shrouded in a flowing cloak of volcanic ridges, valleys and peaks that face seaward. Of the three districts, Inner Chilbo is the furthest pocket from the sea and, it seems, with the most sites to offer.

Inner Chilbo
Small, stumpy mountain ranges and shallow valleys make Inner Chilbo ideal for trekking with towering cliffs, kept upright by evergreen pine trees, tender azaleas and maple trees and offer breathtaking views. Seek out the bizarre

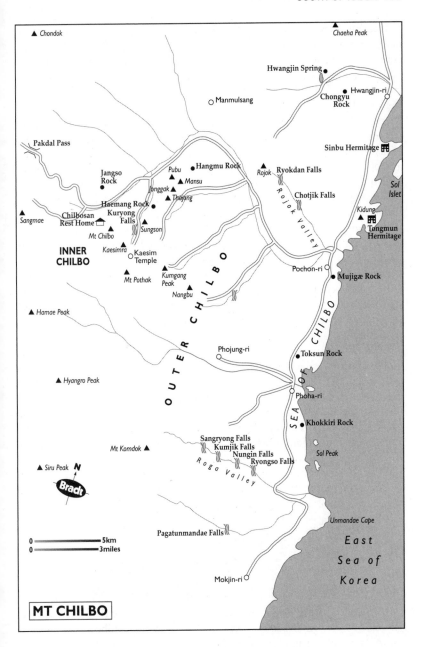

MT CHILBO

cluster of mushrooms that constitutes Pae rock, and the samples of streamlined strata held aloft on Nongbu rock, looked down on by craggy Kumgang rock. Suri peak is frozen mid-launch from a silo of trees, Pubu rock is a gallery of stone monks. Thajong and Hwaebul rocks are the mace and axe-shaped formations that dominate their locale.

Kaesim Temple is on Mt Pothak, and, built in 826, is very notable for being one of the few visitable sites dating from the Palhae dynasty. It comprises the Taeung Hall, Hyangdo Pavilion, east and west monasteries and Sansin Pavilion, with an 18th-century bronze bell. A 200-year-old chestnut tree grows in front of the temple. Inner Chilbo is cupped from the ravages of the sea by the fortress hills of Outer Chilbo. The finest area is the Manmulsang District, with its dense forests crowding over its congregation of waterfalls and pools. On the trekking trails keep a lookout for the lofty Samson rocks and military precision of the Chonyo rock. A finger of rock just touches an opposite pillar to make Kangson Gate, through which can be seen **Sea of Chilbo**.

Hwangjin-ri is a village at the northern end of the Sea of Chilbo, and sits in the shadow of Chonyu rock, guarding the entrance to Hwangjin Valley where the Hwangjin Spa Sanatorium is located. Pochon, Onsupyong and Taho are other spa sites located around Chilbo. A path stretches southwards along the Chilbo coast for about 30km, starting in Hwangjin-ri. The attractions of hermitages and strange rock formations flank the path as it picks through the villages of Pochon-ri, Phoha-ri and Mokjin-ri. These villages are the hubs of the local farms visible from inside Chilbo, and the local people, seemingly steeped in a very traditional rural life, are noted for their warmth and friendliness.

Going south from Hwangjin-ri, the path passes the rocky outcrop with the Sinbu Hermitage, adjacent to Sol Islet. A few kilometres to the south is another raft of rocks with the Tongmun Hermitage and Pochon-ri. Following the river east inland takes you to Inner Chilbo, but a rivulet goes north to Nojok Peak, and the Chotjik and Ryukdon waterfalls descend a worn staircase of rock, between evergreen pine trees holding on to sheer cliffs. Back on the path going south, look for Mujigae Rock and Tal Gate on the way to Phoha-ri, some hours' walk away. Beyond Phoha-ri on the coast appears the dramatic Khokkiri Rock and before the bizarre Unmandae Cape is Roga Valley. In here is a series of waterfalls, and this crevice, effectively the southernmost feature of Sea of Chilbo, is worth an afternoon's scouting by itself.

'Seoul 70km' – the border at Panmunjon

Mt Paektu

42° north, 128° east; in the northwestern part of Samjiyon county, Ryanggang (two rivers) Province, the border with China. Northern end of Paektu range. Janggan peak on Mt Paektu reaches 2,750m above sea level.

The Tuman and Yalu rivers dividing Korea and China source from one mountain, Mt Paektu. This volcanic mass of frozen lava smashed out from the wide, elevated planes of dense forest and bogs surrounding it over a million years ago, and has a powerful spiritual symbolism for the Korean people, as indicated in the local tourist literature:

> When children begin to study language, they are taught to sing song of Mt Paektu and when they begin to draw a picture, they make a picture of the spirit of Mt Paektu. When they attain the age of discretion, they visit Mt Paektu, because they know their real mind by reflecting it on Lake Chon and when their hair turns grey, they climb Mt Paektu with a desire to be reborn as a youth and live a long life. Those that leave the motherland in a state of sorrow for lack of a nation return to visit Mt Paektu first of all.

This is evidenced by a thriving south Korean tourist industry on the Chinese side of the mountain.

Paektusan means 'white-topped mountain', as it's skinned in white pumice and usually crowned with snow. It sits in an extensive lava area of its own doing, and hasn't stopped adding to it. White pumice showered the area and lava flowed many times in the 12th century.

The harsh terrain and remoteness of the mountain meant its environs have remained sparsely populated and it's been sparsely defended for centuries; across its porous border cattle herders, trappers, hunters and loggers pass back and forth. These occupations survive today alongside the slither of a tourist industry that accommodates 'tens of thousands every year' and the KPA activities. The locals are also exceedingly friendly and warm, highly welcome in such beautifully serene desolation.

Koreans once believed that dire punishment befell anyone intruding on the seclusion of the resident Spirit, as Captain Cavendish's companion H E Goold-Adams found out when hunting on the lower slopes in the 1880s:

> Before we could sit down to our magnificent repast, the spirit whose domain we were invading had to be propriated; for this purpose rice had been brought (otherwise difficult to cook properly at altitude). A miserable little pinch was cooked, spread out on the trunk of a fallen tree, and allowed to remain there for a quarter of an hour or so until half cold; my men in the meantime (though professed Buddhists) standing in front, muttering, shaking their hands in the Chinese fashion, and now and then expectorating. Their incantations finished, the rice was brought back to the fireside and solemnly eaten. They explained to me that the spirit being such, could not eat rice, and only required the smell, so there could be no harm in their consuming this tiny luxury … At a later juncture I had to fire both barrels of my shot-gun in the air to appease the spirit.

A more modern mythology has been built around the Great Leader's exploits here, for officially this is where he was based from 1937 to 1943. With mercurial powers, he led his forces into thousands of victorious battles against the Japanese at '200-ri at a stretch to annihilate the Japanese punitive troops and mowed down all the enemy force', a feat the enemy thought only possible through 'the art of land contraction'. Another time before the liberation the Japanese forces surrounded the mountain where hid a small Korean People's Army unit led by Kim Il Sung. A ferocious battle raged all night, but, next day, only dead Japanese were found, and not one single guerrilla. The Japanese had been fighting among themselves all night! This positively spooky occurrence finally scared all the Japanese away. Numerous secret camps and battlegrounds have been rediscovered since the 1970s, with more sites being found all the time, and are on public show.

The average temperature on the mountain is –8°C, the highest being 18°C and the lowest recorded –47°C; Korea's coldest area. The weather changes quickly, some say four times a day, others say four times an hour. The wind is always strong as the Paektu range striding northwards into China provides the battleground for warm air from the mainland blowing into a barrage of cold air. As a result, much of the flora has a distinctive 'blown' shape to it. The freeze begins in September and thaws from late May. Around 2,500mm of rain comes each year, mainly in July. Snow starts falling from early September until mid-June. The harshness of the weather effectively rules out any winter visits, although the scenery is at its most icily barren and empty then, but in spring and summer liquid emerald erupts from the hills and carries down currents of flowers, washing across the area's meadows and valleys.

Within Paektu's thorny crown of petrified lava is cupped the world's highest mountain lake, Lake Chon. Lake Chon used to be known as Ryongdam or Ryongwangthaek because dragons were thought to live there. Should a hurricane be raging around you, the absolute stillness and intense blueness of the lake in its grey-white bowl becomes even more prominent. Snips of alpine meadow and birch trees cling on to the sheer cliffs of young, crumbling pumice which make the crater like a marbled bowl, filled with an eerily blue water. The surface of Lake Chon is at 2,190m, covers an area of 9.16km^2, and has a depth of 384m, making it the deepest mountain lake in the world. Supplied by rain and underground springs, its volume is 1,955 million cubic metres. A DPRK guidebook handily points out that should you ever try to empty Lake Chon, get a pump discharging faster than 1m^3 per second, because that'll take 60 years. The lake's surface ice freezes to 4m thick, and its water temperature never rises above 6°C, so good luck to the hardy ones wading into it.

WILDLIFE
Broadleaf and needleleaf forests smother the planes and valleys up to 2,000m, whereupon alpine grass then makes a belt around Paektusan. The road going up takes in a cross-section of the different flora and fauna of rising altitude, from the temperate lowlands to the tundra highlands. Most of the species around the lake are thought to have arrived in the last 200 years – including Western hunters. Goold-Adams hunted for tigers reportedly over 4m in length, and leopards nearly 3m long. Not so long ago, every third or fourth village north of Wonsan would reportedly be under siege from tigers, raiding houses when snow covered their usual hunting grounds. Wild boar provided easier pickings, which the locals considered pests anyway as the boars snaffled their crops at night. Fauna seen here in more recent times have still included Korean tiger, leopard, lynx, wild boar, deer (including musk deer and Paektusan deer), and at Motojondo (about 50km north of Paektu on the Korean side) black and brown bear, moose, squirrel, fieldmouse, with wild pig, beaver, and sable.

The landscape houses over 200 species of flora, including bracken, blueberry, *Abies nephrolepis*, and 20 species of edible wild vegetables. Blue oval berries (*Lonicera edulis*), evergreen rhododendron, lilies, white angelica, and a hundred or so medicinal plants thrive among the lowland birch and larch trees, and the treeline is finished off at its height by eastern Siberian and Khinghan fir. In the meadowlands are found trollius, blue-violet (*Veronica verticillata*), alpine papaver and red *Lychnis fulgens*. Spying the land from the sky are black cock, hazel grouse, pheasant, nightjar, quail, broad-billed roller, black grouse, hazel grouse, woodpecker, and hedge sparrow. Lake Samji has Samjian crucian carp, red carp and char carp.

GETTING THERE
The only way is a one-hour flight by a chartered Air Koryo propeller plane, costing around €3,000 return for the whole plane that can seat up to 20 in a group. The distance to Mt Paektu from Pyongyang is 385km.

WHERE TO STAY
Pegaebong Hotel A large Swiss-styled hotel at the base of Pegae peak 2km from Samjiyon town. 47 rooms.
Onsupyong Hotel 7.5km northeast of Pochonbo. Second class, 40 rooms.
Hyesan Hotel Hyesan City. Third class, 49 rooms.

WHAT TO SEE

Unless inclined to hike, take the cable-car (if working) to **Lake Chon**. Around the lake, Paektu is the crown of the Paektu range, a third-degree burn of rock with Chilbo at the southern end, so, like Chilbo, Paektu has many spas that, according to local sources, are 'full of ion'. Paektu Spa is 73°C, Paegam Spa is on Lake Chon's northern shore, mild at 46°C, while Jangbaek Spa, nearly boiling at up to 82°C, is 850m from Jangbaek Falls. A double rainbow often appears in front of Sangmujigae Peak (2,626m). The Paektu area can be seen as rectangular, moated in by the Yalu or Amnok River, the Tuman River and the Sobaek stream running south from the edge of the Tuman. The Amnok River gorge at Chongun rock is a cathedral of natural sculpture, but for the DPRK tourist board, the main sites are the **Paektu secret camps**, starting with Paektu Secret Camp No 1. This was officially Kim Il Sung's headquarters from 1936 to 1943, and the biggest of four camps in the area. Here stands the house where the Great Leader expanded the Party and conducted the strategy of liberation. With its weapons' repair shop, hospital, publishing house amongst other buildings, this was evidently a veritable camp to hide out in, and in amazing nick, like new in fact.

All around are screened-off trees bearing slogans like 'our nation is the greatest nation in the world that gave birth to General Kim Il Sung' and 'Successor to General Kim Il Sung was born in Mt Paektu', written by Korean soldiers during the anti-Japanese struggle. More and more of these slogans are being discovered and preserved all the time. Near the camp, across the Sobaek stream, is the house where Kim Jong Il was born (in Khabarovsk, thus dispelling the myth about his birth). Exactly 216m behind the house (2/16 was Kim Jong Il's birthday!) sits the 1,797m Jong Il Peak, with the Dear Leader's name carved on it in red. Other revolutionary sites are pointed out by guides with local literature to regale you with, but the area's natural beauty makes it all worth it.

Mt Kom (Komsan), 'bear mountain', a round, bulky mass covered in moss that staggers up to 1,860m. Four kilometres from Kom is Sonosan Secret Camp, adjacent to the Hyongie (brothers) Falls, two ribbons of water cascading side by side in summer and held frozen in winter. A kilometre away are Paektu Falls and the refined, three-tiered Sagimum Falls. Paektu Bridge and a restaurant are 5km northeast of here.

Around 30km from the Secret Camp No 1 is **Lake Samji**. The tranquillity of this location is all the more affecting, given the desolation of the area. For revolutionary history, Lake Samji is important for the decisive Musan battle allegedly pitched here in 1939, celebrated at the bronze Samjiyon Monument with its 50m-tall Juche torch. Of the two largest groups of figures, one is 'reverence' and the other 'advance'; a smaller group is visible in the lake itself. The lake is adjacent to Samjiyon Town, where you'll probably stay. Another 40km south of Samjiyon is the Amnok riverbank city of Hyesan, opposite China, worth visiting for another China/DPRK comparison that's also a favourite for visitors to Dandong (see page 201). It's the best base for seeing **Pochonbo** town (21km north), famous in DPRK folklore for being the place where the Great Leader won a decisive battle over the Japanese, and with the remains of a Ri-dynasty castle.

The Border with China and Beyond

12

SINUIJU

40.1° north, 124.4° east; on the Amnok/Yalu River, North Pyongan Province, DPRK border city

For many travellers, the last (or first!) they see of the DPRK is at the border city of Sinuiju, through which the Pyongyang–Beijing train trundles. Sinuiju sits on the east bank of the Yalu (Amnok to Koreans) River, opposite China's thriving port-city of Dandong. Sinuiju's substantially smaller than its Chinese counterpart, with a population of 326,000, but has similar industries to Dandong, including paper milling, chemical production, aluminium, alcohol distillation and the processing of soya-bean products, as well as being of course the rail hub of the DPRK and China.

History

Sinuiju was formerly known as Ai-Chiu, a border fortress and 'gate to old Korea' from before the Ri. The drain sluices of its thick granite walls provided the routes for early missionaries to sneak into the city and the country beyond. It's been the capital of North Pyongan Province since 1923, taking over from Uiju that lies 28km upriver. Following the outbreak of the Korean War in July 1950, US commander General MacArthur decided that the flow of troops and supplies from Manchuria into North Korea had to be cut. In November a series of raids by B-29 heavy bombers pounded bridges all along the Yalu, mainly hammering Sinuiju Bridge. As Chinese MiG jet fighters soared up to intercept the bombers and their jet-escorts, Sinuiju earned the dubious distinction of hosting the world's first jet-to-jet combat. Sinuiju briefly became the DPRK capital in October 1950, as Kim Il Sung bestowed that status on the city when Pyongyang was briefly lost to United Nations forces. Much was levelled during the war, and has been rebuilt since.

The most thrilling event in decades came in mid-2002, when it was announced that Sinuiju would be the centre of its own free-enterprise zone, the 'Hong Kong of the North'. Unfortunately, virtually upon announcement the entrepreneur set to organise the scheme was had up for tax evasion amongst other charges; his chance for a DPRK diplomatic passport hastened the closing of the noose. Nevertheless, the plans are there for anyone else

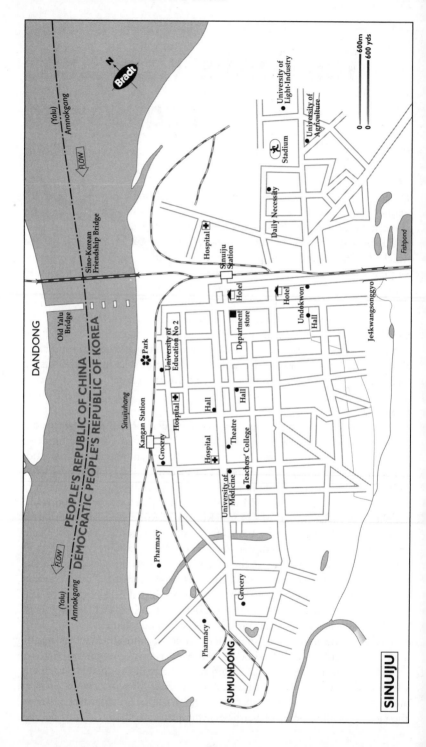

wishing to set up a competitive trade zone opposite one of China's boom cities.

What to see

Being a border town means that Sinuiju's inhabitants are 'privileged' to, but trusted not to, 'wander into China'. Foreigners can come in far more easily than locals can come out, if 'foreigners' is restricted to meaning Chinese. Chinese and 'normal' foreigners (usual restrictions) can come in on one-day tours, the highlight of which is Sinuiju's central square and its Kim Il Sung statue. One half of the square is clean and bright, and you can photograph it. The other half is dirty, derelict, and, in a stunning visual admission, is full of beggars, and can't be photographed. A lot of Sinuiju is fenced off with barbed wire so that the locals can't enter, let alone foreigners. Otherwise, you're likely to come in on the train and on the train is where you'll stay, unless the train gets delayed on the DPRK side by power-failure and humanity dictates you can get off on to Sinuiju station platform. Visitors to Sinuiju are often diverted to the city of Uiju, further north along the Amnok. It was first known as Ryongman, meaning 'a river bend with dragons', but the city's history is largely steeped in battling invaders from every direction, mostly from China. From Koguryo a fort existed here and the city never lost its military significance. Peaceful trade links over the river made Uiju prosperous in times of peace, and it was the provincial capital from 1907 to 1923, when Sinuiju took over. The Uiju Revolution Museum is devoted to Kim Il Sung's father, Hyong Jik. Two hundred metres away is the Uiju Nam Gate, which originates from Koryo times. Another site, 1km north of here, is Thongounjong Pleasure Ground, home to numerous pavilions that date from the Koryo when the area's hills marked it for defensive purposes. Sites like the Thongung Pavilion (1117) were part of the walled city of Uiju.

DANDONG

40.1° north, 124.3° east

From Sinuiju, the train carriages are batted across the bridge into Dandong, a city with two major tourist features for Chinese: first, it's China's only city right on a national border, and a natural border at that; second, and far more alluring, the country across the river is the DPRK. It's mostly Chinese tourists that make the day-trip into Sinuiju, and for everyone unable or unwilling to get over there, there are still many means to get within metres of the world's most secretive, inaccessible country. For those Chinese in their late thirties and older, there is the added poignancy of seeing a land so close that so resembled their own country only a generation ago, and there's the sickening luxury of being able to watch the DPRK's appalling famine strike only a few hundred metres away.

The difference between the two cities' fortunes is painfully obvious. Dandong's commercial towers reflect sunlight on to Sinuiju's smokeless chimneystacks. At night the Chinese side is a jungle of neon, the Korean side, darkness. In winter, the river can scarcely freeze on Dandong's side as its warm waste waters pour into the river. Sinuiju remains behind its shore-long barrage

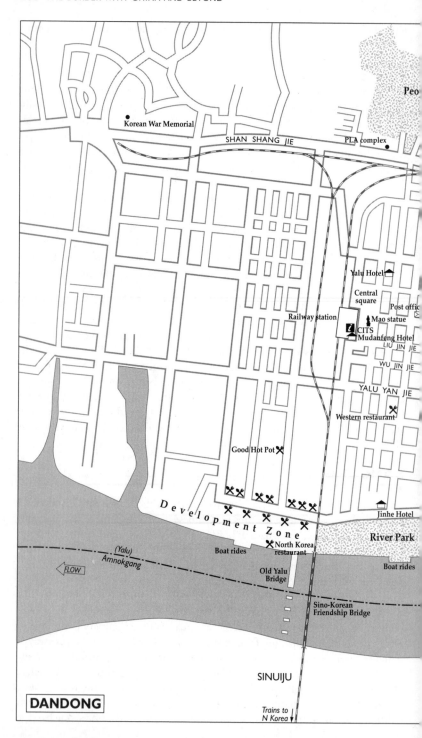

Peo

Korean War Memorial

SHAN SHANG JIE

PLA complex

Yalu Hotel

Central square

Post offic

Railway station

Mao statue

CITS

Mudanfeng Hotel

LIU JIN JIE

WU JIN JIE

YALU YAN JIE

Western restaurant

Good Hot Pot

Development Zone

Jinhe Hotel

River Park

Boat rides

North Korea restaurant

(Yalu)
Amnokgang

FLOW

Old Yalu Bridge

Boat rides

Sino-Korean Friendship Bridge

SINUIJU

DANDONG

Trains to N Korea

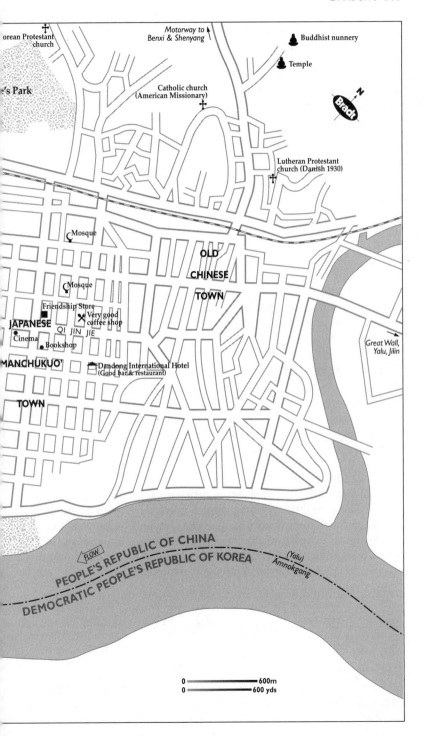

orean Protestant church

's Park

Motorway to Benxi & Shenyang

Buddhist nunnery

Temple

N

Bradt

Catholic church (American Missionary)

Lutheran Protestant church (Danish 1930)

Mosque

OLD

CHINESE

TOWN

Mosque

Friendship Store

Very good coffee shop

JAPANESE

QI JIN JIE

Cinema

Bookshop

MANCHUKUO'

Dandong International Hotel (Good bar & restaurant)

TOWN

Great Wall, Yalu, Jilin

FLOW

PEOPLE'S REPUBLIC OF CHINA

DEMOCRATIC PEOPLE'S REPUBLIC OF KOREA

(Yalu) Amnokgang

0 ————— 600m

0 ————— 600 yds

of ice, perfectly marking the mid-river border of China and the DPRK. It's a measure of how Dandong sees Sinuiju that facing the latter from atop a mighty Dandong Hotel is a huge advert for SPAM.

History

Now the largest city in east Liaoning, Dandong was until the 1960s known as Andong. With the town recorded as under Zhou dynasty administration in the 6th century BC, Andong was built by the timber trade, becoming a major timber-trading centre from the timber floated downriver. In 1903 the Qing dynasty proclaimed it a free-trade port. Rapid growth from 1907 followed the railway link-up to northeast China and further from 1911 when the bridge into Korea was completed. The Japanese industrialised it during their occupation in the 1930s and '40s, and the neat grid-layout around the station is the 'Manchukuo' Japanese quarter of town, so-called from the Japan's colonial name for Manchuria. Following China's entry into the Korean War, the city (along with Sinuiju) was bombed many times by US aircraft, as it was a major rail and river communications and supply link with North Korea. When the bridge was damaged, Korean and Chinese forces valiantly connected the banks with pontoon bridges. Today, Dandong is a flourishing industrial area, processing wood, paper, rubber, chemicals, ginseng and tussah, and a major port for the river and coastal trade.

Getting there and away

Buses 80 and 94 leave Dandong bus station at 06.30 and 08.50 respectively to drive ten hours northwest to Tonghua, a town with connections to the Changbaishan reserve.

Planes to and from Dandong airport cost in the environs of 850Y o/w to Beijing, 850 o/w Shanghai.

Travel agencies

The CITS and KITC in Dandong are very good at making the arrangements to cross into the DPRK, if you're going to catch the train from Dandong to Pyongyang, but if that's what you're going to Dandong for, you need to get the ball rolling at least two weeks before going there (unless you sort out the papers from Beijing or elsewhere) initiated by phone/fax. Never forget that a visa to the DPRK is not a three-day pay 'n' stamp.

CITS 2nd Floor, Mudanfeng Hotel (adjacent to Dandong railway station); tel: ++86 (0) 415/212 0187
KITC Xian Qian Rd, Yuan Bao District Dandong, China; tel: ++86 (0) 415 281 2542, 2810457; fax: ++86 (0) 415 281 8438

Getting around

All buses for the town and beyond go from the square in front of the railway station. Taxis kerb-crawl the streets for Y5 minimum fare and pedi-cabs for half that.

Where to stay
Dandong International Hotel Xin'an St, Dandong 118000; tel: 0415 2137788; fax: 0415 2146644. Three star.
Ya Lu River Guesthouse 87 Jiuwel Rd, Dandong 118000; tel: 0415 2125901; fax: 0415 2126180. Three star.
Mudanfeng Hotel 3 Liujin St; tel: 0415 2132196
Jinhe Hotel Yalu Bridge; tel: 0415 2132771

Where to eat
The development zone along the river front is home to many good and cheap Chinese and North Korean restaurants, serving bountiful food from US$5 per person. An excellent hot-pot restaurant is 200m up on the left of the first road south of the railway bridge that runs into town away from the river. The **International Hotel** is more popular with expats and has prices to match.

What to see
Dandong is an unusually 'do-able' city, compared with other northern Chinese cities, and is quite clean and human in scale (its 700,000 urban population is villagesque compared to other Chinese conurbations). Many sights relate to the border, Chinese-Korean relations and communism. Arriving by train or bus, the first thing you see in the station square is Mao Tse Tung's statue, now in pragmatic salute to the city's bustling capitalism.

The station and square are on the southern side of the 'Manchukuo' town, and in this grid of streets fenced in by the railway are most of the hotels, bars and amenities. The higgledy-piggledy streets north of here are the old Chinese-built town.

From the station square buses (1, 2, 4, 5) can be caught southwest up to the Memorial to Resist America and Aid Korea. This huge white column, well visible to most people in Dandong and pointedly to anyone in Sinuiju, towers over the city. It reminds everyone, Koreans especially, of China's contribution during the Korean War. After paying a Yuan to enter the Jinjiang hill park where the tower is, at its base is the Museum to Commemorate US Aggression (Tuesday-Sunday 08.30-16.00, Y35), an impressive series of halls full of the war hardware of bombs, tanks, fighter-planes, wreckage, and maps, documents and photos of decapitated POWs, etc. One hall has an extraordinary 360° diorama where you're surrounded by communist liberators fighting up a hill towards you. The museum tells the story of the war from the Chinese point of view and makes for an interesting comparison with Pyongyang's own excellent war museum, and for Westerners how 'well' the United Nations comes out of it all, but only if you can read Chinese or Korean!

From the monument follow the Shan Shang Jie road and railway northeast until on the left appears a PLA complex with peculiar Danish 'gingerbread' detailing. Adjacent to that is the entrance to 'People's Park', with pleasant walks and steep ridges to get views of the town and the DPRK. On the park's north side is a Korean **Protestant church**, built in the 1990s by the South Korean Church. Further north just off Shan Shang are two more churches, one **Catholic church** built by American missionaries, and a **Lutheran church** built by the Danes in the 1930s. Tucked into a small valley leading away from this area are a small temple and a Buddhist nunnery.

On the waterfront

Of the two bridges beginning from Dandong's shores, only the Sino-Korean Friendship railway bridge makes it all the way across. The Old Yalu Bridge, a stone's hurl south of the rail bridge, was bombed during the Korean War (first hit in 1950 but it held together until early 1951). The Chinese half of the Old Yalu still stands, on the Korean side only stone bridge stumps protrude from the waters, like furious stelae. For a minimal fee, you can walk out along the bullet and shrapnel scarred Old Yalu Bridge until its girders gnarl to nowhere. In summer here is a mini-café, in winter you can try to lob snowballs on to Korea's frozen riverside.

If this isn't close enough, in fair season from the Yalu River Park and from a pier just south of the Old bridge are slow boats with dragonheads and tails or speedboats that, for Y10–20, take you to the river's mid-way 'border', or, some say, within metres of the DPRK shore. Although Sinuiju is behind a large dyke-type wall, you might see, like many others do, parties of schoolchildren in white shirts and red neckerchiefs trotting gaily along the Sinuiju bank behind groups of fishermen and youthful soldiers.

Back at the River Park, other amusements include shooting at live animals and poultry. On the south side of the old bridge is a development zone, and from the southern end's Culture Square, this is a pleasant place to amble along at dusk, with all Dandong people out strolling, playing, enjoying the breeze. Along here are many little Chinese businesses and excellent restaurants run by Koreans (look out for one restaurant graced by a poster of the Mona Lisa with a great big dope plant). Many Koreans are living and working in Dandong in restaurants or small businesses, and a few businessmen fleet in from Sinuiju to stock up on food, cigarettes and anything else sellable across the water. You can also pick up DPRK stamps, trinkets and Kim Il Sung badges here (debatably real). One enterprising Korean has, rumour goes, set up a casino on a liner-like boat on the Yalu. Anyone who gets to go is welcome to write in about it.

Around Dandong

Lying 52km northwest of Dandong, just outside Fengcheng, is the stunning Phoenix Mountain (Fenghuangshan) set in its own small reserve (open 08.00–17.00, admission 30Y). Taoist worshippers come here to pray for relief from their illnesses, for the God of Longevity occupies the mountain's west ridge. Every April 28 a 'Medicine King Meeting' is held at one of the temples, but, in company with former T'ang and Yuan emperors who pocked the mountain with their own tributes of temples and pagodas, the mountain's scenery and serenity are worth taking in anyway. Take the slow trains from Dandong (1 hour).

Within Dandong's boundaries is the Baishilazi Natural Protection Area, a large reserve committed to protecting China's deciduous broadleaf forests; it is both a natural botanic garden and a zoo. Also of note are the Dagu Mountain with groups of ancient temple structures, the Qingshan gully with natural waterfalls, and Dagshan granite outcropping, with beautiful temples in the vicinity.

SOUTH FROM DANDONG

For more border-related points, go south of Dandong, following the Yalu to the coast, to Donggo town on the Chinese side. There's not much beyond a container park and a permanent Yurt, but here the River Yalu splits around little islands, property of the DPRK. A few kilometres further west along the coast is Dalu Island, a 'pearl on the Yellow Sea', and a splendid natural retreat of caves as well as the Camel Peak. It also offers the chance to splash lazily in Moon Bay. It has a bizarre collection of buildings, from T'ang temples to a Danish church and a British lighthouse. There's also the tomb of Deng Shichang, a Chinese captain killed in 1894 as the Japanese fleet sunk the Chinese fleet en route to 'rescuing' Korea from the Tonghak. Ferries run to Dalu (Y80–90).

Beyond Dandong to South Korea

The ROK is also accessible from Dandong on the *Oriental Pearl* ferry from Dandong overnight to Incheon, the major port next to Seoul (tel: +86 415 315 2666; fax: 315 6131). The ferry leaves Dandong at 16.00 on Tuesday, Thursday and Sunday each week and arrives in Incheon the next morning at 09.00. First-class, two-berth cabin: US$215 per person; second-class: four-berth cabin, US$160 per person.

NORTH FROM DANDONG

North along the Yalu from Dandong is the town of Changdianhekou, unremarkable except for its own rail terminus, but 3km north of here is the Taipingwan hydroelectric dam. Halfway across the dam is a rusted, padlocked metal gate, another border with the DPRK, and noticeable along the DPRK bank are regular sentry points. On this reservoir it's possible to get a speedboat up and down it.

The Yalu is not a deep river, and in summer this natural border becomes especially shallow, a fatal flaw for a natural border. Many small islands surface in the shallows, that are technically the DPRK if you're considering going and standing on them. A well-known point for this is the 'One Step Crossing' that is a short trek downhill from the Tiger Mountain Great Wall. The mountain is where China's Great Wall begins, and its good views into the DPRK makes it a great attraction.

One Italian journalist made the 'One Step Crossing', reached an exposed island and was hailed across by a DPRK guard, which he accepted! The Italian wrote later he was well fed and asked idiot questions for a few days before being sent to drift back into China (far easier than fiddling with visas at controlled border points). Great japes: don't try it!

In the regions running northeast from Dandong along the Yalu, the Korean influence becomes more and more marked. In Jilin and Heliongjiang provinces live 1.8 million ethnic Koreans, 800,000 of whom live in the

Yanbian Autonomous Prefecture, a triangular enclave forming the last section of China's border with the DPRK.

From the southeast of Liaoning Province all the way to Changbaishan are entire Korean villages, visible in the shop-signs, bi-lingual roadsigns, Korean forms of dress, the density of Korean Protestant churches and the highly conscious bi-lingualism of the locals. Korean communities grow in rural and urban concentration the closer to Korea you are. (Unfortunately, Korea's division manifests itself in the peninsula's diasporas abroad, and in Beijing the distinction between the ROK and DPRK communities is clearly defined.)

History

Tides of migration have ebbed and flowed from China into Korea and back for millennia. Some tribes or groups were nomadic, touring the lands before arbitrary borders were defined in search of new lands of plenty when previous habitats were lacking, natural disasters destroyed their crops or ill-treatment posed some kind of threat. They then either resumed their livelihoods elsewhere or formed military forces to resist and possibly oust their homeland rulers. Sometimes, people were given in tribute from one state to another, or were stolen by foreign raiding parties.

The area came under Koguryo control from the late 400s as Koguryo united the Puyo people and ruled all the way up to the Amur River for two-and-a-half centuries. When Koguryo divided into separate states from 668, the northernmost state was that of Palhae. A former Koguryo general formed with the Malgal tribe an army that led a mass migration into Manchuria, settling around today's Jilin. A new state was established, named Palhae in 713, that soon expanded to take over the northern remnants of Koguryo, combining them with the Manchurian gains. The state reached its pinnacle in the first half of the 9th century under King Seon, when Palhae stretched from the Yellow Sea to the Sea of Japan, and from Chongjin in today's Korea up to Yanji, with its capital in today's Chongchun. However, the state was only as stable as its neighbours allowed it to be, and Palhae wasn't exempt from the warring that brought down the Tang dynasty, succumbing to the Khitan in 926. Those of the ruling classes that could escape to their more common kin in the new Koryo state did so. The Koreans joined with the Malgal people and assimilated into Manchurian life, eventually helping found the Jurchen.

Later Koreans were just taken. In 1254, the Mongols returned from Koryo with a booty of 26,000 Koreans. Many returned over the years, and many migrated back, so in 1464, 30,000 Koreans were recorded as living in Liaodong. The 1627 and 1637 Manchu raids on Korea enslaved tens of thousands. Some Korean families somehow earned freemen status and attained minor noble status under the Manchus, but these were the exception.

From 1677, an area one thousand li north of Changbaishan was declared off limits by the Qing dynasty that also established a buffer zone just north of the Yalu and Tuman rivers. Any interlopers were thrown back south of the rivers to the Ri, who built a half dozen garrisons to prevent any concerted northern invasion.

Nonetheless, people continued to migrate across the rivers in fair seasons, dressing down and cutting their topknots to appear more Chinese as they escaped the harsh life of northern Korea. For two centuries this continued until a string of natural disasters in northern Korea caused a sudden upsurge in migration away from famine. From 1865 the Qing officially allowed Koreans to live and farm in Manchuria and later Dunwha, where Korean farmers pioneered and prospered on the land. Immigration to Manchuria eased as trade with Ri was established, and by 1894 there were 20,000 in Yanbian alone.

It's from those decades of migration that the current Korean population's cultural origins are thought to source. Earlier waves and pockets of Koreans saw their own way of life drowned in the sea of Han Chinese culture. The circumstances of their arrival, often destitute and starving, prevented them reaching any position of wealth and influence to defend their culture. As well as happenstance and convenience, their new rulers demanded the migrants' assimilation, to turn them from obstructive aliens to trusty clans people. The Yuan rulers established a governor-general office to rule the Koryo people, as did the Ming. Migrants arriving in early Qing Manchuria were dispersed far and wide. Toleration of Koreans didn't come until the late Qing.

Imperial Japan's attempts to smother Korea's culture were partly what led to a staggering rise in Korean migration in the 20th century. That, and the impoverishment of Korea's peasants, saw migrants into Manchuria surpass 450,000 in number in 1920 to reach 2.1 million by 1945. Many had fled the Japanese but many more were sent there. As Japan's great but subservient brethren, Koreans populating Manchuria secured the territory for their Japanese masters. Only the landscape and sheer numbers allowed for great resistance. Many of the disparate political and military movements that were collectively the Korean National Liberation Movement were based in Manchuria throughout Japan's rule, aiding and abetting Chinese resistance against the Japanese; and thousands of Koreans volunteered for the communist forces in China's civil war of 1946–49, engaging in fighting and liberating cities like Changchun and Jilin.

This assistance to the communist victory was in return for Chinese help in Korea's own struggle against the Japanese and later in the Korean War. Long-term training and support, ideological and material, was also provided by the Soviet Union at this time, where Kim Il Sung refined his leadership skills. The extreme conditions of guerrilla warfare in this part of the world imbued toughness in its veterans that would serve them well.

What to see

The roads pass a landscape of forested hills, gulleys and peaks. From Dandong to Tonghua on route 201 is Huanren town, where there's an odd little theme park. From there you can take a power-boat on to the adjacent lake that stretches over the Liaoning-Jilin border to an artist's colony where Chinese artists go and commune with nature, living in a tiny valley in which sit little gothic-style timber houses. Visitors are welcome to stop off to visit, see their works and hang around for a bizarre but relaxing sojourn.

Further along the way is Huadian, a town on a river where you're almost compelled to stop and try the local fish restaurants.

Tonghua
41.3° north, 126° east; 40km from DPRK border, Jilin Province, China
This sprawling provincial town hangs on to the lower slopes of the Longgang mountain range, with parts over 1,500m altitude. It doesn't serve any great treats for the visitor and is mainly useful for its proximity to Ji'an.

Where to stay
Tonghua Hotel 22 Cuiquan Rd, Tonghua, Jilin 134001; tel: 0435-213798; fax: 0435-213367

Getting there and away
It's an hour's taxi-drive from Tonghua to Ji'an. There is an overnight train to Tonghua from Beijing (19 hours, Y82), then transfer to Jian bus at the long-distance bus station (2 hours, Y15).

Ji'an
41.10° north, 126.05° east; China/DPRK border, Jilin Province, China
This is a small, bi-lingual city of 100,000, stashed in the mountains flanking the Yalu, but is rich in its ancient history and its tourist industry thrives on ROK tourists coming to what was the capital of the Koguryo empire. It was established by the Qin 221BC, and noted sights include the Tianxiang Memorial, the Bailuzhou Institute or the Xiyang Palace. Ten thousand ancient tombs and other historical sites including the General's Tomb are around the city, although many are barred to non-Chinese or Koreans. But it doesn't seem that the tourists spend a lot here: the city still has a slightly run-down appearance that fits its remote setting. From Ji'an station a train runs to the DPRK, for which there is fat chance you can get on, but following the tracks to Ji'an Bridge is one viewing point for those coming in and out of the DPRK. Border guards and railway workers may be amenable to fees allowing you to get very close to the dividing line on the bridge that trains steam over daily. The risk's up to you.

Where to stay
Ji'an Hotel 98 Yingbin Lu; tel: 0435-620-1598. Serviceable rooms for around Y220.

Moving on
Route 201 continues from Tonghua to Baihe, the last port of call for Changbaishan Nature Reserve.

Changbaishan Nature Reserve
42° north, 128° east; China/DPRK border, southeast of Jilin province, China
This is China's largest nature reserve at over 200,000 hectares of virgin forest, a 78 x 53km area across three counties, and has recently become a UNESCO World Biosphere Protection Zone. It is home to the rare Manchurian tiger,

sikas, sables, snow leopards and wild ginseng, and as the ground rises up from 500m above sea-level to over 2,000m, the forests turn from broadleaf coniferous through pine, spruce, stunted fir and then tundra.

The transformation of the landscape forms the backdrop as you plough skywards, towards the heart of the reserve where sits Changbaishan, meaning 'eternally white mountain', practically the same as the Koreans' Mt Paektu, or 'white-topped mountain'. This crown of volcanic rock surrounds a piercingly clear, round lake in its caldera, the Tian Chi Lake (meaning 'heavenly lake').

The final road to Changbaishan is little more than a dirt track. The tourist buses take around three hours to heave towards Changbaishan through a flat wilderness of clearings between forests of birch, towering Korean pine, Scotch pine and Japanese yew, while lorries laden with logs come the other way. The road forks at two huge billboards for Daewoo and Hyundai, a big white modern hotel with Korean buses outside of it. Another 45 minutes further is the national park entrance. Locals and student cardholders pay 15 yuan, foreigners 150! Regardless, you're clearly at the bottom of something steep. Fifteen minutes later, you arrive at the base of Changbaishan itself, evidenced by a car park full of tourists, hawkers, little shops and stalls of T-shirts, medicinal antlers, and ginseng. There's a small hotel good for seeing the area in the evening.

From the car park are a few routes up the mountain. For Y100 a jeep can take you up a series of hairpin bends to the volcano's summit (high above the lake) where the view's terrific if not blocked by fog. To go by foot, the western path is scenic but dangerous enough to entail another charge of 'insurance' and you're given a hard hat to walk up steps sheltered with metal-sheet. Fifteen minutes' walk up these stairs is a beautiful waterfall pouring from the lake, cited as the beginning of the Yalu River, and then comes Tian Chi Lake itself. High winds may be blowing between the sharp peaks stabbing the sky round Tian Chi, but the lake itself will be mirror-flat. Many Koreans wade into the scarcely thawed water and sing songs, while the Chinese take pictures. There are also a hundred-odd little towers of piled stones, impromptu pagodas that tourists build.

Although the lake's half Chinese, half DPRK, there's no sign of the border at all in the crater, and it's not obvious outside of it either – no great electric fences or 'LANDMINE' placards about. Once you're free of the crater, it's a landscape (or moonscape) of Scottish moorlands well scored with paths, but be very careful where you stray. One Bristol chap wandered off and came across a hut where he went to ask directions to the nearest Chinese village. The DPRK border-guards inside took him to the nearest DPRK village, where he wasn't badly treated for the two months of haggling the authorities took to get him out.

On Changbaishan's north side is a group of hot springs, identifiable from the hot, steamy air that wafts from them all year. The waters are supposed to be of great medicinal benefit, and some pools can be entered but be careful as they're mostly over 60°C, with an extreme measured at 82°C.

Getting there and away
One way to get to Tian Chi is to book a three-day tour through the CITS in Jilin (tel: +86 432 244 3442; fax: +86 432 245 6786), for all transport, accommodation

up to and around the lake. There are also ROK specialist firms in Beijing that run tours (they're the organisers of the Korean tour buses you'll see all over the site). Non-Koreans are unusual but most welcome. Contact Beijing Xinhua International Tours Co, Jia 23, Fuxinglu, Beijing China; tel: +86 10 68296533.

By bus
Otherwise, going it alone, the nearest village to Tian Chi is Baihe, which one way or another you have to reach. Jilin to Baihe takes seven hours and costs Y50. Yanji to Baihe takes three hours and costs Y20. There's also a direct bus from Yanji that takes four-and-a-half hours. Dunhua to Baihe takes four hours; there are six buses a day starting at 07.45.

Buses from Baihe to Tian Chi leave opposite Baihe railway station from 06.00 until 12.00. The last buses from Tian Chi to Baihe leaves at 16.00.

By train
One train leaves Tonghua at 08.45 arriving in Baihe at 17.15, another overnighter leaves Tonghua at 21.05, and arrives at Baihe at 04.36.

By car
From Tonghua and Yanji it's possible to hire drivers who will take you to Changbaishan in one-day missions (from Y300) but from any further places you would have to account for their accommodation.

Where to stay and eat
Swimming Pool Hotel Baihe. A family-run establishment, which is good for children.

The only food on offer anywhere is likely to be dog meat.

Yanbian Autonomous Prefecture
Northeast part of the China/DPRK border, Jilin Province, China
Changbaishan sits just on the southernmost corner of Yanbian Autonomous Prefecture (Yonbyon to Koreans). This triangular area on the DPRK's border is home to over half of China's Koreans, who make up half the population, as they have for a century. This population density has meant that Yanbian's Koreans have been able to defend their ethnicity as a coherent community by being more powerful politically and economically, hence China's communist government recognises the Koreans as a distinct nationality, ethnically separate from the dominant Han Chinese. From 1949, Han Chinese began to repopulate the area, in the cities of Tonghua, Wangqing and Yanji. The Korean nationality is the 12th largest of China's 56 minorities, although it makes up under 0.2% of the total population. In Yanbian Chinese and Korean languages are used at varying levels in local government and are taught in schools.

History
For centuries before the late 1800s, Yanbian was off limits, kept by the Ming and Qing as an exclusive reserve of primeval forests and virgin land used as royal hunting grounds. The region was only officially to come under

cultivation from the 1880s, although many migrants, including Koreans, had surreptitiously begun to till the land before this. It was the Koreans who became most noted for their skills in turning huge tracts of apparently useless land over to wet-field agricultural use. Their reputation for changing this wild frontier into usable paddyfields was something on which the Japanese wished to capitalise when they forcibly populated Manchaca with Koreans. Complicit in Japanese suppression of Korean culture from 1910 onwards were the Chinese warlords who filled the post-Qing power vacuum at the time – although even the Qing hadn't been overtly tolerant of Korean culture.

In that decade Yanbian became a centre of anti-Japanese resistance, and 20 towns recorded disturbances during the 1919 March 1 Movement, formulating the first coherent civilian response to Japan's occupation of Korea. In 1920 major battles were fought between the Japanese and forces of the Korean Provisional government (based in Shanghai). A Korean division wiped out a smaller Japanese force in June, and lost 1,000 troops in heavy fighting around Chung-san-ri (northwest of Changbaishan) in October 1920. Japanese forces retaliated by burning 2,500 homes and schools and killed or imprisoned over 10,000 Koreans in the Yanbian area. Thousands of skirmishes occurred in the 1920s, and small groups later formed into Anti-Japanese Guerrillas or Worker-Peasant Righteous Armies, accruing 12,000 Korean troops in Yanbian by 1932. The Northeast Anti-Japanese United Army (NEAJUA) soon formed, the main resistance force among a myriad of other units that sprung up across Manchuria and the Sino-Soviet border. Many stayed on after 1945 to fight Chiang-Kai Shek's forces, and by 1949 14,000 Koreans had died fighting for the Chinese communists. The People's Republic of China established the Yanbian Autonomous Prefecture in September 1952, which remained a backwater for decades as Koreans and Chinese settled into reconstructing their agrarian lives.

Since the early 1990s, two groups of Koreans have been migrating back to the region. One group is ROK Korean business investors (and lately, tourists) keen to plough hundreds of millions into the area as a centre of Korean industry and commerce in China's industrial northeast and on Russia's border. ROK business has grown since China recognised the ROK in 1992, and the average wage in Yanbian is twice the Chinese national average.

The second group is another migration of refugees from the DPRK following the 1990s' agricultural collapse. Hundreds of thousands are estimated to be hiding in China, mostly among the Korean communities that can absorb them and give them shelter and waged work. Whether eking out a living with other Koreans or en route southwards, these illegal immigrants are forcibly repatriated to the DPRK by the Chinese security services, where their fate can be prison or sometimes worse. A steady rise in refugees storming Beijing's embassies from 2000 onwards raised tensions between the two Koreas and caused great political embarrassment for the Chinese government, particularly as the incidents surged in the run-up to the 2002 World Cup in the ROK. The Chinese are taking the DPRK side (it would be difficult for them not to) and there have been incidents of Chinese troops 'invading' embassies with some violence to retrieve refugees. The barbed wire that now bedecks Beijing's diplomatic quarter is one very visible result of this hard-line policy.

For more information on the plight of refugees and what they are escaping, search for North Korea under the United Nations High Commission for Refugees (www.unhcr.org), Amnesty International (www.amnesty.org) or the Human Rights Watch (www.hrw.org).

Yanji
42.5° north, 129.25° east; Jilin Province, China
The capital of Yanbian is Yanji, a small city of 350,000 people of whom 60% are ethnic Koreans, as seen in the bilingual street signs. The Chinese minority speak less Korean, but Koreans typically speak both languages. Investment from ROK businesses into industry and tourism has been pouring into the city, and it is a prosperous-looking city, with wide roads, lots of glass and steel and shopping malls. There are over 500 Chinese-foreign joint-ventures in Yanji. It's easy to get whole-body massages and facials that go on for hours for only 50 Yuan, and Yanji is full of dog restaurants.

In very early September is the Korean folk festival, that exhibits folk arts in painting, dress and food, but also folk customs in song and dance, with song and dance competitions such as wrestling, seesawing and swinging that date back centuries in Korea. But this all takes place at the end of the season when Changbaishan is easily accessible, so time it well. The Tuman River International Art Festival of Yanbian Prefecture is another festival that you should ask CITS about.

Getting there and away
No special permits are needed for the Yanbian Prefecture. Yanji is the nearest big Chinese city to Changbaishan. Flights from Beijing to Yanji cost around US$240 return, and from Yanji one-day tours (Y290) to Changbaishan run, the mini-bus leaving at 05.00 to make the five-hour drive and hammering it back by evening. To Yanji there are daily trains (13 hours, Y322) and flights (2 hours, Y970) operate from Beijing.

Tour operators
CITS 4 Yanxi St, Yanji, Jilin 133002; tel: 0433-271-5018; fax: (0433) 271 7906

Where to stay
Baishan Hotel Yanbian 2 Youyi Rd, Yanji, Jilin 133000; tel: +86 433 515958; fax: +86 433 519493
Yanbian Guest House 3 Yanji Rd, Yanji, Jilin 133000; tel: +86 433 512733
Postal Hotel (3★) 68, Juzi jie, Yanji City; tel: +86 433 2910888
Xinqiao Hotel 96 Guangming Lu, Yanji; tel: +86 433 251 7452

Where to eat
There are a lot of dog-meat restaurants – follow the howling (no, really), or Korean cold noodles are found at 42 Hailan Lu (tel: +86 433 251 3624).

Appendix 1

LANGUAGE
General

	Transliteration
Hello	*Annyong haseyo*
Goodbye	*Annyonghi kyeseyo*
Good morning/afternoon/evening	*Annyonghasimnikga*
How are you?	*Pyonanhasimnikga?*
My name is (I am) John.	*Jega John imnida.*
Yes	*Ye*
No	*Aniyo*
Please	*Juseyu*
Thank you	*Gomapsumnida*
How much is this…?	*Iga olma eyo?*
It's too expensive	*Nomu pissayo*
I'd like to buy…	*… issoyu*
Where is … ?	*….i odi issoyu?*
Excuse me	*Yobosio*
I don't understand	*Modaradurossoyu*
What street is this?	*Yogin musun gorimnikga?*
I'm going to Pyongyang	*Nanun Pyongyang-e gamnida*
doctor	*uisa-sonsaengnim*
hospital	*byong-uon*

Transport

airport	*konghang*
bus	*bosu*
bus station	*bosu tominol*
bus stop	*bosu chongnyujang*
metro	*chihachol*
railway station	*kichayok*
taxi	*taegsi*
Take me to…	*… e kajuseyo*
Turn right	*Oruntchoguro kaseyo*
Turn left	*Wentchoguro kaseyo*
Go straight on	*Dokparo kaseyo*
How much to go to…	*… kaji kanund olma eyo?*

Stop here	*Yogiso seuojusibsio*
What street is this?	*Yogin musun gorimnikga?*
Where can I buy a ticket?	*Pyo odiso salsu issoyo?*
Does this train go to…?	*Ichiga … e kayu?*
What station is this?	*Yogiga mosun yogeyo?*
Does this bus go to…?	*Ibosu … e kayu?*
How long is the tour?	*Yohang hanund omana kollyoyo?*

Hotels and restaurants

hotel	*hotel*
restaurant	*shiktang*
toilet	*hwajangshil*
I'm hungry	*Che paegopun*
I'm thirsty	*Che mongmarun*
I'm tired	*Che pigonhan*
Please show me the menu	*Sigsa annaepyo jusibsio*
Please give me …	*… jom jusipsio.*
Please give me some tea	*Cha jom jusipsio*
I don't eat pork/egg/meat	*Nanun doejigogi/dalgyal/gogi an mogsumnida*
Cheers!	*Konbae!*

Food

beans	*kong*
beef	*sogogi*
beer	*maegju*
bread	*bang*
butter	*bada*
carrot	*hongdangmu*
chicken	*dakgogi*
coffee	*kopi*
cucumber	*o-I*
egg	*dalgyal*
fish	*saengson*
fish soup	*saengson-gug*
meat	*gogi*
milk	*uyu*
omelette	*dalgyalsam*
onion	*pa*
pork	*doaejigogi*
potatoes	*gamja*
rice	*bab*
salad	*saengchae*
soup	*gug*
soya	*ganjang*
spinach	*sigumchi*
tea	*cha*

tomato	*domado*
vegetables	*yacha*
water (sodawater)	*saida*

Drinks

beer	*maegju*
coffee	*kopi*
tea	*cha*
milk	*uyu*
water (soda water)	*saida*

In an emergency

hospital	*pyongwon*
pharmacy	*yakkuk*
embassy	*taesagwan*
doctor	*wisa-sonsaengnim*
Help me	*Towajuseyo!*
Call the police	*Kyongchal pulojuseyo!*
Call a doctor	*Wisa pulojuseyo!*
It hurts here	*Apayo*

Other useful words

post office	*ucheguk*
department store	*pakwajom*
bank	*unhaeng*

Time

What time is it now?	*Jigum myosimnikga?*
What time does (it)… open/close/leave/arrive?	*Mun onje yoroyo/tadoyo/donayo/tochakayo?*
3 o'clock	*Se si*
minute	*ban*
03.05	*se si da ban*
03.15	*se si sibo ban*

Days of the week

Monday	*wolyoil*
Tuesday	*hwayoil*
Wednesday	*swuyoil*
Thursday	*mokyoil*
Friday	*kumyoil*
Saturday	*t'oyoil*
Sunday	*ilyoil*

Months

January	*iluol*	July	*chil-uol*
February	*I-uol*	August	*pal-uol*
March	*sam-uol*	September	*gu-uol*
April	*sa-uol*	October	*si-uol*
May	*o-uol*	November	*sibil-uol*
June	*yu-uol*	December	*sibi-uol*

Numbers

1	*hana*	30	*sorun*
2	*dul*	40	*mahun*
3	*sed*	50	*suin*
4	*ned*	60	*yesun*
5	*dasod*	70	*irun*
6	*yosod*	80	*yodun*
7	*ilgop*	90	*hun*
8	*yodol*	100	*baeg*
9	*ahop*	200	*I + baeg*
10	*yol*	1,000	*chon*
11	*yol + hana*	10,000	*baeg + man*
20	*sumul*	half	*ban*

Some useful phrases

What a fast Chollima speed!	*Cholima-sogdoimnida!*
Fancy abolishing taxation!	*Segumul opsaedani!*
President Kim Il Sung is really the greatest Communist fighter and true revolutionary.	*Kim Il Sung jusongimun chamuro uidaehan gongsanjuitusaisimyo jinjonghan hyongmyongga isimnida.*
Long live the Juche idea!	*Juche sasang-manse*
Korea must be identified independentl.y	*Josunun jajujoguro tong-il haeya hamnida*
Yankees are wolves in human shape.	*Yankingum in gane tarul sun sungnyang-ida*

Co-op farm on the way to Kaesong

Appendix

FURTHER READING

Many of the contemporary titles listed below are available through booksellers or can be found on www.amazon.co.uk or www.amazon.com. Older titles could be obtained through Probsthains, 41 Great Russell St, London WC1, tel: +44 (0)207 636 1096, a specialist bookshop on east Asia, or the School of Oriental and African Studies (SOAS), tel: +44 (0)207 637 2388; web: www.soas.ac.uk.

A comprehensive list of DPRK publications in Western languages can be obtained from the Korean Publications Exchange Association, PO Box 222, Pyongyang, DPRK; fax: +850 2 381 4632, telex: 3-7018 EPB KP.

Contemporary DPRK

Kongdan Oh, Kongdan and Hassig, Ralph C *North Korea through the Looking Glass* Brookings Institution Press, 2000, ISBN 0-8157-6435-9. A must-read dissection of modern North Korea and how its society and economy have come to be.

Choi, Sung-Chul *Human Rights and North Korea* Institute of Unification Policy, Hanyang University, 1999, ISBN 89-86763-05-2

Chol-Hwan, Kang and Rigoulot, Pierre *Aquariums of Pyongyang: Ten Years in the North Korean Gulag* Perseus Press, 2001, ISBN 1-903985-05-6. One man's chilling account of life in a DPRK prison camp.

Cornell, Erik *North Korea under Communism* Routledge 2002, ISBN 0700716971

Cumings, Bruce *Korea's Place in the Sun*, Norton, W W & Co, 1998, ISBN 0-3933-168-15. A comprehensive history of Korea focusing mainly on the tumultuous last century and the origins of both sides' political economies.

Cumings, Bruce and Hoepli-Phalon, Nancy L (ed) *Divided Korea: United Future?* Headline Series, 1995, ISBN 0-8712-416-41

Grangereau, Philippe *Au Pays du Grand Mensonge: voyage en Corée du Nord* Le Serpent de Mer, 2001, ISBN 2-913490-05-0

Harrison, Selig S *Korean Endgame: A Strategy for Reunification and U.S. Disengagement* Princeton University Press, 2002, ISBN 0-691-09604-X 448. Harrison argues that the North is not about to collapse and the path to permanent peace on the peninsula is being obstructed by US policy.

Hayashi, Kazunobu and Komaki, Teruo (eds) *Kim Jong-Il's North Korea, An Arduous March* Institute of Developing Economies, Tokyo 1997. Accessible accounts of the DPRK's economic woes.

Henderson, Gregory *Korea: The Politics of the Vortex* Harvard University Press, 1968

Hunter, Helen-Louise *Kim Il Sung's North Korea* ISBN 0-275-96296-2, Library of
Congress No 98-24560. Easy-to-read section-by-section account of life in the DPRK,
from school to army to workers, based on declassified CIA reports from defectors.

Krause, Lawrence B and Cumings, Bruce *Korea's Economic Role in East Asia – The Great
Game on the Korean Peninsula – Japanese Colonialism in Korea: a comparative perspective*
James Lilley, 1997, ISBN 0-9653935-18

Natsios, Andrew S *The Great North Korean Famine* United States Institute of Peace,
ISBN 1-929223-33-1. In-depth coverage of the collapse of DPRK's agriculture.

Noland, Marcus and Bergsten, C *Avoiding the Apocalypse: The Future of the Two Koreas*
Institute for International Economics, 2000, ISBN 0-881-322784. A droll and
accessible yet broad account of the complex socio-economic and security issues
facing the north and the south.

Ok, Tae Hwan and Lee, Hong Yung *Prospects for Change in North Korea* Regents of the
University of California & Research Institute for National Unification, Seoul,
1994, ISBN 1-55729-045-8

Scalapino, Robert (ed) *North Korea Today* Frederick A Praeger, 1963, Library of
Congress No 63-20152. A readable overview of the post-war DPRK reconstruction
and rebirth.

Scalapino, Robert and Lee, Chong Sik *Communism in Korea* vols 1 & 2, Berkeley:
University of California Press, 1972

Suh, Dae-Sook and Lee, Chae-Jin (eds) *North Korea after Kim Il Sung* Lynne Reiner
Publishers, 1998, ISBN 1-55587-763-X. A broad selection of essays on the DPRK's
economic, military, political and foreign prospects.

The leaders

Baek, Jo Song *The Leadership Philosophy of Kim Jong Il* Foreign Languages Publishing
House, Pyongyang, Korea Juche 88, 1999

Buzo, Adrian *The Guerilla Dynasty* Westview Press, 5500 Central Avenue, Boulder,
Colorado, 1999, ISBN 0-8133-3659-7. This is the Kremlinologists' guide to the
DPRK, a masterpiece of inference.

Ha, Kim Chang *The Immortal Juche Idea* Pyongyang Foreign Languages Publishing
House, Pyongyang, 1984

Lankov, Andrei *From Stalin to Kim Il Sung: The formation of North Korea 1945–1960*
Rutgers University Press, 2002, ISBN 0-8135-3117-9. This charts in detail the first
decades of North Korea when Kim Il Sung's power was forged to be absolute. This
has a complete biography of Kim Il Sung to his death in 1994.

Sung, Kim Il *Kim Il Sung: Works* Foreign Languages Publishing House. The 39
volumes by the Great Man are the clearest DPRK produced texts, for it is himself
and his ideas in his own words.

The True Story of Kim Jong Il The Institute for South-North Korea Studies, Korea
Herald Inc, 1993. Scandalous in every sense, this ROK publication is worth reading
for its extreme view of the DPRK

War

Baldwin, Frank (ed) *Without Parallel: The Korean-American Relationship Since 1945*
Pantheon Books, New York, 1973

Hastings, Max *The Korean War* Pan Macmillan, 1993, ISBN 0-333-59153-4. Well-written account of the conflict but virtually bereft of any Korean civilian or North Korean accounts.

Kirkbride, Major Wayne *A Panmunjom: Facts about the Korean DMZ* Hollym International Corp, USA, 1985, ISBN 0-930878-42-6

Stone, I F *The Hidden History of the Korean War* New York: Monthly Review Press, 1952

Vatcher William H, Jr *Panmunjom Frederick* A Praeger Inc, 1958, LCCCN 58-7887. Hyperbole and vitriol at the armistice talks. A really bad-tempered book by someone evidently too close to the action.

A Practical Business Guide on the Democratic People's Republic of Korea The European Union Chamber of Commerce in Korea, 1998, www.eucck.org

Korean history

Hatada, Takashi *A History of Korea* American Bibliographical Center, Clio Press, LCCCN 69-20450. A very economics-oriented take on Korean history but with some good passages, when not bogged in detail.

Henthorn, William E A *History of Korea* The Free Press, 1971, LCCCN 75-143511

Maidment, Richard & Mackerras, Colin (eds) *Culture and Society in the Asia Pacific* Routledge, 1998, ISBN 0-415-17278-0

Suh, Dae-Sook and Schultz, Edward J (eds) *Koreans in China* Center for Korean Studies, University of Hawaii 96822, 1988, ISBN 0-917536-18-5

Tennant, Roger *A History of Korea* Kegan Paul International, 1996, ISBN 0-7103-0532-X. An enjoyably readable history of Korea.

Pyongyang Pingpong Diplomacy – What Achieved and Not Achieved The Korea Herald, Kwanghuamun, PO Box 523, Seoul, ROK, 1979. Collection of largely speculative articles about what the 1979 Pyongyang Ping-Pong Tournament was to achieve. More interesting for how universally cynical Western journalists can be.

Overview of Korean culture

Hoare, James and Pares, Susan *Korea: An Introduction* Kegan Paul International Ltd, 1988, ISBN 0-7103-0299-1. A rounded and enjoyable introduction to the history and culture of the peninsula.

Howard, Keith, Pares, Susan and English, Tessa *Korea People, Country and Culture* SOAS, 1996, ISBN 0-7286-0266. A highly accessible sectioned breakdown of the major facets of Korean life.

Lee, Hyangjin *Contemporary Korean Cinema* Manchester University Press, 2000, ISBN 0-7190-6007-9. This thesis discusses cinema on both sides of Korea and details what's been shown at the Pyongyang Odeon.

Revolutionary Operas SOAS, London, DKN 782-387-559. A collection of operas produced through the lens of Juche.

Hoare, James and Pares, Susan *Korea* World Bibliographical Series Vol 204, ISBN 1-85109-246-3

Travelogues from the early 19th and 20th centuries

Allen, Horace N, MD *Things Korean* Fleming H Revell Co

Bergman, Sten *In Korean Wilds and Villages* Travel Book Club, London, 1938. A somewhat pro-Japanese travelogue of this ornithologist's expedition around Korea shortly before World War II.

Bishop, Isabella Bird, FRGS *Korea and Her Neighbours* Yonsei University Press, Seoul (reprint 1970). An interesting and warm account of missionary life in the late 19th century, if not a little heavy on the salvation angle.

Carles, W R *Life in Corea* Macmillan and Co, 1888. Quite a dull book for someone with such access to top-drawer chicanery.

Cavendish, Captain A E J *Korea and the Sacred White Mountain* George Philip & Son, London, 1894. A dour account of one man's hunting holiday, but useful to understand how the West saw Korea.

Griffis, William Elliot *Corea The Hermit Nation* Charles Scribner's Sons, New York, 1897. Of the accounts by early venturers to Korea, Griffis' is by far the most comprehensive, detailed and respectful.

Jaisohn, Philip, MD *My Days in Korea and Other Essays* Institute for Modern Korea Studies, Yonsei University, 1999, ISBN 89-7141-497-9-03900. Jaisohn's works give a highly intelligent but personal insight into Korea's history from the run-up to Japanese colonialism, Japanese rule and the post-World War II division.

Sihanouk, Norodom *The Democratic People's Republic of Korea* Foreign Languages Publishing House, Pyongyang, 1980. The King of Cambodia gets a very nice tour of the country and dutifully recorded everything he was told.

Underwood, L H, MD *Fifteen Years among The Top-knots* American Tract Society, 1904

Language
Bear in mind that neither of the following teach the nuances of 'North' Korean:

Vincent, Mark and Yeon, Jaehoon *Teach Yourself Korean* Teach Yourself Books, 1997
Kim, In-Seok *Colloquial Korean* Routledge, 1996, ISBN 0-415-10804-7

North Korean published guides
Few of the following publications can be found easily outside of the DPRK except in some university libraries, but contact the Korean Publications Exchange Association, PO Box 222, Pyongyang, DPRK, fax: +850 2 381 4632, telex: 3-7018 EPB KP

Hyok, Hwang Bong & Ryol, Kim Jong *Korea Tour: A land of morning calm, a land of attractions* National Tourism Administration Juche 86, 1997. Irritatingly vague at times.

Ju, Pang Hwan and Hyok, Hwang Bong *A Sightseeing Guide to Korea* National Tourism Administration, Foreign Languages Publishing House, 1991

Korea Tour National Tourism Administration, Pyongyang, 1998. One of the more recent guides with more factual details.

Kaesong/Mt Paektu/Mt Myohyang/Kumgang Tourist Advertisement and Information Agency, Songuja-dong, Mangyongdae, Pyongyang. Well-written guides to their respective areas, with good maps and details on routes and pockets of interest.

Pyongyang Review Foreign Languages Publishing House, Pyongyang, 1995. A dry mini-encyclopedia on Pyongyang.

Overviews of the country

Lankov, Dr Andrei *Pyongyang and Its People; notes of a Soviet Student* A very good read. This and other works by Dr Lankov can be found through www.google.com, as can those of Aidan Foster-Carter.

Phyo, Jon Won, Gang, An Chol and Su, Ri Pom *Panorama of Korea* Foreign Languages Publishing House

Juche 88, 1999. Very similar in scope to *Pyongyang Review* and filled with maps and pictures to break up a fact-filled but dry text.

Shuhachi, Inoue *Modern Korean and Kim Jong Il* Yuzankaku, Tokyo, Japan 1984

Juche: A Christian's Study This is a religious dissection of Juche but is far more readable than its title suggests, with lots of eyewitness accounts of what life is like in the North.

Magazines

Korea Today
Democratic People's Republic of Korea
Foreign Trade in the DPRK

Websites

Harvard University's www.fas.harvard.edu/~korea/biblio has stacks of further resources.

News

www.kena.co.jp
www.times.dprkorea.com

Current affairs

north-korea.narod.ru/pyongyang_watch.htm
www.fas.org
www.kimsoft.com
www.koreascope.org/eng/main/index.jsp
www.nautilus.org
www.worldperspectives.org/dprk/

Economy

www.eucck.org
www.fao.org/
www.fbda.net
www.kbc-global.com
www.tradepartners.gov.uk_korea
www.unicef.org/emerg/DPFK.htm
www.wfp.org/index2.html

General information

www.budgettravel.com/nkorea.htm
www.cia.gov/cia/publications/factbook
www.fco.gov.uk

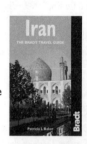

Index

Page numbers in bold indicate major entries, those in italics indicate maps.